Teaching Christianity

Augustinian Heritage Institute

THE WORKS OF SAINT AUGUSTINE
A Translation for the 21st Century

Part I — Books

Volume 11: Teaching Christianity

The English translation of the works of Saint Augustine has been made possible with contributions from the following:

Order of Saint Augustine

Province of Saint Thomas of Villanova (East)
Province of Our Mother of Good Counsel (Midwest)
Province of Saint Augustine (California)
Province of Saint Joseph (Canada)
Vice Province of Our Mother of Good Counsel
Province of Our Mother of Good Counsel (Ireland)
Province of Saint John Stone (England and Scotland)
Province of Our Mother of Good Counsel (Australia)
The Augustinians of the Assumption (North America)
The Sisters of Saint Thomas of Villanova

Order of Augustinian Recollects

Province of Saint Augustine
Mr. and Mrs. James C. Crouse
Mr. and Mrs. Paul Henkels
Mr. and Mrs. Francis E. McGill, Jr.
Mr. and Mrs. Mariano J. Rotelle

THE WORKS OF SAINT AUGUSTINE

A Translation for the 21st Century

Teaching Christianity

(De Doctrina Christiana)

I/11

translation and notes by
Edmund Hill, O.P.

editor
John E. Rotelle, O.S.A.

New City Press
of the Focolare
Hyde Park, NY

Published in the United States by New City Press
202 Comforter Blvd., Hyde Park, New York 12538
©1996 Augustinian Heritage Institute

Library of Congress Cataloging-in-Publication Data:

Augustine, Saint, Bishop of Hippo.
    The works of Saint Augustine.

    "Augustinian Heritage Institute"
    Includes bibliographical references and indexes.
    Contents: — pt. 3, v. 15. Exposition of the Psalms, 1-32
— pt. 3., v. 1. Sermons on the Old Testament, 1-19.
— pt. 3, v. 2. Sermons on the Old Testament, 20-50 — [et al.] — pt. 3,
v. 10 Sermons on various subjects, 341-400.
    1. Theology — Early church, ca. 30-600. I. Hill,
Edmund. II. Rotelle, John E.   III. Augustinian
Heritage Institute. IV. Title.
BR65.A5E53 1990 270.2   89-28878
ISBN 978-1-56548-055-1 (series)
ISBN 978-1-56548-048-3 (pt. 1, v. 11)
ISBN 978-1-56548-049-0 (pt. 1, v. 11 : paperback.)

1st printing: April 1996
8th printing: February 2018

Printed in the United States of America

CONTENTS

INTRODUCTION

Structure and Pastoral Theology
of *Teaching Christianity*

Composition and Structure

Around 396, Augustine, who had been consecrated Bishop of Hippo shortly before, undertook the writing of *Teaching Christianity* (*De doctrina christiana*). The first version ended at Book III, 25, 35; in 426–427 he added the end of the third book and the whole of the fourth; he interrupted his work on the revision of all his writings, the *Revisions*, in order to supply a conclusion to the early books of *Teaching Christianity*, which he regarded as "incomplete."[1] Everything suggests a long-pondered work, the structure of which is outlined by the author himself: "The first three books help in understanding scripture; the fourth shows how one who has understood it should express himself."[2] The heart of the work, and its driving force, is therefore sacred scripture, understood and adopted "as the sole foundation of a truly Christian education."[3] With this in mind Augustine develops a whole series of questions and topics having to do with the twofold purpose he has already identified: to understand the scriptures and to express them.

Here we have, for the first time, a "program of higher studies that provide a complete formation of the mind and are conceived solely in function of the religious purpose which Christianity assigns to the intellectual life."[4] Visible here is the vast difference between the new education proposed by Augustine and the admittedly analogous purpose of secular classical education: the Christian orator is "the bearer of the word of God, the minister of saving truths."[5] On the other hand, the seemingly encyclopedic range of knowledge required by Augustine in the educational program of *Teaching Christianity* follows, in fact, the simple line that inspired the grammatical schools of antiquity in its decline, and leads to the demand (one that would be amply met) for the necessary manuals and repertories so that Christians

---

1. *Revisions* II, 4, 1. On the reasons for the long interruption see A. Pincherle, "Sulla composizione del *De doctrina christiana* di S. Agostino," *Studi in onore di E. Dupré Theseider* 2 (Rome, 1974) 541–559.
2. *Revisions* II, 4, 1.
3. M. Simonetti, *Lettera e/o allegoria. Un contributo alla storia dell'esegesi patristica* (Rome, 1985) 338.
4. H. I. Marrou, *S. Agostino e la fine della cultura antica* (Milan, 1987) 331.
5. *Ibid.*, 334.

might acquire from them the little they needed without excessive effort.[6] If, then, *Teaching Christianity* can be regarded as "the fundamental charter of Christian education" by reason of its restrictive program of research and study and its emphasis on the use of repertories, it also shows itself "a very peculiar testimony in the history of decadence."[7]

But it is in the word "teaching" (*doctrina*) that the very special nature and structure of Augustine's treatise come into view; the word is a pregnant one and has been the subject of a great deal of writing and discussion.[8]

The impossibility of translating the Latin *doctrina* by a single word is due to the several meanings of a term which Augustine uses now to indicate the activity of teaching, now to designate the content of this activity, and, in certain cases such as the title of this work, to convey both meanings at once.[9] It is to be noted, however, that Augustine's specific purpose, namely, to educate people in a faith which by its nature needs to be "thought out," is implicit in the very word *doctrina*, which sums up "the entire field of 'Christian knowledge' that is to be gathered from its three sources: scripture, tradition, and the living authority of the Church."[10] To sum up: in the light of Augustine's statement in the *Revisions*, *Teaching Christianity* is meant both as a guide in learning the truths of faith contained in scripture and as a methodology for teaching others the truths learned.[11]

As for the structure and contents of the work, let me give a quick outline of the essentials, while referring the reader to the fuller expositions found in various other studies.[12] As Augustine says at the beginning of the first book, the treatise is divided basically into two parts: one, which includes the first three books, deals with "a way to discover what needs to be understood," and another, comprising substantially the fourth book, deals with "a way to put across to others what has been understood."

After the Prologue, in which the purpose of the treatise is defined and some possible criticisms are taken up, the first book is divided into four

---

6.   *Teaching Christianity* II, 39, 59.
7.   Marrou, *S. Agostino*, 342.
8.   See E. Kevane, "Augustine's *De doctrina christiana*: A Treatise on Christian Education," *Recherches Augustiniennes* 4 (1966) 122–133; I. Opelt, "*Doctrina* und *doctrina christiana*," *Der altsprachliche Unterricht* 9 (1966) 5–22; G. A. Press, "The Subject and Structure of Augustine's *De doctrina christiana*," *Augustinian Studies* 11 (1980) 101–107; idem, "*Doctrina* in Augustine's *De doctrina christiana*," *Philosophy and Rhetoric* 17 (1984) 98–120.
9.   Press, "*Doctrina*," 103; L. M. J. Verheijen, "Le *De doctrina christiana* de saint Augustin," *Augustiniana* 24 (1974) 12. [*De doctrina christiana* can mean either "On the teaching professed by Christianity" or "On the activity of teaching Christianity." —Tr.]
10. L. Alici, *S. Agostino d'Ippona, La doctrina christiana* (Milan, 1989) 31; Marrou, *S. Agostino*, 314.
11. Press, "*Doctrina*," 114.
12. See Kevane, "Augustine's *De doctrina christiana*," 112–117; Press, "The Subject," 112–116; idem, "The Content and Argument of Augustine's *De doctrina christiana*," *Augustiniana* 31 (1981) 165–182; Alici, *S. Agostino d'Ippona*, 33–41.

parts dealing with the contents of the faith: principles and basic distinctions between things and signs, means and ends (1, 1–4); dogmatic contents (1, 5–19); principles of Christian ethics (1, 20–38); principles of biblical exegesis (1, 39–44).

The second book is devoted to studies having to do with the Bible and has three sections: remarks and general principles on "signs" and on the canon of scripture (2, 1–13); knowledge of the biblical languages and an appraisal of the translations of the Bible (2, 14–23); the aid given by the natural sciences, the humanistic disciplines, and philosophy in the study of scripture (2, 24–63).

The third book, likewise in three sections, has for its subject the interpretation of sacred scripture: ambiguities in the text due to problems of grammar (3, 1–8); ambiguities in the scriptures due to a metaphorical use of words, and charity as a hermeneutical criterion (3, 9–41); a discussion of the seven rules of Tychonius (3, 42–56).

The fourth book, which might be entitled "the Christian teacher and preacher," explains, in four sections, how to expound and teach the truths that have been learned: basic principles of oratory (4, 1–10); examples from scripture (4, 11–26); the three aims and corresponding styles of oratory, with examples from Paul and the Fathers (4, 27–50); ten rules for Christian oratory; prayer (4, 51–64).

The way in which *Teaching Christianity* is arranged has focused attention on some expressions used by Augustine that, along with the pregnant term *doctrina*, make it possible to define more closely the shape and structure of the treatise. Press has studied the use of *tracto-tractatio* ("treatment")[13] and the special character of the rhetorical element in *Teaching Christianity*; he sees this as being in the line of the classical tradition and he defines it as "an account of *tractatio scripturarum*," in which "classical rhetorical theory has been transformed to meet the needs and serve the purposes of a new community and a new culture."[14]

Theology and Pastoral Activity

The relationship of theology to pastoral activity, to which only passing references are made in the various studies that analyze *Teaching Christianity* and pass judgment on it, deserves some further attention. After all, it is a relationship that pervades the whole of Augustine's activity, and it can be said that, unlike our own age, there were no periods of real crisis in this relationship nor did it become especially problematic throughout a large part of the patristic age, when theology and pastoral activity ordinarily collaborated and influenced each other.

The reason for this necessary connection was recently pinpointed by the Church's Magisterium in an Instruction that has given rise to debate. The

13. Prologue 1; 1, 1; 4, 1.
14. Press, "The Subject," 113–124; idem, *"Doctrina,"* 115.

essentially exegetico-theological activity of the Fathers (it was said) took place *in medio Ecclesiae* ("in the midst of the Church"); the Fathers were active participants within a setting of liturgy and the Church and they were animated by a genuinely apostolic faith in their thinking and speaking.[15]

In *Teaching Christianity* Augustine intends to instruct Christians how to practice a "faith that has been thought out" and to avoid and surmount the obstacle created by a particular educational tradition that had become rigidified in the form of rhetoric. To this end, he skillfully places his pastoral concern within the framework of biblical theology. This fruitful interrelationship, which for centuries nourished the faith and "Christian education," comes down to us in its richly relevant reality and provides the key for reading "a very modern book."[16]

Let us therefore look again at the essential lines and most salient stages of the work.

1) The sections most directly dealing with theology are to be found especially throughout the first book of *Teaching Christianity*, and Augustine gives the reason for this while at the same time delimiting the scope and extent of what he has to say: "I have wished to talk about things to do with faith, as much as I judged sufficient for the moment; because much has already been said on the matter in other volumes, whether by other people or by myself."[17] What he is offering, then, is a concise review, a "short inventory," of truths in the area of dogma and morality[18] that constitute as it were the essence of Christianity according to biblical revelation[19] and that are here placed in the pedagogical and educational perspective proper to the treatise. In this setting, the area of the "disciplines," rather than being subordinated, is closely connected with the requirements of "doctrine"; thus to know and to teach are two complementary phases of a single theological and pastoral activity.[20]

Fundamental to this pastoral didactics is the assertion of God's absolute transcendence[21] and resulting ineffability.[22] It follows from this that God is truly sought beyond the ladder of created living things and even beyond the

---

15. *Instruction on the Study of the Fathers in the Formation of Priests*, issued by the Congregation for Catholic Education (November 10, 1989), in *Origins* 19 (1989–90) 549–561. See also *Instruction on the Ecclesial Vocation of the Theologian*, issued by the Congregation for the Doctrine of the Faith (May 24, 1990), in *Origins* 20 (1990–1991) 117–126. In the present situation this latter document calls for a close collaboration between the Magisterium and theology. See the description of the true theologian in Gregory of Nazianzus, *Or.* 27, 7 (PG 36:20B; ed. Gallay, SC 250:286).
16. P. Brown, *Augustine of Hippo: A Biography* (Berkeley, 1967) 267.
17. I, 40, 44.
18. Marrou, *Saint Augustine, and his influence through the ages* (London, New York, 1957)
19. Verheijen, "Le *De doctrina christiana*," 12–14.
20. Alici, *S. Agostino d'Ippona*, 23.
21. Prologue, 8–9.
22. I, 6, 6—7, 7.

life of the intellect, which by its essence is immersed in the realm of what is mutable. In God, wisdom, which is identified with what is immutable, is infinite.[23] But if God is completely ineffable, then it is impossible to affirm even his ineffability. The only way of escaping from this paradoxical aporia is by silence,[24] but a silence that is swiftly overtaken by the need and compelling desire to speak of God, who "has accepted the homage of human voices," which express praise and thereby bring immense joy.[25]

At the outset, there is a connatural intuition that impels the mind to think of a being "than which there is nothing better or more sublime."[26] In this way, the truth of God that emerges from the bosom of this fruitful silence becomes the object of a joy that eventually leads to the fullness of enjoyment; it offers an exciting prospect that opens upon the "way" of the human being to the homeland; everything else, the *res*, is simply a means which one "uses" in order to attain to the "enjoyment" of the supreme Good. The dialectical distinction between "using" and "enjoying" (*uti—frui*) is already anticipated here.[27] The fullness of this enjoyment is to be found in the relationship with the Trinity, the one substance in which the Father is distinct as unity, the Son as equality, and the Holy Spirit as "the harmony of unity and equality."[28] In addition to the repeated emphasis on the equality of nature in the three divine Persons, we glimpse a reassertion of the doctrine of substantial, because immutable, relations that grounds the principle of the trinitarian distinction of Persons. This is the line taken in *The Trinity*, which, even chronologically, moves in parallel as it were with *Teaching Christianity*.[29]

All this requires that human beings undertake a journey of enlightenment and purification that would be impossible for them if their weakness were not offset by the very "wisdom" of God, which manifests itself "in mortal flesh" and draws them to itself in a process of assimilation. This wisdom is the Word "who became flesh and dwelt among us."[30]

The identification of Wisdom with the Word made flesh, which is later taken up explicitly,[31] recalls the personification of *sophia-sapientia*-wisdom

---

23. I, 8, 8—9, 9.
24. *Order* II, 16, 44: "of that supreme good that is better known by not knowing"; *Ans. Adimant.* 11: "before which [the majesty of God] a respectful silence is more fitting than any human words." See E. Gilson, *The Christian Philosophy of Saint Augustine*, trans. L. E. M. Lynch (New York, 1960), Part III.
25. I, 6, 6.
26. I, 6, 7. On this probable source of Saint Anselm of Aosta's ontological argument see Alici, *S. Agostino d'Ippona*, 109, note 1.
27. See Marrou, *S. Agostino*, 288; G. Istace, "Le livre 1er du *De doctrina christiana* de saint Augustin," *Ephemerides Theologicae Lovanienses* 32 (1956) 292–301; W. R. O'Connor, "The *Uti-frui* Distinction in Augustine's Ethics," *Augustinian Studies* 14 (1983) 45–62.
28. I, 5, 5.
29. See *Trinity* V, 5, 6.
30. See John 1:14.
31. I, 34, 38.

in the Book of Proverbs and, in particular, the tortuous Christological exegesis of the famous passage, Proverbs 8:22, an exegesis that had a long life, especially in the East.[32] Augustine develops a sagacious line of reasoning that reveals his pastoral concerns, as in the light of 1 Corinthians 1:21 and John 1:10 he applies the biblical idea of incarnate wisdom to the history of salvation. "Wisdom" was already in the world, but human beings did not recognize him; the resultant impossibility of their knowing God through wisdom became part of the wise plan of God, who sent the Word-Wisdom into the world to save believers "through the folly of preaching."[33] This conception sums up the Augustinian doctrine of the mediation of Christ in its various aspects: it is one, because the mediator, the God-Man, is one;[34] it is the cause of freedom and salvation for human beings;[35] it is universal.[36]

Characteristic of Christological references in *Teaching Christianity* 1, 11 is the recourse, frequently practiced by Augustine, to the analogy with human thought, the intention being to shed light on the mystery of the Word who became flesh "in order to dwell amongst us" "without being changed in the least." As thought achieves communication by taking the form of sound and yet in the process undergoes no change but remains "undiminished in itself," so the Word of God takes flesh in order to manifest himself, but his nature remains unchanged. This image helped an essential formula of faith enter into and spread through the stream of tradition and thus to become a bit of the patristic riches inherited by the liturgy: *Quod fuit permansit, quod non erat assumpsit* ("What he was he remained; what he was not he assumed").[37]

The incarnate Word effects redemption by "curing some of our ills by their contraries, others by homeopathic treatment," just as medicine does, that is, applied to the illnesses of the body. Humanity fell through pride and is cured by humility; the supposed wisdom of the tempter caused humanity's ruin, and the "folly" of God saves it; the corrupted soul of a woman caused the disease, but we are saved from this by "a woman's body preserved intact." Conversely, the man who was led astray by a woman is set free "by one born of a woman"; human beings are saved by a human

---

32. See M. Simonetti, *Studi sull'arianesimo* (Rome, 1965) 9ff.
33. 1, 12, 12.
34. *Confessions*. 10, 43, 68; *City of God* IX, 15, 2; Sermon 47, 1.
35. *Trinity* IV.
36. *City of God* X, 32, 2; X, 47.
37. *Liturgia Horarum* I. Octava Nativitatis Domini, Ant. ad Bened. [In the English translation of the Liturgy of the Hours the verse is translated: "He remains what he was and becomes what he was not." — Tr.] See the comparable formula in the so-called "Faith of Damasus": "He did not lose what he was, but began to be what he was not" (DS 72; trans. in J. Neuner and J. Dupuis [eds.], *The Christian Faith in the Doctrinal Documents of the Catholic Church* [rev. ed.; Staten Island, NY, 1982] no. 15, p. 11). The analogy with thinking recalls Augustine's teaching on the *verbum cordis* (Sermon 119, 7). See Leo the Great, Sermon 27, 1; H. Rahner, *L'ecclesiologia dei Padri* (Rome, 1971) 19.

being, mortals by a mortal, and the dead are redeemed by his death.[38] The ultimate goal of the redemption is assimilation to Christ, the uncreated and ineffable Wisdom of God, which while being our home also becomes the way to that home, the way to the Father.[39] In keeping with Pauline soteriology,[40] Augustine sees in the resurrection and ascension of Christ the source of a great hope that nourishes and sustains the faith of believers. Not only that: the theologically indestructible support of this faith is the fact that the resurrection shows us "how willingly he had laid down his life for us, by having the power in this way to take it up again."[41]

In short, Christ's free choice of the supreme sacrifice (his free will was a subject of lengthy debate before and during the Councils of Ephesus and Chalcedon) is the act of love that united the death and resurrection of the Lord into a single mystery of salvation.

When seen from a viewpoint dear to Augustine and expressed, here again, by an analogy that links the process leading to resurrection with the interior life of the human person, the resurrection of the flesh is part of the mystery of Christ: After death, which is due to "the chains of sin," the body will be "refashioned for the better" by putting on immortality,[42] just as the soul, in virtue of repentance and conversion, is transformed for the better and renewed.

This line of thought includes an indispensable reference to the nature and final destiny of the Church. The gifts which human beings receive from God on their journey to resurrection are meant for the building up of his Church. Referring explicitly to Saint Paul,[43] Augustine says that the Church is both body and spouse of Christ and gathers into a healing unity the many members who have been purified by numerous temporal trials, "so that, once it has been snatched from this world, he may bind his wife the Church to himself for ever, *not having any stain or wrinkle, or any such thing.*"[44] The unity of the Church as thus conceived implies the reality of a "body" whose members receive a life-giving solidarity from the head, which is Christ.[45] On its journey through time the Church possesses "the keys" of forgiveness and mercy that have been entrusted to it by Christ; faith in this power obtains a forgiveness of sins that is ratified by heaven.

Augustine's explanation delves once again into the intricacies of religious psychology and brings to light a disconcerting aspect of this psy-

---

38. I, 14, 13.
39. I, 11, 11 and 34, 38. See Istace, "Le livre 1er," 312.
40. 1 Cor 15:1ff.
41. I, 15, 14.
42. See 1 Cor 15:50–53.
43. Eph 1:23; 5:23–32; Rom 12:4.
44. I, 15, 4—15.
45. This is the well-known Augustinian conception of "the whole Christ." See Sermon 45, 5; S. Grabowsky, "Saint Augustine and the Doctrine of the Mystical Body of Christ," *Theological Studies* 7 (1946) 72–125.

chology: those who do not believe that their sins can be forgiven them are trapped in a despair that renders them worse, as though they were convinced that without this faith "nothing better remains for them than to be evil."[46] This paradox expresses Augustine's conviction that for the exercise of the power to absolve that has been granted to the Church there is an essential condition, namely, a heartfelt repentance that is "the habitual practice of every authentic spiritual life."[47]

But the primary and basic task of this power of the keys is to give an authentic interpretation of the scriptures, one that reveals "the kingdom of charity" and guides those who have received the "key" of forgiveness and of the spiritual life.[48] Augustine's thinking thus broadens and extends to the universal mediatory role of the Church, a role mysteriously connected with the universal salvific love of Christ. Augustine's ecclesiology, while taking account of the dynamic co-presence of Christ, the Church, and human beings, lays a greater emphasis on the doctrine of the "birth of God in the heart of the believer," the interiority of the heart, as compared with the rest of the patristic tradition, especially the Greek.[49]

2) The ethical content of *Teaching Christianity*, which is primarily and closely connected with the truths of faith and therefore with dogma, which forms as it were the basic fabric,[50] is inspired by the key distinction between *uti* and *frui*, "use" and "enjoyment," both of which are understood on the decisive ontological level,[51] even though the distinction is situated on the level of "scientific knowledge about *res* and *signa*." The use-enjoyment pair is the point of convergence for the fundamental motifs of Augustine's theology of Christian love with its two branches: human love and the love of God for human beings. Augustine locates the relation between the Good and goods, between divine Love and human loves, beyond the realm of "things." At the same time, he limits human use to created things understood as "instruments" for reaching the supreme goal, which is God, who alone is the proper object of enjoyment because he is the only reality that is to be loved "for itself."[52] Augustine uses a fine comparison to explain the dialectic of these relationships: As "exiles in a foreign land," people on the way to our own country, we cannot lose ourselves in "the pleasures of the journey" and stop to "enjoy" what we can really only "use," but "we have to use this world, not enjoy it, so that we may behold *the invisible things of God*," which are made understandable through created things.[53]

---

46. I, 17, 18.
47. H. Chadwick, *Augustine*, (Oxford, 1986) 60.
48. III, 15, 23; see II, 8, 12.
49. Rahner, *L'ecclesiologia dei Padri*, 97.
50. See Istace, "Le livre 1er," 298.
51. See O'Connor, "The *Uti-frui* Distinction," 43–62.
52. 52. I, 22, 20.
53. I, 4, 4 and 1, 22, 21. See Marrou, *S. Agostino*, 288; A. Di Giovanni, *La dialettica dell'amore. "Uti-frui" nelle Preconfessioni do S. Agostino* (Rome, 1965) (on the

Some have thought to find in the Augustinian conception of love a kind of "egocentrism" and resultant "instrumentalism."[54] Nygren had made a thorough study of this question and formulated a double answer.[55] In its object the Augustinian conception is definitely theocentric, because "no object can vie with God for our love"; but if we consider the kind of love, the conception is clearly egocentric, because "even in God I seek my own good." O'Connor even says: "This, of course, violates the well-known Kantian principle of always treating persons as ends and never merely as means."[56] The weak point of this statement, however, is that it does not take into account the difference in perspective: Kant's is immanent ("the realm of ends"), Augustine's is transcendent and metaphysical.[57] It is in this particular perspective that we must view the hierarchy of ends established by the *ordo amoris*, in which "the enjoyment of God includes both love of neighbor (and forgiveness as an act of a will that is strengthened by memory and not by forgetfulness) and a virtuous self-love."[58]

The epicenter and full motivation of this "theology of Christian love" are found in God's love for humanity, in the unfathomable depths of the "metaphysics of God as Love."[59] Since God is by nature love, he cannot but love either by way of enjoyment or by way of use. He cannot love human beings with enjoyment, since that would represent an absurdity, inasmuch as God would have to love a being "outside of" himself as an ultimate and finalizing object; in the final analysis he would be not-God.[60] Therefore God, who is the fullness of being, loves human beings insofar as he "uses" them, but not in the way that we "use" others in our love of the neighbor. The analogy brings into focus the vast difference between God and human beings and the absolute ontological divine transcendence: God loves as creator, humans love as creatures; God's love is changeless, the love of human beings is subject to the mutability of their nature; the love of human beings spurs them to the enjoyment of God, while God loves them because they enjoy him.[61] It is this "theocentric perspective" that governs

origin of the *uti-frui* distinction in Augustine). On the special relevance of this doctrine for ethics see O'Connor, "The *Uti-frui* Distinction," 43.

54. K. Holl, "Augustins innere Entwicklung," *Gesammelte Aufsätze zur Kirchenge-schichte* 3 (1938) 54–116.
55. A. Nygren, *Agape and Eros*, trans. P. S. Watson (Philadelphia, 1953) 449–562.
56. O'Connor, "The *Uti-frui* Distinction," 45.
57. See O. O'Donovan, *The Problem of Self-Love in Saint Augustine* (New Haven, 1980) 158–159; in the author's view the criticism of Augustine's opponents is directed against the hedonism which they find in the Augustinian conception.
58. R. Bodei, *"Ordo amoris." Conflitti terreni e felicità celeste* (Bologna, 1991) 153. See Augustine, Sermon 301/A, 6.
59. A. Di Giovanni, "Metafisica del Dio-Amore nel *De Doctrina Christiana*," *Augustinianum* 6 (1966) 294–300.
60. *Ibid.*, 296.
61. I, 31, 34—32, 35. See Di Giovanni, "Metafisica del Dio-Amore," 299–300.

Augustinian anthropology, the original contributions of which enrich the fundamental elements of the patristic tradition.[62]

Having received from God "both their very existence and their love for him,"[63] human beings are taken up and elevated to the level of "participation," which makes them be "in the image and likeness" of God; and this elevated "nature" of theirs flows out and finds expression in the dynamic love that is the essence of the image-likeness, which is in constant tension toward the Infinite.[64] What is brought to light here is the true, that is, interior, character of our journey of purification, in the footsteps of Christ, toward the beatifying union with the changeless Truth.[65]

The complex subject of the Christian freedom that presides over this journey of purification and salvation is the subject of a rapid but important reference in connection with signs,[66] that is, with "things" that signify other things and refer to these. Among these signs are the sacraments, such as baptism and the Eucharist "so awesome to understand and so pure and chaste to celebrate." These we venerate "not in a spirit of carnal slavery, but rather of spiritual freedom," so that we will not be slavishly bound to the letter and will avoid substituting the "signs" as such for the things signified.[67] The reference to and broad distinction between sign and thing signified are an indispensable element in any discussion of the sacramental teaching of Augustine, in which *sacramentum* is normally connected with sign.[68]

A further original touch is to be found in the context of the subject under discussion: freedom thus understood is also a liberation that is expressed in

---

62. See V. Grossi, *Lineamenti di antropologia patristica* (Rome, 1083) 63, 103, 137–139; A. G. Hamman, *L'uomo immagine somigliante di Dio*, Italian ed. under the general editorship of E. Giannarelli (Milan, 1991) 54.

63. I, 29, 30.

64. See I, 33, 36—34, 38. This is an echo of the characteristic *epektasis* ("stretching out; reaching forth") of Gregory of Nyssa.

65. I, 10, 10 and I, 17, 16. On the relationship to the analogous theme in Plato see Alici, *S. Agostino d'Ippona*, 112, note 1.

66. II, 1, 1; III, 8, 12—9, 13.

67. III, 9, 13. See *Teacher* 9: the knowledge of the *res* is "worth more" than the knowledge of the *signum*.

68. Augustine follows the line taken by the Roman and African tradition, not that of his teacher, Ambrose. The *res sacramenti* belongs to the order of symbolism, while the *virtus* or *vis sacramenti* has to do with the efficacy of the sacrament. The *res sacramenti* is Christ and indirectly grace. See H. M. Féret, *"Sacramentum, res, dans la langue théologique de S. Augustin," Revue des sciences philosophiques et théologiques* 29 (1940) 232–240. See N. Bobrinksoy, "L'Esprit du Christ dans les sacrements chez Jean Chrysostome et Augustin," in *Jean Chrysostome et Augustin* (Actes du Colloque de Chantilly 22–24 Sept. 1974), ed. Ch. Kannengiesser (Théologie historique 35; Paris, 1975) 263–264.

and made a reality by the resurrection of the Lord,[69] which thus advances and guides the eschatological journey of sacramental grace.[70]

A subtle and widespread snare endangers human freedom: the superstitious practices more or less connected with magic. An especially harmful practice is astrology with its resulting astrological fatalism.[71] Writers before or contemporary with Augustine attacked the foolishness of this "birthday science," which imagined that it could predict the fate of the newborn child on the basis of mysterious calculations of the position of the stars at the moment of its birth.[72] But, using the well-known and widespread argument of Carneades, they attacked more explicitly the disturbing results of astrological fatalism, which strangled personal freedom and destroyed the foundation of social life.[73]

With the dialectic of freedom and with the theology of Christian love is connected the theme of love of self and of one's own body, as part of the problematic relationship of body and soul.[74] In dealing with this problem here Augustine remains "closer to the Pauline reading of it than to the dualistic presuppositions of Neoplatonism"[75] that are to be seen in other Augustinian contexts. The view expressed here is a reasonable balance in which the writer asserts the positive value of the body but at the same time its subordination to the life of the spirit in a relationship of integration and harmony that is pursued in this life and rendered complete and comprehensive in eternity after the resurrection.

In this view there is implicit a theological perspective involving creation and the incarnation and resurrection of Christ, and, at the same time, the theology of the mystical body.[76] The theology of the incarnation, in particular, brings out the positive value of the human body and the unsustainability of any depreciation of and attack upon the body.[77] The resurrection will renew the substantial union of body and soul, ensuring an indestructible existence for both; but it will bring death to the wicked and eternal life to the just. In the first case, there is a clear reference to the "second death" that definitively and permanently separates the soul from God. This death is due to the attitude of those who do not renounce the world or undertake

---

69. It is in this sense that I understand the pregnant meaning of "freedom" as used by Augustine in III, 9, 13: "the clearest indication of our freedom has shone upon us in the resurrection of our Lord."
70. See C. Couturier, "Eschatology in the Sacramental Teaching of Saint Augustine," *Studia Theologica* 1 (1947) 5–26.
71. II, 20, 30—23, 35.
72. II, 22, 33–34.
73. See Basil of Caesarea, *Hexaem.* 6, 7; D. Amand, *Fatalisme et liberté dans l'antiquité grecque* (Amsterdam, 1973) 382.
74. I, 24, 24—25, 26.
75. Alici, *S. Agostino d'Ippona*, 126, note 1.
76. I, 11, 11—16, 15.
77. I, 11, 11—12, 13. See *City of God* X, 29, 2; Alici, *S. Agostino d'Ippona*, 126, note 3.

the journey of conformity to the truth and are therefore "dragged down by the death of the body into a more grievous death still."[78]

These are the most important "fragments" of theology that are strewn especially throughout the first book of *Teaching Christianity*; but the fragments are solidly connected with the dominant idea, namely, "the theology of Christian love" that is revealed in the scriptures.

Dogmatic Exegesis

In a short essay entitled "Exegesis and Dogmatic Theology,"[79] Karl Rahner brought into focus the not always peaceful relationship between exegetes and dogmatic theologians and pointed out the attitude of mutual coldness and distrust and even, at times, of resentment that prevailed between them. The result was a certain distance between the two camps of exegesis and dogmatic theology. To bridge this gap Rahner proposed a method and a basic objective, namely, to do both exegesis and dogmatic theology as a "service" to the Magisterium and therefore to all human beings, to whom the gospel message is addressed. This is a very pastoral outlook, in which tasks of a rather overwhelmingly scientific and technical nature are directed to facilitating the teaching of the faith to modern human beings.[80]

As in the case of the earlier-mentioned relation between theology and pastoral practice, the problem of exegesis and dogmatic theology calls for a return to the experience of the Fathers, for whom exegesis and dogmatic theology normally worked hand in hand. Augustine is a typical example of this collaboration: his dogmatic works show a solid basis in biblical exegesis, and in his specifically exegetical works, especially those that are wide-ranging, we see exegesis firmly directed to the service of a dominant doctrinal concern.[81] But a critical appraisal of Augustinian exegesis in its various aspects, on which a great deal has been written, is a complicated matter, since it must take into account, first and foremost, a vast activity that was carried on over a lengthy period of time and thus made room for a succession of understandable second thoughts and nuanced changes of view.[82]

From the viewpoint of the long-lasting controversy between literalists and allegorists Augustine's exegesis is quite balanced: while he gives a sometimes exclusively literal interpretation of many pages of scripture,

---

78. I, 20, 19. See Alici, *S. Agostino d'Ippona*, 119, note 1.
79. K. Rahner, "Exegesis and Dogmatic Theology," *Theological Investigations* 5, trans. K.-H. Kruger (Baltimore, 1966) 67–93.
80. H. Rahner, *Ecclesiologia dei Padri* (Rome, 1971) 38.
81. See Simonetti, *Lettera e/o allegoria*, 342–344, 354. The main doctrinal themes discussed in Augustinian exegesis are given in M. Pontet, *L'exégèse de S. Augustin prédicateur* (Paris, n. d.); M. Comeau, *Saint Augustin exégète du quatrième évangile* (Paris, 1930).
82. See B. De Margerie, *Introduzione alla storia dell'esegesi* 3. *Sant'Agostino*, Italian trans. ed. by V. Grossi (Rome, 1986).

his predilection for the spiritual meaning makes him an exegete who is "ready to engage in allegorizing, but in moderation," all the more so since he understands allegory in a broad sense as "an interpretation based on figures" and usually uses such words as "figure" in referring to the idea.[83]

Teaching Christianity is a basic text for understanding the methodology and motifs that are typical of Augustinian exegesis. A foundational principle is the superiority of the scriptures over every other rich text and even over the very treasures of pagan culture,[84] the reason being that the scriptures "contain everything that a Christian, whether layperson or cleric, needs to know."[85] But the scriptures often put difficulties of various kinds in the way of understanding, although, on the other hand, these are providential means of overcoming pride through committed toil and of refreshing the mind when it experiences boredom.[86] Augustine had had personal experience of these difficulties: the bare simplicity and great modesty of the scriptures, which intellectual pride rejected as "unworthy of being compared with the dignity of Cicero";[87] embarrassment at inconsistencies in the text, or the "disagreement" between some narratives, such as the two genealogies of Christ in Matthew and Luke.[88]

A further difficulty is due to the polysemy, or plurality of senses, in the scriptures, a problem that engaged Augustine in various forms and for a long time and that finds definitive formulations and "real progress" in *Teaching Christianity*.[89] The "different" sense extracted from a biblical passage is legitimate if it is confirmed by other passages of scripture and is therefore "in agreement with the truth": this falls under the action of God's Spirit and of providence, which thus reveals the full, generous fruitfulness of the scriptures.[90] Only a person "well equipped and well furnished" will

---

83. Simonetti, *Lettera e/o allegoria*, 341–342, note 404; 354. See the analysis by M. Marin, "'Allegoria' in Agostino," in *La terminologia esegetica nell'antichità* (Atti del Primo Seminario di antichità cristiana, Bari, 25 ottobre 1985; = Quaderni di *Vetera Christianorum* 20) 135–161; G. Ripani, "L'allegoria o l'*intellectus figuratus* nel *De doctrina christiana* di Agostino," *Revue des études augustiniennes* 18 (1972) 219–220.

84. II, 42, 63.

85. Marrou, *Saint Augustine, and his influence through the ages* (London, New York, 1957)

86. II, 6, 7. There are difficulties in understanding this passage. Green's text in CSEL 80: *ad.... intellectum a fastidio renovandum*, which the codices support, has been corrected and apparently normalized by other editors: *ad.... revocandum (removendum?)*. For the reading of the codices and Green, which I follow, see Quintilian, *Inst.* 6, 3, 1: *risus animum.... a fatigatione renovat*.

87. III, 5, 9.

88. De Margerie, *Introduzione* 3:16–17.

89. III, 25, 25—27, 38. See De Margerie, *Introduzione* 3:68.

90. Urged by his pastoral sense Augustine does not offer Christians a training in criticism but "endeavors to arouse in them a spiritual yearning" (Pontet, *L'exégèse de S. Augustin prédicateur*, 148).

be able to discuss and resolve the obscurities and many ambiguities contained in the scriptures.[91]

In dealing with signs, the ambiguities of which are due to sin,[92] it will be necessary above all to distinguish between the "proper" and "metaphorical" senses[93] and to allow oneself to be guided by the Spirit who gives life and to avoid being enslaved by the letter that kills.[94] Even the seven exegetical "rules" set down by Tychonius for the allegorical interpretation of difficult or ambiguous biblical passages—rules which Augustine acknowledges to be of great help in understanding the scriptures—are used under the standard and with the attitude of spiritual freedom that allows the person to rise above the rigid formulations of these rules and to find new "rules" beyond them. In any case, it will be useful and even necessary to have recourse at every moment to the authority of the Church, to which Christ has entrusted the Bible as a "sign."[95]

Charity is the essential and supreme hermeneutical criterion in Augustinian exegesis. Exegesis is thus linked to the central theology of love, and Augustine can, even as an exegete, be called the "Doctor of charity."[96] The study of scripture must be done with a diligent and unremitting attention, "until your interpretation of it is led right through to the kingdom of charity."[97] This is accomplished in the light of five fundamental principles involving the three theological virtues of faith, hope, and charity; while the first two fade away in eternal life, charity "will abide, more vigorous and certain than ever."[98]

In this way, every error will be avoided, especially the error of loving one's own interpretation to the detriment of the scriptures themselves, the result then being a vacillating faith and a consequent drying up of charity. Augustine's insight sees in this process an evangelical paradox: those who have firm possession of the three theological virtues have no need of the scriptures except "as a means of forming others." Many, in fact, are able to live in solitude "without books," because what the apostle says[99] in an eschatological perspective that applies to the here and now has already come to pass in them: *"As for prophecies, they shall be done away with, as for tongues, they shall cease, as for knowledge, it shall be done away with."*[100]

---

91. 3, 1, 1.
92. II, 4, 5.
93. II, 10, 15; III, 10, 14.
94. See Alici, *S. Agostino d'Ippona*, 230–231, note 1.
95. See IV, 8, 22.
96. De Margerie, *Introduzione* 3:33, 44, 178.
97. III, 15, 23.
98. I, 36, 40—40, 44. See 1 Cor 13:8 and 13.
99. 1 Cor 13:8.
100. I, 39, 43.

Scripture is thus "the means by which we are carried along" and is destined to disappear when we have reached the final goal.[101] The image of a journey, which has already been applied to the ongoing ethical tension in human life, returns now as an exegetical journey through the seven degrees or stages of love:[102] fearful knowledge of the divine will; modesty and piety in the presence of scripture; true knowledge that teaches us to love God for his own sake and the neighbor for the sake of God; fortitude; "counsel which goes with mercy"; love of neighbor with eyes purified; and, finally, "wisdom," the last and most important stage on a journey that starts with fear of God[103] and reaches the joy of a full and serene contemplation of changeless love.[104] Love thus guides and coordinates all the stages of this biblical ascent in accordance with a dynamic that becomes exemplary for the relationship between knowledge and charity.

Augustine devotes a lengthy section, in which he also takes up difficulties and deviations, to the role of knowledge in relation to the scriptures, knowledge being seen both as careful study and as a necessary store of wide-ranging information.[105] Knowledge inspired by love builds up; otherwise it is empty, as the apostle says: *Knowledge puffs up, love builds up* (1 Cor 8:2). Only when accompanied by love does knowledge pierce the mystery and reach a level that is "existential and experiential." Paul's profound words to the Ephesians supply the key to this kind of knowledge,[106] for they enable us to glimpse and "know" the mystery of the cross, the dimensions of which embrace the universe.[107] Two inseparable elements form the center and high point of this "existential experience": the hearing of the word and the Eucharist.[108] It is chiefly in the privileged area of the New Testament dispensation that Augustine's exegesis, which is characteristically Christocentric and ecclesial, forms a solid biblical theology.[109]

Apart from the limitations noted and the reservations voiced by critics,[110] these are the most important and original results of Augustinian exegesis. It is these that the few references to *Teaching Christianity* were meant to set forth and reconfirm.

---

101. 101. On the theme of the transitoriness of the scriptures as such see de Margerie, *Introduzione* 3:38, 42, and 52, with the implicit application of the *uti-frui* theory to the scriptures.
102. II, 7, 9–11.
103. See Ps 110:10; Sir 1:16.
104. The journey described is that of the purification of wisdom, an idea that goes back to Plato (*Phaedo* 99c-d). See *Teaching Christianity* I, 10, 10; Alici, *S. Agostino d'Ippona*, 112, note 1; 159, note 4.
105. 105. II, 7, 9—41, 62.
106. Eph 3:18–19.
107. II, 41, 62. See H. Schlier, *Lettera agli Efesini* (Brescia, 1965) 208–212. The Pauline idea of the cosmic significance of the cross had long inspired patristic soteriology. See Justin, *Apol. I*, 55.
108. Sermon 56, 6, 10; 58, 4, 5; see de Margerie, *Introduzione* 3:182–85.
109. De Margerie, *Introduzione* 3:139, 179.
110. *Ibid.*, 174–81.

Theology of Oratory

The fourth book of *Teaching Christianity* is devoted, as Augustine himself says, to "a way to put across to others what has been understood"[111] or, to put it even more briefly, to the subject of Christian eloquence. While prescinding from the properly rhetorical aspects, which will be considered separately, it seems appropriate to call attention here to the underlying theology that characterizes and defines Augustine's explanation.

First of all, the basic assertion Augustine makes is that rhetoric, whose devices are useful but not indispensable, must serve the truth, defend it against error, and advance it.[112] Following this line of thought, we reach a close relationship, even a kind of unification, of eloquence with "wisdom,"[113] but a union in which "content controls form."[114] On the other hand, the supreme and unquestionable source of truth and "wisdom" is the scriptures. Consequently, the contents, the very form, and the explanatory tools will be modeled on what the scriptures dictate, since these proclaim the great truths of salvation. Thus for the Christian orator everything he says will always be of great importance.[115]

The three functions of eloquence—to teach, to delight, to sway[116]—will also draw their substantial inspiration from the requirements of the scriptures. Teaching, which is a response to the Lord's categorical command,[117] predominates and justifies the other two. But, as has been said elsewhere, all this, once again, presupposes and requires love as guide and standard of pedagogy.[118] Moreover, the determining motif in which the true teaching—oral or written—of a Christian "orator" is summed up and brought to completion is prayer; this is the last and most important of the ten rules governing Christian eloquence:[119] let the preacher trust more in "the piety of prayer" than in oratorical resources; "let him be a pray-er before being a speaker."[120]

This final exhortation, which "certainly does not sound like a mere passing thought,"[121] is evidence once again of the typical Augustinian linking of theology and pastoral practice with exegesis; it also sums up what may

---

111. I, 1, 1; IV, 1, 1.
112. IV, 2, 3.
113. IV, 5, 7—6, 10.
114. M. Marin, "Retorica ed esegesi in Sant'Agostino," in *L'umanesimo di Sant'Agostino* (Mari, 1988) 216.
115. IV, 18, 35.
116. IV, 18, 35.

116. IV, 12, 27—14, 31.
117. Mt 28:19.
118. See *The Instruction of Beginners* III, 6, 4.
119. IV, 22, 51—30, 63.
120. IV, 15, 32. See Letter 130. See *The Teacher* 7 for the connection between prayer and teaching.
121. Alici, *S. Agostino d'Ippona*, 360, note 1

be called the vertical and transcendent theological orientation of *Teaching Christianity.*

Mario Naldini

Sign and Language

"Through Material Things to Immaterial"

Following an obviously classical model,[1] Augustine identifies "three classes of seafarers" in the introduction to his youthful dialogue *The Happy Life*. The first "consists of those who, having reached the use of reason, with but little effort and a slight stroke of the oars, go only a little distance away. There they establish themselves in such tranquillity that they erect for as many other citizens as possible a very bright sign of their own work." The second class includes all who let themselves be fooled by the apparent state of the sea, head out into the deep, and sail far from their homeland, driven by an uncontrollable wind. The third class, finally, in which Augustine places himself, consists of all who, "on the very threshold of youth, or after being already long tossed about, still perceive some familiar signs and remember, even amid the waves, the great sweetness of home.... They take the direct course, in no way deceived, and without delay reach home again."[2] The image is not simply a vague literary reminiscence; it already contains, in a nutshell, an idea that will leave a deep mark on Augustine's interior journey in search of truth, giving it that special combination of faith lived and faith thought out that has made it in many respects emblematic of the human condition itself and has given it a classical, perennially valid status.[3] Above all, the image expresses the conception of a quest in which the subject himself is called into question, to the point of laying siege to the roots of his being. Thus Augustine will exclaim in the *Confessions*: "I have become for myself a soil which is a cause of difficulty and much sweat."[4]

Sailing, then, is a disquieting metaphor for human confusion, in which the ups and downs of a life are interwoven with the labor of reflection: the nostalgia for a safe harbor, which the reading of Cicero awakened in

---

1.   See, among others, Plato, *Polit.* 518c-d; Aristotle, *Nicom.* 1095b17.
2.   *The Happy Life* I, 2. L. Pizzolato emphasizes in detail the importance of this passage in his "Il *De beata vita* o la possibile felicità nel tempo," in *L'opera letteraria di Agostino tra Cassiciacum e Milano* (Palermo, 1987) 53–55.
3.   I refer the reader to my essay "Agostino tra fede e ricerca: la conversione del'intelligenza," *Agostino e la conversione cristiana* (Palermo, 1987) 35–53.
4.   *Confessions* X, 16, 25; see X, 28, 39; X, 33, 50. Citing this passage in his *Being and Time*, Heidegger would observe: "That which is ontically closest and well-known, is ontologically the farthest and not known at all" (M. Heidegger, *Being and Time*, trans. J. Macquarrie and E. Robinson (New York, 1962) 69.

Augustine, is not enough by itself to bring him out of the darkness that condemns him to drift, although it is a first and indispensable way of orienting himself. Enthusiasm and disillusionment alternate as long as he has not yet glimpsed the polar star that will show him the irreversible course his life is to take. But long-standing resistances hinder the sailing and render its progress uncertain; among these, is "a huge mountain that rises in front of the harbor."[5] This is in a certain sense the final temptation, for it represents "the proud quest of an utterly meaningless glory (*superbum studium inanissimae gloriae*)."

The image Augustine uses of a hollow mountain, of a crumbling but enticing ground that swallows up the traveler now close to his native land by blinding him and causing him to plunge from light into darkness, is not only an effective picture of the gap between authority and reason that is characteristic of his early writings. It also provides an interpretive key to two different ways of conceiving the journey to truth: a proudly and abstractly rationalist way that abandons human beings to captivity by the immediate and suffocates their understanding; the other, that of those who are disposed to let faith guide them by providing what are at best mediated ways of understanding.

The nautical metaphor allows the author to take his own demand for meaning and salvation and to articulate a rereading of it in terms of the pattern of going astray and rediscovery. This in turn is reinforced by a set of appropriate parallels: life as a quest in which the subject is put in the first person and becomes a "great question" to himself; the value of the final goal, which must be identified and reached while overcoming the recurring temptation to let oneself be led astray by false objectives; the importance of the intermediate means of orienting oneself; the necessity of jettisoning all useless clutter.

The outlook is still one of vibrant joy, dominated by the central event of the return to God and by the determination to consecrate himself entirely to God's service. Even at this point it is already possible to catch a glimpse of the guiding lines along which future works will develop, especially the determination not to isolate the event of conversion as a nonrepeatable individual experience that is to be retold simply for edification, and the resultant effort to rethink it in universal terms by discovering in it the source of a structural tension proper to human beings. In this perspective, the problem of the relation between the search for truth and the possession of it, around which much of the *Answer to the Academics* is structured, will arise again and converge with its parallel, the faith that tends toward truth just as time does toward eternity.[6]

The Cassiciacum dialogues thus seem to reach a first, delicate balance between faith and searching, in which the problems inherent in a philo-

---

5.　*The Happy Life* I, 3.
6.　See *The Trinity* 4, 18, 24.

sophical sea journey, though necessary and difficult,[7] are linked with the newness of a "happy life" already glimpsed as the final landfall and even already savored at each stage of an ever more demanding advance in a personal history. These works exist for the most part under the sign of a twofold confidence. The first is confidence in the possibility of rethinking the Christian message in an organized way, in which it is seen as the completion and explicitation of the truest demands of classical culture, from the Neoplatonic idea of a philosophical life as a spiritual asceticism to the combination of authority and reason, through which the inheritance of Latin culture may be filtered. The second is a human confidence in the practicability of this idea, a confidence based on the conviction, initially rather simplistic and, as it were, prepelagian (even according to Pizzolato[8]), of the easy victory of reason over bodily conditions, a thesis, this, that was probably conditioned by the Plotinian idea of the goodness of existence and by a strong will to achieve emancipation from Manichean dualism.

Along with this trend, and partially as a corrective of it, there gradually emerges in the reflection of the now converted Augustine an attention to concrete problems of education. Here a fund of solid pedagogical realism, reinforced to some extent by his not always positive professional experience as a young rhetorician, is combined with the new perspective opened up by his journey in the Christian faith, which he now accepts completely.

This formative intention seems to take concrete form essentially along two lines: on the one hand, in the attempt at an organized rethinking of the whole of the liberal arts, as he plans to devote a series of treatises to each of these;[9] on the other, in starting to think about the communicative potentialities of language and the implications of language in the realm of

---

7. See *The Happy Life* I, 5.
8. See Pizzolato, 31–112: between 394 and 397 Augustine explicitly holds the thesis that, as long as it is in time, the body invincibly resists the spirit and therefore happiness cannot be attained within history (see 109). This judgment is very different from that of Flasch who maintains, on the basis of other arguments, that the Augustinian "exaltation of rationality was entirely rhetorical and external or, to put it better, was the result of a Stoic and Neoplatonic philosophy that had been reduced to mere edification and taken from its context" (K. Flasch, *Agostino d'Ippona. Introduzione all'opera filosofica* [Bologna, 1983] 133).
9. The projected works on the liberal arts were to be divided into seven treatises: grammar, dialectics, rhetoric, arithmetic, music, geometry, and philosophy (see *Revisions* I, 5, 6). In opposition to Marrou, who sees formulated in this division the basis of classical culture and the meeting point of Isocrates' literary model and Plato's philosophical model (see H.-I. Marrou, "Les arts liberaux dans l'antiquité classique," in *Arts liberaux et philosophie au Moyen Age* [Montreal-Paris, 1969] 12), there are those who hold that the idea of a cycle of liberal arts as the first and fundamental stage in the establishment of the Trivium and Quadrivium appeared for the first time in Augustine himself, where it is clearly derived from Neoplatonism and from Porphyry in particular (see I. Hadot, *Arts libéraux et philosophie dans la pensée antique* [Paris, 1984] 25–60). On this point I refer the reader to some reflections in my introduction to: *San Agostino. La dottrina cristiana* (Milan, 1989) 16–17.

teaching.[10] Starting with the dialogues, Augustine outlines an educational project that can lead human beings through material things to immaterial (*per corporalia ad incorporalia*). In this plan, the encyclopedic structure, as it appears in, for example, *Order*, which contains a kind of "miniature encyclopedia,"[11] already has a first philosophical support in the Neoplatonic problematic of the mediation between the intelligible and sensible orders; this problem will later receive a complete, Christocentric solution, but even at this early point it contributes to the sketching of a theory of signs as the essence of this ascent to immaterial things.

From Dialectic to The Teacher

The semiotic practices that had developed in various areas of life in the ancient world, from divination to medicine, had served as a point of convergence for various needs and problems and had fed a theoretical reflection that runs through the whole of Greek philosophy after being given basic form in the work of Plato and Aristotle. "But," Manetti points out, "in the transition from the Greek to the Roman world the semiotic paradigm leaves the field of philosophy in the strict sense of this term and takes a central place in the areas of rhetoric and law."[12] In particular, the fact that in judiciary matters signs came to be regarded as investigative pointers had given rhetoric new tasks in the classification of signs, calling upon it to determine their various degrees of probative worth and of value in argumentation. When the question was faced by the Stoics in a rationalist perspective and by the Epicureans in a more empirical perspective, the challenge put to the legal craft became henceforth an unavoidable point of reference.[13]

Through the study of evidence pointing to guilt broader theoretical implications soon surfaced, beginning with the possibility of moving from a set of sensible data to a set of meanings that are reconstructed through imagination and inference. The problematic character of this movement brings an awareness, according to Crapis, "of the varying epistemological values of signs and of the fact that their capacity to convey meaning is often based on social conventions rather than on scientific laws." Orators

---

10. On this subject see C. P. Mayer, *Die Zeichen in der geistigen Entwicklung und in der Theologie des jungen Augustinus* (Würzburg, 1969) 109–110.
11. U. Pizzani, "L'enciclopedia agostiniana e i suoi problemi," in *Atti del Congresso internazionale su S. Agostino nel XVI centenario della conversione* I (Rome, 1987) 332. The very dialectical movement from the corporeal to the incorporeal displays echoes of Varro according to A. Solignac, "Doxographies et manuels dans la formation philosophique de Saint Augustin," *Recherches augustiniennes* 1 (1958) 122.
12. G. Manetti, *Le teorie del segno nell'antichità* (Milan, 1987) 201.
13. See A. Giuliani, *Il concetto di prova* (Milan, 1961).

are therefore urged "to point out the inherent polysemy of signs when there is question of refuting an adversary's argument."[14]

In this context, Augustine's semiology occupies a crucial position, for he developed a synthesis that was new by comparison with earlier positions, while in other respects he anticipated some tendencies that would show up fully only in modern thought.[15] Augustine seems especially aware of some characteristic elements of Stoic logic, especially of its interest in hypothetical syllogisms and in dialectics.[16]

As early as his youthful work *Dialectic,* which was composed around 387 and the authenticity of which today seems definitively established, he had explained the relationship between dialectic ("dialectic is the science of good argument"[17]) and grammar, saying that the latter is concerned primarily with the study of words as sounds.[18] In the Stoic perspective, the heart of philosophical discourse is to be found in the logical structure of the *sêmeion* or sign,[19] thus giving rise to a conception of language as a formal structure of meaning, a conception in which the proposition provides the connecting link between signifier and signified. But this perspective did not seem to offer the fusion between theory of signs and theory of language that appears for the first time, in an explicit and conscious form, in Augustine himself.[20] Augustine's attention is now focused on the *verbum simplex,* which serves as the starting point for an analysis of words as signs; the latter affect not only sense perception but mental understanding.

In *Dialectic,* therefore, there already seems to be present a triadic conception of signs, one that distinguishes between meaning (*dicibile*), signifier (*vox articulata, sonus*), and referent (*res*).[21] Augustine will retain the same

14. C. Crapis, "Il concetto di segno nelle teorie retoriche: La *Retorica ad Alessansro* di Anassimene di Lampsaco," *Segni e comprensione* 5/12 (1991) 15.
15. This is the position of Eco, among others; he sees Augustine as moving toward a new "instructional" model of semantic description, according to which the meaning of a term "is a block (a series, a system) of instructions for its possible insertion into contexts and for its various successful semantic uses in various contexts (all of which, however, can be registered in the terms of the code)" (U. Eco, *Semiotica e filosofia del linguaggio* [Turin, 1984] 34). This judgment is reported and shared by Manetti, *Le teorie del segno,* 241.
16. See G. Verbeke, "Augustin et le stoïcisme," *Recherches augustiniennes* 1 (1958) 77. On Stoic logic see M. Baldassarri, *Introduzione alla logica stoica. Testimonianze e frammenti. Testi originali con introduzione e traduzione commentata* (Como, 1985); S. Bobzien, *Die stoische Modallogik* (Würzburg, 1986). On the development of these doctrines see M. Colish, *The Stoic Tradition from Antiquity to the Early Middle Ages* (2 vols.; Leiden, 1985).
17. *Dialectic* 1, 1.
18. See J. Pépin, *Saint Augustin et la dialectique* (Villanova, 1976) 9–10.
19. See G. Preti, "Sulla dottrina del *sêmeion* nella logica stoica," *Rivista critica di storia della filosopfia* 11 (1956) 5–14; reprinted in *Saggi filosofici* II. *Storia della logica e storiografia filosofica* (Florence, 1976) 3–16.
20. See Manetti, *Le teorie del segno,* 226–27.
21. In *Dialectic* a distinction is made between the *verbum* (the word that designates itself), the *dicibile,* that is, what the mind understands, and the *dictio,* that is, the

approach later on, and the majority of interpreters have emphasized, with varying nuances,[22] his dependence on Stoicism in this matter, although others urge that equal account be taken of the Aristotelean conception.[23] In particular, we already find in Augustine, thanks to the notion of *dictio*, a direct connection between sign and language,[24] with a resultant substantial unification of perspective in which language displays new potentialities that finally transcend the semantic limits of early theories, which were restricted to nonverbal signs.

Not by accident, the Augustinian encyclopedia seems to be based on a fundamental interconnection between language and reality, between the sphere of signs and the sphere of things, an interconnection which medieval education will repeat in the well-known distinction between the Trivium and the Quadrivium. Within this basic system, then, a study of the structure of the liberal arts requires a further investigation into the genesis, nature, and limits of language as a tool. This is the context of *The Teacher*, a dialogue between Augustine and his son Adeodatus; its focus is the role of the interior teacher, and it attempts to outline an initial philosophical and theological synthesis by combining the invitation to open the self to the teaching of the only real teacher with a more properly methodological problematic that sheds new light on the possibility of learning, of interpersonal communication, and on the profound dynamics of interior understanding.[25] Eco says

---

word insofar as it points to something other than itself. The *res*, finally, is everything that is not the *verbum*, the *dicibile*, or the *dictio*. On this see G. Bouchard, "La conception augustinienne du signe selon Tzvetan Todorov," *Recherches augustiniennes* 15 (1980) 312–317.

22. See, for example, T. Todorov, *Theories of the Symbol*, trans. C. Porter (Ithaca, 1982) 37, who agrees with Pépin in emphasizing the correspondence between the terms *dictio*, *dicibile*, and *res*, on the one hand, and the respective Stoic terms *lexis*, *lekton*, and *tynkanon*, on the other. As the reader will know, according to Stoic dialectic there is a difference between signifier and signified, this last being distinct, however, from the really existing thing; from this point of view, Markus says, the Stoics placed an intermediary of a conceptual kind between sign and thing (see R. A. Markus, "Saint Augustine on Signs," *Phronesis* 2 [1957] 60–83), while other interpreters, who stress the Aristotelean origin of a connection thus conceived, prefer to speak of an incorporeal entity (the *lekton*) that exists only in thought (see E, Brehier, *La théorie des incorporels dans l'ancien stoïcisme* [Paris, 1970⁴; 14–36).

23. See, among other, Pépin, *Saint Augustin et la dialectique*, 67–81, who emphasizes the exact correspondence in Augustine with the terminology of Aristotle as well as with that of the Stoics. According to Darrell Jackson, too, who maintains the thesis that it is words that express meanings, Augustine is closer to Aristotle than to the Stoics; see B. Darrell Jackson, "The Theory of Signs in Saint Augustine's *De doctrina christiana*," *Revue des études augustiniennes* 15 (1969) 38.

24. See M. Baratin, "Origines stoïciennes de la théorie augustinienne du signe," *Revue des études latines* 59 (1981) 260–268. The thesis is cited and shared by Manetti, *Le teorie del segno*, 228.

25. See G.-H. Allard, "Arts libéraux et langage chez Saint Augustin," in *Arts libéraux et Philosophie au Moyen Age*, 481–492. I refer the reader to my own work, *Il*

that in *The Teacher* "Augustine will effect a definitive fusion between the theory of signs and the theory of language."[26]

The idea of an "interior teacher," which has already made its appearance in Augustine's first writings,[27] receives here its fullest explicit form. As Pieretti observes, "The basis of the ability to convey meaning is not in the signs but in the things to which they refer or, more accurately still, in the truth that renders them intelligible. For this reason, the speakers in the dialogue proceed to ascertain whether and how it is possible to teach. The result is the pedagogical aspect of *The Teacher*."[28] Augustine himself says:

> As for all the things which we "understand," it is not the outward sound of the speaker's words that we consult, but the truth which presides over the mind itself from within, though we have been led to consult it because of the words. Now He who is consulted and who is said to "dwell in the inner man," He it is who teaches us, namely Christ.[29]

In *The Teacher*, reflection on the dynamics of teaching is concerned essentially with finding a Christological basis for the doctrine of the interiority of truth,[30] although the theme seems to be already filtered through a confrontation with the pedagogical culture of the pagan world and, in particular, with the disciplines by which this culture was transmitted in institutionalized and methodologically articulated forms.

Toward a Christian "Doctrine"

Ratzinger writes that in regard to the contemplative ideal which had been revised and tested during the retreat in Cassiciacum and which was in large measure dominated by the idea of limitless progress in wisdom, "the year 391 created a completely new situation for Augustine."[31] First his priestly ministry and then his episcopal consecration a few years later gave

linguaggio come segno e come testimonianza. Una rilettura di Agostino (Rome, 1976).

26. Eco, *Semiotica*, 33.
27. See *The Happy Life* IV, 35; *Soliloquies* I, 1, 1.
28. A. Pieretti, "Introduzione," in *S. Agostino d'Ippona. Il Maestro* (Milan, 1990) 50.
29. *The Teacher* 11, 38.
30. Pieretti, again, comments: "That which comes last in *The Teacher*, that is, truth in the interiority of human beings and therefore God as sole teacher is in fact first when it comes to the treatise's logico-conceptual articulation" ("Introduzione," 53).
31. J. Ratzinger, *Popolo e casa di Dio in sant'Agostino* (Milan, 1971) 57. Among others who emphasize the importance of this event in the development of Augustine's thought are M. Wundt, "Ein Wendepunkt in Augustins Entwicklung," *Zeitschrift für die neutestamentliche Wissenschaft und die Kunde der älteren Kirche* 21 (1921) 53–64; H. Hagendahl, *Augustine and the Latin Classics* II (Göteborg, 1967) 714.

him new reasons for concerning himself with, and a new attentiveness to, the tradition of the Church, the works of the Fathers, and the theological positions that were emerging in Africa. As Marrou, too, has brought out, unforeseen pastoral responsibilities henceforth draw Augustine away for good from the intellectual mold of "a minority that led an artificial and impoverished existence" and opened his heart to the concerns "that make up the rough and simple life of human beings."[32]

A priest at thirty-six and a bishop at forty-two, Saint Augustine had already received his intellectual formation, and it was not possible for him to turn himself into a tabula rasa and rid himself of the intellectual baggage and mental habits he had acquired. But in Hippo his study became more focused and at the same time broadened; according to Marrou, this development "can be summed up in a few words: a deeper interior understanding of Christianity."[33] Naturally, the works he continued to write reflect this changed state of life; he broke off his projected series on the liberal arts and committed himself to a labor of deeper theological understanding that had formidable ramifications: from philosophical reflection to biblical exegesis, from spirituality to catechesis.

As a result, the gulf between the pagan and Christian authors also widened: the view that attributed to the former an exclusive competence in the matter of signs and to the latter an exclusive competence in dealing with things[34] is followed by a less black-and-white and more complex one that can be glimpsed in the *Confessions*. Without going into the theological questions that were preparing the slow gestation and composition of *Teaching Christianity*, since this would distract us from our specific concern here, we cannot fail to note how the Christian message is henceforth dealt with across the entire range of its theological, cultural, and pastoral potentialities.

In the letter to Dioscorus, written soon after Augustine's episcopal consecration, this vision is already outlined in a rather detailed way: the supreme and immutable good is something close to us and unmerited, nor should human beings try to attain to it by winding and misleading ways. It is therefore necessary to submit one's whole life, including the intellectual life, entirely to God. Jesus Christ is truth personified and only "a blindness of mind brought on by the filth of sin and the love of the flesh"[35] could make the learned waste all their time in empty debates. For this reason, the disciplines must be subordinated to the requirements of doctrine, that is, of what is to be taught. Neoplatonic philosophy with its powerful spiritual inspiration and Roman culture with its pragmatic awareness of institutions

---

32. H.-I. Marrou, *Saint Augustin et la fin de la culture antique* (Paris, 1958)
33. *Ibid.*, 281.
34. See *Answer to Adimantus* 11: "For as our authors, that is, the writers of the divine scriptures, thought chiefly of things, so almost the entire concern of secular authors is with words."
35. Letter 118, 5, 32.

are now placed in the service of a new project: the development of a global plan for education in the faith.

The primary point of reference here is the scriptures. "The Bible," Jaspers writes, "is [for Augustine] the sole source of essential truth."[36] When dealing with the sacred text one must therefore move beyond the idea of a rhetoric that is the science of persuading people regarding truth and falsehood[37] and undertake a new synthesis of wisdom and eloquence. During this period Augustine in fact devotes himself with greater intensity to the writing of exegetical works, such as the commentaries on the psalms, the gospel, the first letter of John, and Genesis, while at the same period attempting some theologico-pastoral syntheses.[38]

It is also important to note how in a letter to Jerome in 415 Augustine attacks the Stoics for their inability to grasp the element of perfectibility in the moral life and for imagining instead an immediate and painless passage from folly to wisdom. He defends rather the idea of a gradual progress in wisdom and of a love that is proportionate to the nature and degree of the virtues. We must not think, therefore, he writes, "of someone who as he passes from the water into the air, no sooner breaks the surface than he suddenly begins to take in all the air he needs, but rather of someone who as he advances from darkness toward the light, is more illumined, the closer he comes to it."[39] The text is a significant one, and Verbeke is right to stress its importance; he points out that for Augustine virtue has an essentially analogical character and by comparison with it Stoic ethics can only be rejected as inadequate, since it does not take account of human weakness and the constant need of divine grace. Consequently, human beings cannot find the source of their true happiness and perfection within themselves, but only in God.[40]

The idea of a progress in wisdom that depends on history and is subject to moral weakness and sin constitutes the philosophical ground on which Augustine erects his projected *Teaching Christianity*. In working on this project he revises some fundamental theses of Platonic and Neoplatonic anthropology and cosmology, which he had accepted in his youthful works and applied to the crucial problem of the soul's location intermediate between

---

36. K. Jaspers, *The Great Philosophers*, ed. H. Arendt, trans. R. Mannheim (2 vols.; New York, 1962, 1966) 1:186.
37. See, on the subject, M. Manzin, "Il problema della persuasione in Agostino d'Ippona," *Verifiche* 16 (1987) 3–27.
38. An example is *The Instruction of Beginners*, in which a model of elementary instruction in the Christian life is outlined, based on an analysis of the various stages in the history of salvation: Adam's sin, its punishment, the Old Testament as preparation, redemption brought by Christ, end of the world, last judgment. Other syntheses can be found in *Faith and the Creed, The Christian Struggle*, and *Handbook*. See A. M. Kleinberg, *"De agone christiano*. The Preacher and His Audience," *Journal of Theological Studies* 38 (1987) 16–33.
39. Letter 167, 3, 13.
40. See Verbeke, "Augustin et le stoïcisme," 72–73.

the body and God. Plotinus had discussed this question in *Enneads* IV, 8 ("The Soul's Descent into the Body"), where he reflected the tension felt by Plato himself between the more familiar idea of the soul as prison of the body and the idea which emerges especially in the *Timaeus*, namely, that the soul contributes from within to the elevation of the world.[41]

It was on this basis, then, that the question was raised of an intermediary (*medium*) that would make it possible to unite and cross over between the sensible and the intelligible worlds in virtue of what may be termed the ambivalent structure of the created world, a structure capable of joining within itself various orders of reality. Faced with this question, Augustine draws upon the technical baggage that came with his formation as a rhetorician, a formation that combined various elements in the culture of the age. Along with the inheritance of Quintilian's classical rhetoric, there was his scholastic and literary education with its important debt to Varro and Virgil; there was the reading of Cicero,[42] which merged with the rethinking of Plotinian and Porphyrian themes and with traces of Pythagoreanism.[43] Following these paths he would reach the point of looking to language itself for the keys to a true and proper semantic ontology that would enable him to move from a view of signs as simply the tools of rhetorical manipulation to an interpretation of them as the ontological key to a fundamental hierarchical *klimax* (ladder) uniting body, soul, and God.

Following this line, the thesis that thought is internal discourse (a thesis already present in Plato[44] and shared in its essentials by the Stoics, for whom the *endiathetos logos* [immanent word; mental conception] is what properly distinguishes human beings from animals[45]) is combined with the Neoplatonic primacy of the interior dimension and, more particularly, with the assertion of a constitutive weakening of the mediational capacities of expression. If it be true, moreover, as Johnson has pointed out, that Augus-

---

41. In this context Pizzani points out the emergence as early as the work on *Music* of "a kind of dialectical contrast between, on the one hand, an ascensional 'intention' aimed at the complete liberation of the soul from slavery to the senses in order to achieve a pure contemplation of what is changeless and, on the other, a tension in the opposite direction that leads the soul to work within its relationship to the body": U. Pizzani, "Intentio ed escatologia nel sesto libro del 'De musica' di S. Agostinmo," in the collective work, *Interiorità e intensionalitin S. Agostino* (Rome, 1990) 50.

42. On this see J. J. O'Donnell, "Augustine's Classical Readings," *Recherches augustiniennes* 15 (180) 156–167, where he analyzes, among other works, Cicero's treatises on rhetoric, traces of which can be seen in *Teaching Christianity*.

43. On the sources of these ideas see J. Doignon "Le 'De ordine,' son déroulement, ses thèmes," in the collective work, *L'opera letteraria di Agostino tra Cassiciacum e Milano* (Palermo, 1987) 138.

44. See Plato, *Timaeus* 189e-190a (when the soul thinks, it converses with itself) and *Soph.* 263e (the discourse that goes on within the soul is thought).

45. See Sextus Empiricus, *Adv. math.* 8, 275–176. This point is emphasized by Manetti, *Le teorie del segno*, 142–143.

tine "was also a man of words"[46] and that this remained a factor creating continuity between his youthful profession of rhetorician and his mission in later life of proclaiming the gospel and commenting on the scriptures, then the entire process of his spiritual maturation could not but be deeply influenced by the way in which he conceived of communication.[47]

Theological Investigation

This nucleus of ideas offers, therefore, the theoretical scaffolding for a theological rethinking that seems to move in at least three directions. First of all, and especially beginning with the work *Commentary on Genesis, against the Manichees,* moral reflection on original sin and on the consequent obscuring of God's direct interior presence to the human person provides new justifications for the necessity of external communication. Second, the recognized centrality of Christ the incarnate Word provides a theological foundation for the theory of linguistic signs. Finally, Augustine's pastoral concerns commit him to a deeper biblical and ecclesiological study of Christian revelation. The work *Teaching Christianity* will provide a place for the gradual sifting and clarification of these several deeper understandings.

From this point on, Augustine looks upon the biblical episode of the Tower of Babel as describing not so much the act by which language in the proper sense was born,[48] but rather a fundamental experience of division between peoples that resulted from a breaching of the original communion of humanity with the creator.[49] At the origin of language, therefore, there is a profound distortion that shows itself not only in the difficulty of achieving an honest interpersonal communication but also in a much more radical kind of split between language and thought.[50]

In this context the mediating function of signs is burdened with an ambivalence and a new tension by comparison with the elitist and optimistic voluntarism of Neoplatonic asceticism[51] as well as with the naive anthro-

---

46. D. W. Johnson *"Verbum* in the Early Augustine (386–397)," *Recherches augustiniennes* 8 (1972) 29.
47. This approach is taken not only by Todorov, according to whom Augustine transformed the materialistic doctrine of the Stoics on the basis of an analysis of designation together with a doctrine on communication (*Theories of the Symbol,* 54), but also by K. Kuypers, *Der Zeichenund Wortbegriff im Denken Augustins* (Amsterdam, 1934); J. Finaert, *Saint Augustin Rhéteur* (Paris, 1939); Mayer, *Die Zeichen.*
48. See U. Duchrow, *"Signum* und *superbia* beim jungen Augustin," *Revue des études augustiniennes* 7 (1961) 369–372.
49. See *Teaching Christianity* II, 4, 5.
50. See G.-H. Allard, "Arts libéraux et langage," 491. This split, Augustine says, gave rise to Babylon, the city whose name means "confusion" (*City of God* XVI, 4).
51. As O'Meara emphasizes, Augustine "considered in 386 that it was possible by reason alone to arrive at the truths revealed by authority, since God was the source of illumination for both coordinated, though independent, sources of illumination" ("Augustine and Neoplatonism," *Recherches augustiniennes* 1 [1958] 102).

pocentrism of Stoic ethics. This is true even though Augustine remains especially open to the Stoic thesis, which inspired even Varro, according to which, says Pizzani, "the giving of names is the result of a conscious, rational initiative of human beings with a view to reciprocal communication."[52] The historically conditioned proclamation of Christian truth seems in Augustine to be as it were suspended between the unfathomable mysteries of sin and grace, which sum up the alternating experiences of humanity itself on its journey to salvation. When we compare *Teaching Christianity* with *The Teacher* we can gauge the distance traveled by the author in rehabilitating the mediational function of language, which is now seen less as a degraded manifestation of the spirit's life than as a positive, intentional projection of the created universe.[53]

In parallel fashion, again in comparison with *The Teacher*, the person of Christ and the primacy of the one Teacher are rethought in the context of a fallen humanity that is marked in a radical degree by a kind of inability to effect any direct interior contact with God the Truth and thus a need of a structured and reliable doctrinal support that is based on the positive message of the scriptures and guaranteed by the authority of the Church. I cannot agree on this point with all those interpreters, from Trapè[54] to Madec,[55] who have seen the Christocentric orientation as the decisive factor in the very experience of conversion and therefore as the basic interpretive key for the whole of Augustine's thought.

It is just as true, finally, that as Augustine pursued his studies he gradually acquired a deeper biblical and ecclesial understanding of the doctrine of the incarnation. This can be verified in, among other things, the gradual emergence of the idea of "word" (*verbum*), which is now seen in a perspective that is more open to Pauline pneumatology and Johannine Christology.

---

52. U. Pizzani, "La dottrina agostiniana dell'origine del linguaggio e l'esegesi di Gen 2, 19–20," in the collective work *Polyanthema. Studi di Letteratura cristiana antica offerti a Salvatore Costanza* (Messina) 400–416. On this point see also idem, "Schema agostiniano e schema varroniano della disciplina grammaticale," in the collective work *Studi su Varrone, sulla retorica, storiografia e poesia latina. Scritti in onore di Benedetto Riposati* (Rieti, 1979) 397–411.

53. Johnson, *"Verbum,"* 32, emphasizes Augustine's gradual reassessment of the material structure of discourse.

54. See, among others, A. Trapè, *Saint Augustine. Man, Pastor, Mystic,* trans. M. J. O'Connell (New York, 1986); idem, *S. Agostino. Introduzione alla dottrina della grazia* I. *Natura e grazia* (Rome, 1987) 43.

55. In *"Christus, scientia et sapientia nostra.* Le principe de cohérence de la doctrine augustinienne," *Recherches augustiniennes* 10 (1985) 82, Madec writes: "I believe, then, that from the day of his conversion Augustine identified the wisdom of the *Hortensius* and the divine intelligence of Plato with the Word of John's Prologue, the Christ; and that he was convinced that his entire teaching was based on the Christ, the Word who is God and the Word made flesh." Among others, Pizzolato, "Il *de beata vita,*" 11, likewise stresses the central place of the theology of the incarnation in the development of Augustine's thought.

Johnson differs from other critics[56] in pointing out that the increasing use of *verbum* is accompanied by a personalization of Augustinian Christology, in which the person of Christ is gradually removed from the Neoplatonic categories of truth/wisdom. In the works composed from 386 to 389 Augustine never uses "Word" (*Verbum*) as a proper name, whereas from the *Commentary on Genesis, against the Manichees* to *Teaching Christianity* this term, despite the irreducible complexity of its meanings, acquires an ever more explicit reference to the incarnation.[57]

As Gadamer among others has pointed out,[58] the theological use of *verbum* in close connection with the theology of creation and of the incarnation is the springboard for moving completely beyond Platonic dualism. It is on this basis that in his *Trinity* Augustine will propose the well-known thesis regarding the interior germination of the word, having reached the point of recognizing that there is an irreducible gap between external communication and interior word: "Thus the word which makes a sound outside is the sign of the word which lights up inside, and it is this latter that primarily deserves the name of 'word.'"[59] Thus there is a doubling of levels: the level of de facto communication, which plays a fundamental role in integration into society, and the level of expressive potentiality, where thinking and speaking combine to form a kind of "dwelling-place of thought," meaning a primitive nucleus of self-conscious and spiritual life.[60]

There is thus a close analogy between the process of articulating meaning that is expressed in the external order of the human voice and the process that goes on in the interior order of the mind. The analogy seems to be based precisely on the relationship between thing and sign. That is: as the activity of communication, taken globally in its reified exteriority, is a sign

---

56. See, for example, A. Schindler, *Wort und Analogie in Augustins Trinitätslehre* (Tübingen, 1965), who does not regard the linguistic implications of the use of *verbum* as central but sees them rather as originating in speculation on the Logos, and U. Duchrow, *Sprachverständis und biblisches Hören bei Augustin* (Tübingen, 1965), who prefers to connect the term with the problem of enlightenment in the order of seeing rather than in that of speaking/hearing.
57. See Johnson, *"Verbum,"* 33–41.
58. H. G. Gadamer, *Truth and Method*, trans. J. Weinsheimer and D. G. Marshall (2nd rev. ed.; New York, 1989), writes that "the incarnation is closely connected to the problem of the word" (418). In Augustine, therefore "the 'true' word, the verbum cordis, is completely independent of such an [sensible] appearance. It is neither prolativum (brought forth) nor cogitativum in similtudine soni (thought in the likeness of sound). The interior word is thus the mirror and image of the divine word" (420). On this subject see G. Bavaud, "Un thème augustinienne: Le mystère de l'Incarnation, à la lumière de la distinction entre le verbe intérieur et le verbe proféré," *Revue des études augustiniennes* 9 (1963) 95–101.
59. *The Trinity* XV, 11, 20 (Hill 409).
60. On the subject see J. Mader, *Die logische Struktur des personalen Denkens* (Vienna, 1965) 193; L. Alici, "Linguaggio e tempo in S. Agostino," *Miscellanea Mediaevalia* 13/2. *Sprache und Erkenntnis im Mittelalter*, 1047–1045; I. Sciuto, "Verità della parola e interpretazione in Sant'Agostino," in the collective work *Parola e senso. Studi di ermeneutica* (Padua, 1984) 87–89

of a power of thought that goes beyond the level of empirical fact, so the interior act that embodies meaning is a sign and image of the ontological status of the human person which gives intentional existence to, while also transcending, its own acts: the word as "offspring of the mind."[61]

This analogical structure, though not made the subject of a formal theory, grounds the possibility of a "step back" from phenomenological recognition to a true and proper transcendental reflection, and makes it possible to establish a dialectical connection between exteriority and interiority, semantic horizon and ontological horizon. Thus the idea of "word," understood in its essential structure as a dialectic of immediacy and ulteriority, makes explicit the twofold intentionality that determines the intermediate character of a sign. The condition for the possibility of its reaching beyond the objectivity of things, by establishing a relation of meaning with other signs or things, is, in fact, to be looked for "behind" the sign itself, in the ontological intentionality that is constitutive of the human creature.

Finally, the revealed truth of the incarnation is the decisive theological contribution when it comes to facing, on a different terrain and in new terms, the Neoplatonic problem of mediation. In *Teaching Christianity* this approach is thematized in a systematic and explicit way: the incarnation means that the Word of God became flesh in order to dwell in the midst of us but "was not changed"; in the same way "when we talk...the word which we have in our thoughts becomes a sound, and is called speech. And yet this does not mean that our thought is turned into that sound, but while remaining undiminished in itself, it take on the form of a spoken utterance by which to insert itself into their ears, without bearing the stigma of any change in itself."[62]

The difference that makes it possible to see human word and divine word as having a relationship of participation within a context of transcendence is to be found in the different nature of the divine Person who lives in a perfect communion in the Trinity but at the same time cannot remain alien to the world.[63] In comparison with the Word of God who becomes flesh without ceasing to be part of the trinitarian unity[64] but even fulfilling

---

61. Augustine maintains that in a personal act memory, intellect, and will activate one another, and words are the sign of this fruitful exchange, being the the the manifestation of a presence that brings with it traces of a spiritual world. See *Trinity* IX, 7, 12; 9, 9, 14; XIV, 7, 10; XV, 10, 17–19. I refer the reader to my article, "Il linguaggio come segno e come testimonianza," 93, 104.
62. See *Teaching Christianity* I, 13, 12.
63. Referring to the Wisdom of God, Augustine says that "she came where she already was, because she was in the world, and the world was made through her" (*ibid.*). In this connection, E. S. Lodovici, *Dio e mondo. Relazione, causa, spazio in S. Agostino* (Rome, 1979), emphasizes the fact that Augustine rises above any and every substantialist opposition between God and the world.
64. See *Expositions of the Psalms* 3, 3. Johnson, "'Verbum,'" 50 comments that "it is precisely this unity that makes the Incarnate Word preeminently and uniquely God's Word!"

this unity completely in the trinitarian plan of salvation, the word of human beings is born in a setting of sin and division. Christ, the true mediator, became a human being because "in the Wisdom of God.... the world was unable to come to know God through wisdom."[65]

For this reason, in *Teaching Christianity* the relation of Christ to human beings, without losing its interior depth, is thematized primarily in light of its biblical foundations and as mediated by the Church: the Church is the body and spouse of Christ, and he puts her to the test and purifies her through trials.[66] The human journey, which is interrupted by the weight of sin, is restored to continuity within the Church, where every sinner can find forgiveness and a refuge.[67] Moreover, the development of Augustine's own thought on original sin[68] appears explicable not so much in relation to contingent influences (such as a supposed residue of Manicheism, or contact with the African theology of Tertullian and Cyprian) as in the framework of a much more organized theological reflection that focuses on the figure of Christ the redeemer.[69]

Augustine's consciousness of the catholicity of the Church, which he recognizes as having a universal vocation that corresponds to the common destiny of humanity, has for a consequence that he passes, in principle, beyond any purely sociological or methodological perspective as well as any relativistic vision of culture and communication.[70] This being the case, his attention to signs takes on a meaning that goes beyond the linguistic dimension to which the work is chiefly attentive.

---

65. *Teaching Christianity* I, 12, 12. On Christ as Mediator and the difference between him and the analogous figure in Neoplatonism see G. Madec, "Connaissance de Dieu at action de grâces. Essai sur les citations de l'Ep. aux Romains I, 18–25 dans l'oeuvre de saint Augustin," *Recherches augustiniennes* 2 (1962) 291.

66. See *Teaching Christianity* I, 16, 17.

67. See *ibid.*, I, 18, 17.

68. Only in the second period of his literary activity (397–411) does Augustine clearly focus on the idea of a hereditary fault, while after 412 his interpretation of it becomes more profound and specific: every human being born acquires, by way of propagation, a situation of sin that depends on the sin of Adam. On this subject see A. Sage, "Péché originel. Naissance d'un dogme," *Revue des études augustiniennes* 13 (1967) 211–248, and Trapè, *S. Agostino. Introduzione alla dottrina della grazia*, 200–208, who in conparison with Sage emphasizes the continuity in the development of Augustine's thought.

69. So also M. Flick and Z. Alszeghy, *Il peccato originale* (Rome, 1972) 97–110.

70. As P. Prini writes, Augustine came to realize that "the coming of Christ marked the beginning of a new age with an all-embracing plan and a radical commitment of humanity to itself." See P. Prini, "Temi agistiniani nel pensiero storico contemporaneo," in the collective work *Atti del Congresso internazionale su S. Agostino nel XVI centenario della conversione* (note 11, above) I, 287.

Things and Signs

As Todorov has rightly remarked, *Teaching Christianity* has a claim to be considered "the first semiotic work."[71] We may add, with Eco, that in it Augustine "develops what we today would call a textual semiotic and, certainly, a hermeneutical methodology."[72] But, to speak frankly, I find it difficult even in undertaking simply an inquiry that is meant to be introductory, as this one is, and to provide only a key to the reading of Augustine's work and some elementary tools of interpretation, without locating the problem within a broader speculative, theological, and pastoral perspective.

It is perhaps this fact, moreover, that presents a first and fundamental difference between Augustinian theory and modern semiotics, which arise out of an inquiry that is from the outset neutral in its philosophical implications, and this not always as a simple methodological option. It is precisely this neutrality that often prevents readers from grasping the metaphysical perspective in which Augustinian semiology is located, thereby turning the metaphysical element in Augustine's analysis into a simple set of psychological observations.[73]

In *Teaching Christianity*, then, Augustine's semiology undergoes a profound theological and philosophical amplification, in which, however, the pastoral intention leads to a special emphasis on the mediational function of signs themselves—this, in comparison with other works, such as *The Trinity* and *Homilies on the Gospel of John*, which tend rather to support the idea that the *verbum* is completely irreducible to any form of exterior signification.

The overall plan of *Teaching Christianity* contains two fundamental thematic units, which are enunciated at the beginning of the first book: the first unit, which includes the first three books, is devoted to the identification and understanding of the truths of faith ("a way to discover what needs to be understood"); the second unit, which is developed chiefly in the fourth book, is concerned rather with the setting forth of these truths ("a way to put across to others what has been understood").[74] The first book, which offers an elementary introduction to the Christian life and gives first place to the truths that are to be looked for in the scriptures (that is, the doctrinal and moral content of the faith, and the teachings which every believer is

---

71. Todorov, *Theories of the Symbol*, 40.
72. U. Eco, "L'epistola XIII e l'allegorismo medievale," *Carte semiotiche* 1 (1984) 20. He goes on to say: "Textual semiotics and contemporary hermeneutics still move along the main lines set down by Augustine, even when they are secularized semiotics or hermeneutics, even when they do not recognize their origin, and even when they look upon a worldly poetic text as sacred and a repository of infinite wisdom."
73. Thus, for example, Todorov, in whose view Augustine was "guided by a tendency to inscribe the semiotic problem within the framework of a psychological theory of communication" (*Theories of the Symbol*, 56).
74. *Teaching Christianity* I, 1, 1.

obliged to follow), already contains three important and careful definitions. The first is the thesis that "all teaching is about either things or signs, but things are learned about through signs";[75] to this is added a further division within "things," in light of the categories of "enjoying" and "using"; finally, these categories in turn are made more specific in the "third distinction."

It is important to note that the Augustinian theory of signs, with the linguistic suppositions that lie behind it, is contained within the first unit (discovery). As a matter of fact, attention is focused chiefly on things as they are ("what has to be considered about things is that they are").[76] The latter in turn are divided into things we are to enjoy (*frui*) and things we are simply to use (*uti*). Signs in particular are things that can mediate knowledge of other things "that are not mentioned in order to signify something."[77]

Anthropocentric teleology, of the kind proper to a Stoicizing Platonism,[78] is thus rehabilitated in light of the doctrine of creation: no created nature has within itself the source of its own subsistence, but presents itself to the human intellect as an essence that is drawn out of nothingness and finds its proper good in God, that is, in the supreme being who formed it as such.[79] As a result, there is no place for hypothesizing an ontological dualism, much less for a rupture between semiology and ontology, since signs are not placed in a closed and, as it were, neutralized limbo. Rather there is a single created nature that has different valences according to the meaningful intentionality it can acquire in human society. On the one hand, then, some objects can be regarded as signs;[80] on the other, words, "which are used only for signifying," are also "something." Conclusion: "Every sign is also a thing, because if it is not a thing at all then it is simply nothing. But not every single thing is also a sign."[81]

The connection between signs and things, then, is an expression of a still more primitive connection that tends to interpret in terms of analogy the distance between creation and the creator. It is in relation to this perspective that the difference between use and enjoyment is defined, for this difference is not regarded as an extrinsic notion but is one that traverses the entire order of things as the expression of a primitive ontological difference between the "being toward" of humans and the "supreme being" of God.

---

75. *Ibid.*, I, 2, 3. The statement echoes Quintilian (see *Inst. orat.* 3, 5, 1).
76. See G. H. Allard, "L'articulation du sens et du signe dans le *De doctrina christiana*," *Studia patristica* 14 (1976) 388–89.
77. *Teaching Christianity* I, 2, 2.
78. On this subject see J. Pépin, *La tradition de l'allégorie de Philon d'Alexandrie à Dante. Études historiques* (Paris, 1987) 114, who points out echoes of this conception in the works of Cicero.
79. On this see C. Boyer, "La notion de nature chez Saint Augustin," in idem, *Essais anciens et nouveaux sur la doctrine de Saint Augustin* (Milan, 1970) 215–228.
80. Augustine mentions in this context the wood that Moses threw into the water, the stone on which Jacob rested his head, and the animal that Abraham sacrificed in place of his son.
81. *Teaching Christianity*, I, 2, 2.

"Things used," says Todorov, "are transitive, like signs, and things enjoyed are intransitive.... This distinction has an important theological extension. In the last analysis, nothing other than God deserves to be enjoyed, to be cherished for itself alone."[82]

What emerges here is a fundamental parallelism between epistemology, ethics, and ontology: the gap between thing and sign, as thematized in a philosophical theory of meaning and language, decides the difference in ethical tonality between use and enjoyment and reflects the infinite distance between history and eternity. The grace of God transforms this distance into a space for salvation, a space that is intelligible to and traversible by human beings, on condition that an ordered love[83] plans the concrete itinerary by which human beings on pilgrimage—*homo viator*—are effectively raised above their condition.

The second book turns directly to signs themselves. In the background is the three-stage formulation sketched back in *The Teacher*. The first hypothesis had been to consider the relationship to a sign that is mediated by another sign, a phenomenon made possible by the very nature of signs, which as signs can signify and as things can be signified. The second hypothesis concerned the relation to the thing that is mediated by a sign, and confirmed that knowledge of the thing comes before knowledge of the sign as such. The third hypothesis had to do with the direct relationship to the thing.[84] It is against this background that *Teaching Christianity* makes its contribution, which takes the form essentially of delving more deeply into the idea of sign and attempting to clarify its semantic status.

First of all, signs as such constitute the special class of things that are able to signify something other than themselves. In fact, a sign is defined as "a thing, which besides the impression it conveys to the senses, also has the effect of making something else come to mind."[85] A sign, therefore, is distinguished by a kind of semantic intentionality that is attributed to the thing; a sign is a thing but viewed in its ability to activate, through the

82. Todorov, *Theories of the Symbol*, 41.
83. According to R. Bodei, *Ordo amoris, Conflitti terreni et felicità celeste* (Bologna, 1991), in a love thus understood as an "ascending stream" and an "order open to the Other than us who is in us and in whose nature we participate" (92) "there is inherent both order and freedom" (117).
84. In dealing with the first hypothesis Augustine distinguishes first of all between signs whose meaning does not apply to themselves (the word "conjunction" is not a conjunction) and self-referential signs (for example, "word" and "sign," both of which can be regarded as words and as signs). Second, the various kinds of relationship between semantic content and possibility of use led him to distinguish between nonequivalent signs (for example, "sign" and "word," where the meaning of the former is wider but less comprehensive than the meaning of the latter), equivalent signs ("name" and "word," where the meanings are equivalent but they are used differently), and identical signs ("name" and *"onoma,"* which have the same meaning and use, though in different linguistic settings). On this subject see especially the summary in *The Teacher* 7, 19–20.
85. *Teaching Christianity* II, 1, 1.

indispensable mediation of thought, a relation of meaning with some other thing; it thus becomes part of a circuit of expression and interpersonal communication that transcends the purely empirical horizon of "things."[86]

With this idea of sign as a starting point, the author launches into a series of further clarifications and distinctions, which have been given different interpretations according to different classificatory hypotheses.[87] In any case, there seem to be three levels in Augustine's analysis, corresponding to three different orders of factors. First of all, as far as their nature is concerned, signs are either natural or intentional ("given," "conventional"). Second, in relation to the understanding of them, signs that are recognized are distinguished from those not recognized or ambiguous, the latter being the principal reasons for the failure to understand.[88] Finally, depending on their meaning, signs are either proper or transferred.

To begin with, a sign is natural if, instead of manifesting a relation of meaning that had been established by the human community, it "signals," in a univocal way, a relation of continuity/affinity between things. Here again a type of spiritual understanding is required on the part of the human mind, which is called to recognize the meaning of things in relation to the capacity for grasping their degree of relatedness to the Absolute.[89]

---

86. The definition was not new and even has clear Aristotelean and Stoic forebears; here, however, even by comparison with the statement of the problem in *The Teacher*, something more is said about the specific character of the relationship of meaning. This is the thesis of Darrell Jackson in particular ("Theory of Signs," 12), who analyzes the Augustinian definition and compares it with the theory of signs developed by Aristotle, especially in his *Categories* and his *On Interpretation*, and by the Stoics (see *ibid.*, 41–49). According to Holte, *Béatitude et Sagesse. Saint Augustin et le problème de la fin de l'homme dans la philosophie ancienne* (Paris, 1962), 329–331, the relation between sign and thing is the same as that described in *Order* II, 9, 26, as the relation between "authority" and reason: just as one passes from sign to thing, so one passes from authority to reason. On the relation between thing and sign in Varro see J. Collart, *Varron grammarien latin* (Paris, 1954) 258–278.
87. For example, according to Todorov, *Theories of the Symbol*, 45–56, in Augustine's work signs may be distinguished 1) according to their mode of transmission (sight and hearing); 2) according to their origin and use (natural and intentional signs); 3) according to their social function (natural/universal signs and institutional/ conventional signs; 4) according to the nature of the symbolic relationship (proper and metaphorical signs); and 5) according to the nature of what is designated (a sign or a thing). Darrell Jackson, "Theory of Signs," 15–29, introduces a further division within given signs that takes account of psychological and semantic factors: 1) things; 2) perception; 3) understanding; 4) meaning; 5) communication. Of special interest, finally, is the scheme proposed once again by Manetti, *Le teorie del segno*, 235–36, who sees in Augustine a "classification that includes genus and species," close to the model of Porphyry's tree (on this subject see Eco, *Semiotica e filosofia del linguaggio*, 91).
88. See *Teaching Christianity* II, 10, 15.
89. On this see P. Godard, "Notes complémentaires," *Oeuvres de Saint Augustin* 11. *Le magistère chrétienne* (Paris 1949) 564.

In comparison with natural signs, Augustine's book devotes special attention to "given signs," that is, those consciously produced in order to externalize and communicate what arises in the mind.[90] This class contains verbal signs and, as a subclass, written signs with the limitless possibilities of communication that they provide but also with the inevitable difficulties of understanding them due to the diversity of languages.

These two kinds of signs, then, are distinguished by the presence or absence of an intention to convey meaning.[91] According to Todorov, given signs are characterized by their origin and use: "Intentional signs are things that have been produced for the purpose of serving as *signs* (origin) and that serve only to this end (use)."[92] The definition, already sketched in *The Teacher*,[93] is now subjected to a reworking that preserves the same conceptual contours but explores more fully the constitutive elements and the fundamental motivations. The author seems to be interested here in calling attention chiefly to two levels: the first is that of a kind of phenomenology of communication, which is invoked to prove the semantic functionality of given signs: "Given signs...are those which living creatures give to one another in order to show, as far as they can, their moods and feelings, or to indicate whatever it may be they have sensed or understood."[94] Thus understood, a given sign is a means of interpersonal mediation, its function being to render visible what is interior.

A second level, to which Augustine looks for the conditions that render the communication of meaning possible and the motivations that make it a reality, is the level established by a true and proper ontology of interiority: "Nor have we any purpose in signifying, that is in giving a sign, other than to bring out and transfer to someone else's mind what we, the givers of the sign, have in mind ourselves."[95] The emphasis placed on the goal of communication, so that signs are regarded as mediating between the thing and the intention of producing a meaning ("the will to signify"),[96]

---

90. Given signs should be called "intentional" rather than "conventional": "The term 'given,' which is opposed to 'natural,' implies all that the word 'give' expresses, and that means a subjective intention to signify as indicated by a specific will to communicate something" (G. Ripanti, *Agostino teorico dell'interpretazione* [Brescia, 1980] 39–40). Others who agree with this view are Darrell Jackson, "Theory of Signs," 14, and Manetti, *Le teorie del segno*, 239.
91. This is the thesis of, among other, J. Engels, "La doctrine du signe chez saint Augustin," *Studia patristica* 6 (1962) 371, whereas according to Markus the distinction is based on a difference in the relationship of dependence: a subject-object relation in the case of natural signs, and a sign-subject relation in the case of given signs; see Markus, "Saint Augustine on Signs," 72.
92. Todorov, *Theories of the Symbol*, 47.
93. *The Teacher* I, 2: "Those who speak give an external sign of their intention through articulated sound."
94. *Teaching Christianity* II, 2, 3.
95. *Ibid.*
96. Among others who agree on the existence of this triadic scheme in Augustinian semiology are Darrell Jackson, "Theory of Signs," 22–25, and Sciuto, "Verità

allots first place to the idea of an "interior self," conceived essentially as a spiritual subject which assigns and interprets signs while keeping an eye on prevailing linguistic conventions.

Language and Interpretation

In approaching the question in this twofold perspective, the author could only confirm, as a corollary already implicit in his analysis, the primacy of the linguistic sign which he asserts in studying signs according to the nature of their symbolic relationship.[97] His assertion is based not only on factual observation (of all signs those addressed to the ear are in the majority) but also on a much deeper reason: "Words...are far and away the principal means used by human beings to signify the thoughts they have in their minds."[98] They are, in fact, the only signs that can represent all others and therefore even themselves, while the converse is not true.

We might say that theoretical status is being given here to those properties of verbal language which are called, in modern terminology, "semantic omnipotence" and "metalinguistic reflexivity or capacity."[99] Simone insists that

> Augustine is the first not only to point out the peculiar (semiotic) character of words by identifying the properties that distinguish them from all other kinds of signs, but also...to realize that, unlike other signs, the linguistic sign has the supreme capacity of being able to say everything... that is, it is "stronger" (in the logical sense) and "more powerful" than other signs and at the same time...can function as a metasign in relation to them.[100]

The focus on the linguistic sign, instead of limiting the scope of the inquiry, makes it possible to broaden further the entire problematic into a more general vision of the processes involved in understanding and interpretation. Here the problem of the nonunderstanding of written texts due to the presence of unknown or ambiguous signs intersects, as I said earlier, with the further distinction between proper and metaphorical signs.

---

della Parola," 85. See note 21, above.

97. On this point see also A. Maierù, "'Signum' dans la culture médiévale," in *Sprache und Erkenntnis im Mittelalter* (*Miscellanea Mediaevalia* 13/1; Berlin-New York, 1981) 55.
98. *Teaching Christianity* II, 3, 4.
99. See A. Pieretti, *Il linguaggio* (Brescia, 1984) 20.
100. R. Simone, "Semiologia agostiniana," *La cultura* 7 (1969) 97–98. It is even possible to see in the text of *Teaching Christianity* an anticipation of the theory of the "twofold articulation" of these signs; according to this theory it is only in verbal languages that there is a level made up of minimal units having meaning (monemes, morphemes), these being further reducible only to a level of minimal units that lack any meaning (phonemes). On this question see A. Martinet, *Elementi di linguistica generale* (Bari, 1977) 21–26.

The former correspond in substance to given signs, but the latter have a complex structure: signs "are metaphorical when the very things which we signify with their proper words are made use of to signify something else."[101] Such signs, therefore, says Todorov, "instead of being used for their original purpose…are redirected toward a second function, just as things were when they became signs."[102]

Given these foundations, the dynamics of understanding seem to operate continually on two levels: the level of knowledge and the level of interpretation. When we are faced with proper signs that are unknown to us, certain things are indispensable: knowledge of languages, attention to sources, a continual expanding of our fund of information, and an ability to compare texts and the different ways in which they are translated. But when it is metaphorical signs that are unknown, readers "need to investigate them partly by a knowledge of languages, partly by a knowledge of things."[103] Always with the aim of a better understanding of the revealed text, Augustine reflects on the usefulness of the sciences, the arts, and human institutions, reviewing the most important values of ancient culture and judging them according to their usefulness as prerequisites in the formation of the Christian.[104]

The third book, in contrast, adopts a markedly more hermeneutical perspective and opens a still more explicit dialectical investigation of knowledge and interpretation. To the forefront now are ambiguous signs which oblige the interpreter of scripture to face up to the more controverted passages (Augustine recommends that these interpreters be given a fundamental preparation that looks to both content and methodologies). The author studies the ambiguities connected with signs used in their proper sense, these ambiguities being for the most part reducible to the ways in which words are phrased or pronounced or to grammatical construction,[105] but he pays greater attention to ambiguities arising when terms are used in a metaphorical sense.[106]

As a matter of fact, the Christian faith helps liberate readers from enslavement to the carnal meaning of the scriptures, of which the Jews have continued to be victims, and from enslavement to useless signs, by which

---

101. *Teaching Christianity* II, 10, 15.
102. Todorov, *Theories of the Symbol*, 51.
103. *Teaching Christianity* II, 16, 23.
104. See *ibid.*, II, 16, 24—42, 63. In analyzing the sciences of nature, number, and music, Augustine carefully distinguished revealed truths from the disciplines established by human beings; within the latter he draws sharp lines between science and superstitious practices, and urges his readers to exercise careful discrimination. Finally, he turns to the mechanical arts and to the disciplines having to do with human rationality, especially dialectic.
105. See *Teaching Christianity* III, 1, 1—4, 8.
106. "In the first place," according to Augustine, "you have to beware of taking a figurative expression literally. And this is where the apostle's words are relevant, *The letter kills, but the spirit gives life* (2 Cor 3:6)" (*ibid.*, III, 5, 9).

the pagans have continued to be imprisoned. To this end one must be able to distinguish between the proper sense and the metaphorical sense and to grasp, in all passages that cannot be interpreted according to the letter, the meaning hidden in many figurative expressions that are used to fight against selfishness or to nourish charity. The building up of "the kingdom of charity"[107] is the principal goal and supreme interpretive criterion for exegetical activity.[108] In the last part of Book III Augustine then sets himself to explain the seven rules of the Donatist Tychonius,[109] which Augustine regards as useful in understanding the more controverted passages of the scriptures, provided one exercises an ever watchful and cautious judgment.[110]

The identification of metaphorical signs, which constitutes the basic theoretical core of the hermeneutical problem, was in Augustine's time a heritage shared by both the pagan and the Christian ways of thinking, from the Stoics to the Jews of Alexandria and from Philo to Plotinus.[111] In Augustine's book, in which the distinction is made for clearly hermeneutical purposes, "proper signs" express the literal meaning of the scriptures (Origen's "somatic" sense), while "metaphorical signs" embrace everything that is not directly understood through the immediate meaning of the words,

---

107. *Ibid.*, 2,15, 23.
108. As applications of this criterion Augustine mentions: the ability to distinguish between what is said for all and what is said for only a few; attention to the historical context; the exhortation not to apply one's own measure to others; the interpretation of immoral actions; humility before sinners; respect for a legitimate plurality of interpretations.
109. On Tychonius—an important personage among the Donatists and in a position of considerable authority among them, to the point where Augustine makes use of him in rejecting their idea of the Church as a community of the perfect—see H. A. Van Bakel, "Tyconius, Augustinus ante Augustinum," *Nieuw Theol. Tijdschrift* 19 (1938) 36–57. On the intersecting of the thought of Augustine and that of Tyconius see A. Casamassa, *Il pensiero di Sant'Agostino nel 396–397* (Rome, 1919); A. Pincherle, *Vita di Sant'Agostino* (Bari, 1980) 160–162, 361–163; J. S. Alexander, "Tyconius' Influence on Augustine: A Note on Their Use of the Distinction corporaliter/spiritaliter," in the collective work, *Atti del Congresso internazione.... conversione*, II, 205–211. Around 370 Tyconius had drawn up some exegetical rules for correctly interpreting the relation between prophetic texts and the coming of the kingdom of God (see Tyconius, *Liber regularum*, ed. F. C. Burkitt [Texts and Studies 3/1; Cambridge, 1894). What the rules provided, however, was not so much a method for dealing with allegory but primarily a method for dealing with typology, which tended to interpret personages and events of the Bible, sometimes in an ingenious and forced way, as "types" or prefigurations of the Church and its history.
110. The rules have to do with: the mystery of the union of Christ with the Church; the mystical sense in which we speak of the body of the Lord; the value of the promises and the law; the ability to understand genus and species; the importance of times; the presence of digressions and recapitulations; the meaning of the hidden presence of the devil among believers (see *Teaching Christianity* III, 30, 42—37, 46).
111. See J. Pépin, *Mythe et allégorie. Les origines grecques et les contestations judéochrétiennes* (Paris, 1981²).

and include what in a different theological terminology is the figurative literal sense and the true and proper spiritual, or allegorical, meaning.[112]

Insofar as allegory yields "an intellectual understanding mediated by a concept,"[113] it points to a capacity to rise above the horizon of the senses, and it is precisely in this horizon that Augustine locates it, drawing from it an essential exegetical principle. The semantic foundation of this Augustinian conception derives from "the twofold intentional structure of signs," by which one moves from sign to thing signified and then to the thing's further symbolic meaning, and, according to Ripanti, "corresponds to Augustine's way of conceiving revelation as a *sacramentum*, as a veiling/unveiling, in a degree proportionate to its object's transcendence, by reason of which this object has no choice but to manifest itself 'in the obscurity of allegories.'"[114]

Ancient rhetoric had, of course, been quite familiar with the civilizing function of allegory, as Pépin shows,[115] but in *Teaching Christianity* this attention to allegory becomes central, and the author provides a formal treatise on it.[116] According to Augustine, it is God himself who has placed within the human person zones of greater semantic density that can hide his mysteries as in a casket.[117] Allegory, Pépin writes, "has as its providential purpose to humble human pride,"[118] while stimulating the desire and search for truth.

Consequently, the very nature of a sign, by reason of the stock of meaning that makes it a sign, calls for the continuous mediation provided by interpretation, which, according to Augustine, must be done on the basis of the literal sense. But the unity of this last, as De Margerie notes, "is not completely monolithic but relative to a set of other unities and to the overall unity of the total meaning of all the scriptures."[119] Even more complex, of course, will be the exegesis of metaphorical signs, which seeks understanding of the figurative, allegorical meaning. This understanding

---

112. See E. Moirat, *Notion augustinienne de l'Herméneutique* (Clérmont-Ferrand, 1906) 27–31, 44–45; M. Comeau, *Saint Augustin exégète du IV e Évangile* (Paris, 1930) 103–105.
113. H.-G. Gadamer, "Simbolo e allegoria," *Archivio di filosofia* (Padua, 1958) 32.
114. Ripanti, *Agostino teorico*, 61. In addition to Ripanti's book, which studies the ontological, epistemological, and theological structure of allegory in Augustine, see M. Simonetti, *Lettera e/o allegoria. Un contributo alla storia dell'esegesi patristica* (Rome, 1985) 341, note 404, and 358, where he maintains the theory of a rather sparse use of allegory in Augustine; this thesis needs revision, says M. Marin, *"Allegoria* in Agostino," in the collective work *La terminologia esegetica nell'antichità* (Bari, 1987) 148, note 33.
115. See Pépin, *La tradition de l'allégorie*, 134,
116. See *ibid.*, 92.
117. See, for example, Sermon 52, 4, 5.
118. See Pépin, *La tradition de l'allégorie*, 99.
119. B. De Margerie, *Introduzione all storia dell'esegesi 3. S. Agostino* (Rome, 1986) 74. "The same words, while carrying the same overall meaning for the majority of people, can nonetheless, depending on time and place, take on new nuances of meaning, thanks to a richer set of connotations. What comes into play here is the entire phenomenon of successive rereadings of the same texts" (75).

requires not only knowledge of the entire apparatus of rhetorical figures but also a full store of information about the Bible and, more generally, about the world of "things."[120] Allegorical exegesis thus appears possible and legitimate, but under certain conditions, such as unwavering acceptance of the Church's outlook, fidelity to the Christian message in its entirety, readiness to complete a full course of formation, and possession of an elementary competence in textual and literary criticism. Only under these conditions can the interpreter of the scriptures gradually make all their spiritual fruitfulness to emerge, to the advantage of the entire community of believers.

The acknowledgment of a multiplicity of spiritual senses[121] sets in motion a hermeneutical dynamism that is literally inexhaustible. According to Studer, at this point the Augustinian conception of allegory fuses with a theory of the sacramentality of the Bible and creation.[122] In *Teaching Christianity*, in particular, Christian exegesis is directed toward a search for the "things of faith" and the "things of charity": "The first of these two goals corresponds in the last analysis to the 'mystery' (*sacramentum*), for the aim is in fact to find in the Bible, and this means especially in the Old Testament, both Christ and the Church, the things that are to be believed, the means of purification, the *sacramentum*."[123] What we see here is once again the structure of belonging and subordination that Augustine had identified in the relationship between use and enjoyment, between knowledge and wisdom; that is, the letter is regarded as the basis of the spiritual understanding, and history is open to prophecy, just as the New Testament is the key to the understanding of the Old.[124]

On this point it is possible to measure concretely the way in which Augustine's thought matured. The process began with the discovery of the

---

120. *Teaching Christianity* II, 16, 23. De Margerie observes: "It is through the search for the sacred writer's intention that readers and exegetes hope to find the divine will. This is Augustine's voluntarist and teleological way of emphasizing the great principle of any sound exegesis: the spiritual sense is to be explained on the basis of the literal sense" (*Introduzione* 3:35).

121. See P. C. Bori, *L'interpretazione infinita. L'ermeneutica cristiana antica e le sue trasformazioni* (Bologna, 1987) 99–100.

122. B. Studer, *"Sacramentum et exemplum chez saint Augustin,"* *Recherches augustiniennes* 10 1975) 119.

123. *Ibid.*, 123. He continues: "The second aspect, on the other hand, that is, the search for the love of God and neighbor, is helped especially by *exemplum*, because here there is question of things useful for living, demands to be met, models to be followed."

124. "The New Testament is hidden in the Old, the Old Testament is revealed in the New" (*The Instruction of Beginners* 4, 8). "Augustine has, in fact, a predominant concern: to defend the holiness of the Old Testament against deliberate condemnation. Allegory helps in this defense by uncovering 'certain great secrets' beneath the letter of certain passages.... Well, then, at least in some cases, the secret uncovered by allegory is a meaning that brings the Old Testament closer to the New" (H. de Lubac, *Esegesi medievale* [Rome, 1962] 231–243).

spiritual sense of the Bible, a discovery originally fostered by the preaching of Bishop Ambrose but in turn drenched in Neoplatonic elements. The result was that the original allegorizing tendency, which had enabled Augustine to combat in a thorough way the errors of the Manichees, henceforth reached a balance, despite the persistence of some forms of naive allegorism,[125] and was bound over to coexist with the determination to "hold steadfast to the historicity of the *res gestae*."[126]

The exhortation to look beyond the letter to the deeper spiritual meaning[127] that had been issued by the more moderate representatives of the Alexandrian school reappears therefore in Augustine, but it is made here in the name of charity rather than of wisdom. The fundamental exegetical principle of "understanding metaphors," which is an expression of the process of ascent from the sensible to the intelligible that marks the human journey toward the happy life, is consistent with that vision: "So this rule should be observed in dealing with figurative expressions, that you should take pains to turn over and over in your mind what you read, until your interpretation of it is led right through to the kingdom of charity."[128]

Luigi Alici

---

125. See, for example, J. Ries, "La Bible chez saint Augustin et chez les manichéens," *Revue des études augustiniennes* 7 (161) 231–243.
126. Marin, *"Allegoria* in Agostino," 155. This essay, to which I refer the reader for further study, examines Augustine's notion of "allegory" and analyzes his theory and practice, while studying the influence on him of scripture, the patristic tradition, and classical pagan culture.
127. De Margerie, in particular, emphasizes the fact that Augustine rises above the limitations of Origen's allegorism, as well as his agreement with the theses of Cyril of Alexandria and Isidore of Pelusium; see *Introduzione* 3:55.
128. *Teaching Christianity* III, 15, 23.

Unity of Language and Faith in Biblical Exegesis.
States of Mind and Styles (Genera dicendi)

Chapter 1

While the subject material on which "invention" is exercised is sacred scripture, the "arrangement" (*dispositio*) of the ideas cannot be separated from it, and style (*elocutio*) plays a clarifying role. Of these first three divisions of rhetoric the one most subject to variation is the style that characterizes an author. By way of its vast array of models it involves morphology and syntax. Through grammatical variations and innovations in the choice of words a speaker looks for "colors," no longer as mere adornments but to provide illumination and help understanding of the discourse. Style also indirectly involves diction, which is part of the fifth division, the "action" or actual speaking. From the moment an orator begins to speak, the entire person becomes involved: from the gaze to bodily postures, gestures with the hands, and the use of the voice. Different tones of voice will express a call for help or emotion or enthusiasm, exhortation, threat, or prayer. In saying that style has a large field of models to choose from, my aim is to call attention to the fact that Christian rhetoric, too, makes use of these. The process whereby examples from the pagan classics were replaced by others from the Bible was a lengthy one.

The unqualified principle that the models followed should be spontaneous excludes exercises in "transference" (*traiectio*), the affectation that deadens the spontaneous movements of the heart and leads to complexity. Spiritual attitudes that find expression in words are learned through words.

The models, which transcend lexical limits and are open to meanings that the mind seeks to adapt to reality, have rational and psychological bases. They are not a series of means of verbal expression but have a life of their own and are suited to well-defined and precise situations. Together with all the other factors, such as the human face, they combine to implement the particular style of expression.

No Latin writer has succeeded as Saint Augustine has in the development of models. One follows the other like conceptions scattered about by the mind, and we are faced with an artistic prose, as it were, that produces models. An attempt to single out the formal values of this unusual prose would be a lengthy task. Saint Augustine calls attention to the figures of speech in a process which he had developed along with his thesis on the connection between wisdom and eloquence. The theory is one which he continues to develop in almost all his works, especially in the biblical commentaries, and reaches its culmination in *Teaching Christianity*, which we may describe as a treatise on biblical exegesis growing out of almost thirty years of reflection (397–428). There is still need of giving due importance to this treatise that sums up the teachings of the past and opens the way to the future.

Quintilian[1] rejects the thesis of those who regard our way of speaking and writing as more pleasing when it is natural and simple. According to him, in addition to natural talent, there was need not only of instruction in rhetoric but also of the education which only literature could give.

According to Cicero,[2] literature nourishes us in our youth, is the adornment of our prosperity, and is our refuge in times of adversity; it delights our old age and never abandons us; it gives human beings freedom and dignity. According to Seneca,[3] occupations and affairs can never be allowed to hinder education, because without study a human being is like a corpse: "Leisure without literature is death and a tomb for a person while still alive."[4] Saint Augustine, for his part, as a result of reflection on the behavior of human beings, on the exact sciences, and on the reading of the Bible, is led to take into account the universal values contained in things that have some relation to the human mind.

It is to be observed that many human attitudes are shared by people in different times and places. So too are people's observations of natural phenomena. Striking examples of this can be found in a tradition stretching through the centuries. To look to the dependence of one writer on another as the explanation for this repetition is a useless task. It is not such a dependence that should capture our attention but the inner freedom that directs the words and persuasions of human beings.

One of the aspects neglected by students of late antiquity has been the biblical language of the Christian community. Playing on similar-sounding words in a sentence with parallel halves (paronomasia), Augustine notes that "the sacrament of the New Testament give salvation, the sacraments of the Old Testament promised a savior." Then, continuing the parallelism, he confirms a general opinion:

> The Old Testament is concerned with the image of the earthly man, the New Testament with the image of the heavenly. But lest anyone think that the earthly man was made by someone other than the maker of the heavenly man, when God showed himself to be the creator of both, he also willed to be the author of both Testaments,

---

1. *De instit. orat.* 12, 14, 25.
2. *Pro Archia* 7, 14.
3. *Ep.* 62, 1.
4. *Ep.* 82, 4, in *Epistulae Morales* II, trans. R. M. Gummere (Loeb Library; New York, 1930) 243.

so that in the Old Testament he might promise things earthly and in the New Testament things heavenly.[5]

The faithful should not be ignorant of the sacred scriptures, which in their entirety hinge on Christ. The lowly slave, the peasant, the artisan, the young and the old, men and women of whatever social condition can live Christ, which means understanding the scriptures.

With the coming of Christ a new world has opened up that is independent of "liberal studies"; these are neither excluded nor required. There are many ways of reaching Christ: through manual labor or through study. As a result, the community is a composite body: alongside the educated rhetorician are the uneducated folk. Many forms of classical culture run through the life of the Christian community, some because they are inherent in the communication of the human mind, others because they are more congenial to educated Christians.

Christian homiletics in the early Church could not help but develop exegetical principles for dealing with sacred scripture. Preachers had to speak the language of everyday life; this was true of Christians who spoke Latin or Greek and Christians who spoke the Eastern languages. In a homily on the gospel of John Saint Augustine speaks again of that moment in exegesis when the souls of the preacher and believers meet through recollection and meditation: "I am about to close the book, and you will be returning to your homes. We have been at ease in the light we share, we have enjoyed a good deal of pleasure together, and we have been built up. But when we leave one another we do not distance ourselves from him [Christ]."[6]

Saint Augustine speaks frequently of exegesis: in his sermons, in his theological and philosophical writings, in his commentaries, and in his books on catechesis.

Chapter 2

It is Saint Augustine's experience that when our words are natural and spontaneous they manage to make a deeper impression on the minds of others and to persuade them. In my own research I have on quite a few occasions been able to show how in Augustine's case his thought patterns display a logic and expressivity that flow from a natural rhetoric, the rhetoric that is universal. This is the sore point in his controversy with those whom he calls "educated people" (*litterati*).[7] This last is the term he uses to mean grammarians, rhetoricians, and literary critics, while we today understand it to mean everyone with a general education.

---

5. *Expositions of the Psalms* 73, 2.
6. *Homilies on the Gospel of John* 35, 9.
7. *Teaching Christianity* III, 29, 40.

The people he has in mind did not regard the sacred scriptures as worthy of their consideration because these books did not seem to be written according to the rules of classical pagan rhetoric. Saint Augustine thinks these educated people to be short-sighted because they lack the ability to compare. He himself chooses not to teach by giving instruction in the principles of rhetoric, although he does look for the full meaning—overt or supposed—of words, as in many figures of speech. The use of such figures is in his view a native trait of human language and not limited to professors practiced in the liberal arts.[8]

Even ordinary people easily use figures of speech without having devoted any special study to them.[9] The real problem for Saint Augustine is always to understand the language of the scriptures, in which figures of speech are especially frequent. For this reason, as he writes in *Teaching Christianity*, it is necessary to be very alert to the ambiguity of metaphors, which "call for no ordinary care and attention." Here the apostle's words are relevant: "The letter kills but the spirit gives life" (2 Cor 3:6). If something expressed in a metaphor is taken literally, "we are being carnal in our way of thinking."[10] Those who take metaphors literally and do not realize that they are dealing with a figure of speech, which conveys a different meaning, go astray. They are unable to look at corporeal creatures with the eye of the mind, so as to reach the eternal light: "This, precisely, is the wretched slavery of the spirit, treating signs as things, and thus being unable to lift up the eyes of the mind above bodily creatures, to drink in the eternal light."[11]

To investigate the senses of the Bible was the great task which Augustine the exegete set himself. He sought to call the attention of critics to the eloquence of the sacred scriptures. In his view, the human word is unable to keep up with the speed and liveliness of thought.[12] To some extent this was a torment to him and he tried to conquer it. He was not content to know things for himself but wanted to communicate them to others. He recognized the inadequacy of rhetoric as currently taught, calling it a market of useless words and lies.[13] Thinking of the harm done by the schools of rhetoric, he asked himself whether oratory could still be taught in that way.[14]

Augustine was a highly educated man. He never saw things from a narrow angle but in a broad setting and in continuity with other things. He reflected a great deal on the phenomena of the natural world in order to see in them possible links with what human beings use in order to act and to express themselves. As Della Corte has clearly shown, in Milan

---

8.   M. Marin, "La definizione agostiniana di antifrasi e la sua 'fortuna,'" *Augustinianum* 25 (1985) 329–341.
9.   *Teaching Christianity* III,29, 40.
10. *Ibid.*, III, 5, 9.
11. *Ibid.*
12. *The Instruction of Beginners* X, 4, 4.
13. *Confessions* IX, 2, 2.
14. *Ibid.*, VIII, 6, 13.

Saint Augustine encountered the phenomenon of fog, which he had never met in such density and frequency either in his native Africa or in Rome.

Because the fog was so dense he was no longer able to see the streets, though these were still there since they had not disappeared. Only when the fog began to dissipate was he able to see anything. Hardly had the air become clearer when he began to distinguish how the various streets led off from the main avenue, which itself gradually became clearer.[15]

We cannot imagine the extent to which the phenomenon of fog influenced Augustine's deeper grasp of the principle at work in figures of speech, a principle always to the forefront of his mind. As he himself says, the failure to familiarize oneself with the metaphorical language of the sacred scriptures leads to misunderstanding and consequently breaks the continuity of biblical discourse. He speaks often of this, as, for example, in the antiphrasis (expression by opposites) in *On Lying* 10, 24,[16] in connection with the arguments against the Priscillianists and with the theses on the patriarchs, prophets, and apostles.

According to Saint Augustine, the passages of the Old and New Testaments cited by the heretics are not correctly interpreted. They contain prophetic locutions and references to time that must be properly understood, that is, as metaphors. The attitude of Jacob when he appears to be deceiving Isaac, his father (Gen 27:1–36), is "not a lie but a mystery (*non mendacium sed mysterium*)."

If incidents of this kind are taken as examples of lying, then the parables and figures of speech as well as all the metaphors in which one thing is said but another is signified are also lies. Saint Augustine had accustomed himself to an integral and not fragmentary vision of the literary genres. His starting point was always the word, which is an expression of order and freedom.

Saint Augustine knew the New Testament in its entirety, and at the level of words this follows an uninterrupted line. Paul (Col 4:6) exhorts his readers to let their speech be wise and courteous. In his view, there could be no good morals if speech is perverted (1 Cor 15:33). According to James the apostle, if persons are careful in their speech, they are able to restrain not only their tongues but their whole bodies.

I do not emphasize this point because I have dwelt on it at length in the chapter entitled "Word and Freedom" of my book, *Paideia antenicena* (Brescia, 1967). It is the theme of Saint Augustine on which he builds his thesis of a universal rhetoric. From *Longinus on the Sublime* and, later, Quintilian down to Augustine there is a development among Christian authors who gradually, without lengthy disquisitions, in practice observed

---

15. On this section see F. Della Corte, "Agostino e il progetto 'encyclopedico,'" in *L'umanesimo di Sant'Agostino* (Atti del Congresso internazionale di Bari, 28–30 ottobre 1986) 89–117 and especially 90–91.
16. See Marin, "La definizione"; and see idem "Retorica ed esegesi in Sant'Agostino," in *L'umanesimo di Sant'Agostino*, 215–223.

the difference between classical pagan eloquence and Christian eloquence. The end point of this development is defined in Augustine's *Teaching Christianity*.

If we are to understand Saint Augustine from within, as it were, we must follow his prose through the cosmic harmonies which he hears and translates and by means of which he communicates his faith. He is the theologian of the beauty of number as a universal set of relations. His interior life flowers in the soil of an intense spiritual experience. We have to approach him without breaking the unity between thought and action that shapes and binds together all the Fathers of the Church. The modern world cannot understand him because it has separated theology from science and made it something alien to the Christian people. How can they read Justin and Irenaeus, Origen and Gregory of Nyssa, Ambrose and Augustine?

By deciding to pursue the culture of science as a method of experimentation, without which nothing is regarded as true and believable, we have lost the dimensions of the human person. We need only think here of computers. The dimensions of the human being are interwoven; if one is lost, all are lost. For us nowadays a symbol is a fanciful linking of two ideas, an expressive device that adds nothing to reality. For the ancients, on the contrary, symbols were one of the many means of heightening awareness. By means of symbols they could gain insight into many things that could not be reached by cold reasoning.

For the ancients, symbols guided the mind into areas which ordinary language is unable to penetrate directly.

Saint Augustine is familiar with the logical processes used in scientific research, because geometry and astronomy should, by means of arithmetic, help in grasping many areas of reality that are reflected in the Bible. They are, so to speak, an exegetical necessity. In biblical exegesis an element of recollection is combined with series of images in order to open the door to other spiritual horizons.

With his gaze this man who turned the sacred scriptures into a book of the interior life embraced the various aspects of this book in unbroken succession. One of the elements recalled, one that appears frequently as a sign in the pages of the Bible, is number. Exegesis was to be a service to those who desired to draw near to the word of God in order to hear and assimilate it to the point of living it and sharing in it.

In a prayer for understanding of the sacred scriptures Saint Augustine asked that he might not be deceived in them and might not lead others astray.[17] In *Teaching Christianity* he expressly states that ignorance of numbers hinders the grasp of the metaphorical and mystical sense of much that is found in the Bible: "Unfamiliarity with numbers is…the cause of

---

17. *Confessions* 11, 3.

one's not understanding many things, which are put down metaphorically and mystically in scripture."[18]

This statement of Augustine reveals a quite specific method. According to sacred scripture the creator has arranged everything "by measure and number and weight" (Wis 11:20). Clement of Alexandria regards geometry as a science that helps lead us into things divine and into the Holy of Holies.[19] Plato, too, had said that God always "geometrizes."[20] Anticipating the direction taken by analytic geometry, Saint Augustine regards number as the foundation of mathematics and the natural sciences. He was a keen observer, to the point of grasping the principle of mathematical and philosophical infinity. In his view, memory contains the countless relations and laws of arithmetic and geometry, none of which is impressed on the mind by the external senses.[21]

Our eyes can see even the finest lines, such as the threads of a spider's web, but geometric lines are quite different, because they are invisible to the eyes of the body. We know them in our minds, but without thinking of any object whatsoever. We can indeed have sensations of numbered objects through the five senses of the body, but these objects are different from pure numbers and are not even images of these. Pure numbers are absolute realities.

The third to the sixth century saw advances in the mathematical sciences. The reason why the Fathers were aware of this progress was that number summons up geometry and geometry number. Lest we get lost in abstractions, let me give an example. In the language of Augustine's numerology we must take into account that numbers and geometric figures are interchangeable. In his usage the number four, which signifies the entire world as divided into east and west, north and south, becomes a symbol.

The number four is a reminder of the square and the square of the number four. Four is to be related especially to the square which a human being signifies by the horizontal line of the outstretched arms and the vertical line of the upright body. In other words, a person in this posture inscribes a cross within a square. This is one of the factors that leads to regarding the cross as an element of the cosmos.

When Saint Augustine supposes the Church, the apostles, and the prophets to be a cornerstone, he is trying to persuade his readers that the form of the square is connatural to Christians. In temptation Christians do not fall and, if pushed, they will turn but not fall, like the cornerstone which remains solidly grounded from whatever side it is approached. Augustine applies Psalm 36:24 in an exhortation: "So, then, you have been made four-

---

18. *Teaching Christianity* II, 16, 25.
19. *Stromata* 6, 11, 86 (GCS 15:474).
20. *Symposium* 8, 2.
21. *Confessions* X, 12, 19.

square and ready for all temptations; whatever assails you, let it not throw you back. Let everything that happens find you standing."[22]

As the number four refers to the square, so the number eight, which is the sum of seven and one, refers to the octagon. There is no point to my dwelling here on the ogdoad, since I have spoken of it elsewhere. I must simply note the picture of the "bending of the fingers" to indicate numbers (using the fingers in counting), along with the various images this could call up; it is one of the vivid sources of symbolic language that appears in exegesis. But of this, too, I have often spoken.

Following the lead of Archimedes, Augustine distinguishes between science and technique.[23] In music the technique consists in the use of instruments; instrumentation seeks material effects and the applause of the public; it is not the spirit that inspires the composition. In his *Music*, after dealing with technique, which is not science, Saint Augustine moves on to the essential part: the power of number, which controls every movement and every rule for the succession of sounds. Number that results from measure in the relationship of the sounds is the soul of music because it gives rise to all the sensations. It gives value to tempo and establishes the relations between the various movements and their parts. Saint Augustine uses number to explain the variety of movements.[24]

In his view, primacy in all the sciences belongs to number, which is classified in arithmetic, while arithmetic proceeds independently of the other sciences. This is a principle that Boethius later borrows from Saint Augustine.[25] For Boethius, too, music makes use of arithmetical principles to express its own relationships. In the measurement of lines and figures geometry necessarily makes use of arithmetic.

With the help only of number and geometrical figures astronomy is able to study the movements of the stars. In Saint Augustine's view, number, which underlies rhythm, is connected not with the world of matter but with the world of the soul. It tends to infinity; it shares in the incorporeal reality of the spirit; and it is an operation of the soul.[26]

As for the law governing rhythm, the series of numerical relations—equal or multiplied or one-and-a-half—keeps returning endlessly, like number itself; by "one-and-a-half" is meant a number that contains another

22. *Expositions of the Psalms* 86, 3.
23. See my study, "Le scienze e la numerologia," in *Atti del Congresso internazionale su S. Agostino nel XVI centenario della conversione, Roma 15–20 settembre 1986* I (= *Studia Ephemeridis "Augustinianum"* 24) 419–438; idem, "La sicilianità di Firmico Materno, i suoi *Matheseos libri* e la cultura cristiana delle scienze nel IV secolo," in the collective work, *Il cristianesimo in Sicilia dalle origini a Gregorio Magno* (Caltanissetta, 1987) 127–167.
24. See G. Marzi's introduction to his translation of *On Music* in Collana di Classici della filosofia, ed. at Gallarate (Florence, 1969) 11–68.
25. See F. Di Mieri, "Il *De institutione arithmetica* di S. Boezio," *Sapientia* 37 (1984) 179–202.
26. *Music* VI, 6, 16.

one and a half times (as three contains two). The eternity and immutability of numbers depends on one, which is eternal and immutable. And as one is in a direct relationship with all other numbers, so every nature tends to unity.[27]

The spheres, whose movement we see with the help of our senses and of everything that is included in them, can receive and retain their arrangement in space only if preceded by a succession of times, which are a matter of movement. In turn, vital movement precedes and measures, in a succession of intervals, the numbers whose rhythms define time. And to these the rational and intelligible rhythms of souls transmit the very arrangement decreed by God, including the order established on earth and beneath it.[28]

With his comprehensive vision of the physical world and the world of human beings, and in an effort to bring the one closer to the other, Saint Augustine looks for common denominators, which he finds in number. He starts from areas which have become excessively separated in our minds and therefore seem disparate and distant from one another, whereas in reality they are all linked. He looks for a guiding thread that will help him to narrow the gap between science and the interior life.

This is the reason for enormous difficulties in Augustinian research, and it is a fundamental reason. Saint Augustine, then, sees all the disciplines as interconnected, but his major concern is the passage from the one to the other in their universal functionality despite the human tendency to get lost in details. He even shows how the wicked and the impious can devote themselves to studies. Using the reflection of John: *If the Son frees you, you will be truly free* (Jn 8:36), he tells such people that they are inconsistent, because whatever is in agreement with freedom is also in agreement with truth.

The incarnate Word says: *The truth will make you free* (Jn 8:32). Therefore neither the impious fables of the poets nor the elegant lies of the orators nor the elucubrations of the philosophers that darken the heart and lead it to folly are consistent with Christian freedom. They are sophistries that seek to substitute corruptible mortals for the incorruptible God; they represent the proud error of those who seek to pass off as science that which is fact has nothing to do with science.[29]

Number is for Saint Augustine the starting point for both astronomical calculations and the harmonies of sound. It is precisely the concept of rhythm that constantly postulates a relationship that is inseparable from the concept of number. The alternations of short and long sounds in the various tempos lead us to the temporal values which the soul projects into the metaphysical world. From the earth the soul rises to God, from time to eternity. We must hark back to the great mystery of the number one. Saint

---

27. *Ibid.*, 1, 7, 13—13, 28.
28. *Ibid.*, VI, 17, 58.
29. Letter 101, 2.

Augustine looks at the relations of the various feet not with the senses but with the mind. Syllables are long in relation to short syllables, and short in relation to long ones.[30] He has a clear concept of melody and rhythm.

As everyone knows, rhythm is obtained through an arrangement in which long and short syllables follow in a determined order; this causes the listener (according to Augustine) to perceive a rational alternation of long and short beats. This succession of long and short beats gives rise precisely to rhythm. Melody arises out of the modulated utterance of syllables that are sung on different notes, some lower, others higher: *flexus* or *inclinatio vocis* (variation in pitch; inflection of the voice). Rhythm is the principle, the active element, the soul of the arrangement of the words; melody is the passive element, a kind of resistant matter. Saint Augustine had intended to write six books on melody, but his responsibilities as a churchman prevented him.[31] Thus we are without a work that would have explained a great deal to us.

We cannot simple indulge in inferences, but we may say this much: the subject would have led Augustine to discourse on natural harmonies and the common denominators found in these, thus enabling him to rise to the metaphysical plane. He would have continued to speak of number as he had already done in dealing with metrical feet. He sees the large picture, and every detail has the important role of being an element that helps in the reconstruction and understanding of things. In emphasizing the rhythmical movement he does not neglect "the measured intervals of silence," that is, the beats between various syllables, better known as the "empty beats" (*inania tempora*).[32]

He is concerned about the obstacles that hinder the understanding of the sacred scriptures, but he cannot be always dealing with insulting objections, although he does refute these. He wants to take a rational approach and help others to learn from experience how natural and fulfilling it is to read the Bible.

Chapter 3

In writing the fourth book of *Teaching Christianity*, Saint Augustine went back to the values contained in the formal rhetoric of his time; this meant to the stichometric manner of speaking that was used in the schools of the grammarians and rhetoricians of that age. Saint Augustine's problem was to work out the relationship between wisdom and eloquence while going back to the Bible; he sought a radical resolution of the problem.

He starts from the principle that wisdom is something that cannot be manufactured, and he tries to prove this with examples from the scriptures. The analysis is one which this master of rhetoric makes in a clear and per-

---

30. *Music* VI, 14, 4.
31. Letter 101, 3.
32. Quintilian, *De institut. orat.* 9, 4, 51.

suasive manner. He draws his reader's attention to the fact that the relation between wisdom and effective speech has been the subject of lengthy discussions among rhetoricians and philosophers,[33] but for the sake of brevity he limits himself to a statement of Cicero as an example: "Wisdom without eloquence is of little use to society, while eloquence without wisdom is frequently extremely prejudicial to it, never of any use."[34] In Augustine's eyes, the idea of wisdom was so precious that it could not escape the attention of those who were fully aware of what rhetoric taught, of those "who thought the art of rhetoric... worth teaching," that is, men like Cicero.[35]

Contrary to appearances, Saint Augustine always prefers brevity in presenting an argument; this was a gift which Cassiodorus attributed to him.[36] Thus after citing the statement of Cicero he immediately turns to the subject of the scriptures without any further discussion of the point he has made. He cites a passage from Paul (Rom 5:3–5) in order to show the indissoluble bond existing between wisdom and effective speech. Here is the passage as Saint Augustine read it:

> We glory in tribulations, knowing
> that tribulation results in patience,
> patience in approbation,
> approbation in hope,
> while hope does not confound,
> because the love of God has been poured out in our hearts
> through the Holy Spirit
> which has been given to us.[37]

I have divided the passage into clauses (*kôla*) and phrases (*kommata*) in order to follow the system which Saint Augustine explicitly applies in his formal rhetorical analysis. First of all, he sees in the passage the figure of speech known in Latin as *gradatio* (a series of increasingly forceful propositions), in Greek as *klimax* (ladder). Then, careful to make the ideas clear, he explains what a *gradatio* is: it does not call up the image of a ladder, since the steps are not arranged one above the other, but are here inserted one within another. Patience is connected with tribulation and approbation, and hope with approbation. He does not tell us what the correct name of this figure of speech might be, but simply calls attention to the fact that the Latins did not want to call it a "ladder."[38]

33. *Teaching Christianity* IV, 5, 7.
34. *De inventione rhetorica* 1, 1, cited in *Teaching Christianity* IV, 5, 7.
35. On the relation between wisdom and eloquence see my study *"Sapientia ed eloquentia* nell'insegnamento e nella prosa di S. Agostino," *Conv. studio e aggiorn. Facoltà di Lettere crist. e class. Pontif. Instit. altioris Latinitatis Rome 20–21 marzo 1987* (Biblioteca di sienze religiose 80; Rome, 1988) 165–182.
36. See my essay, "La *elocutio* di S. Agostino nella riflessione di Cassiodoro," in *Miscellanea A. Trapè* (= *Augustinianum* 25 [1985]) 385–403.
37. *Teaching Christianity* IV, 7, 11.
38. *Ibid.*

He has passed from the general to the particular, as though reticent lest he lose the thread of his discourse in the labyrinth of the figures of speech and their variations.

Continuing his exegesis of the passage from Paul, he calls our attention to the different tones of voice that are needed in order to capture each nuance of the image throughout the circuit of propositions which we today call principal and secondary, or coordinate and subordinate, but which the ancients simply called "clauses" and "phrases." In the teaching of rhetoric rules concerning the use of the voice were given in the fifth division of the subject, namely, the oratorical action or delivery of the speech.

But these precepts are connatural to human discourse and implicit in it, and Saint Augustine does not mention them. He does however say that in order to avoid all misunderstanding when reading the Bible aloud, the necessary balance must be observed between the phonetic value of the words and their expressive value. (We must not forget the important role played by the lector in the reading of the sacred texts during the liturgy in the early centuries.) This kind of reading is one of the "embellishments" of which Saint Augustine often speaks.

> There is also another embellishment to be observed, that after some phrases, each terminated by a pause, which our people call "clauses" or just "phrases," while the Greeks call them *kolons* and *kommas*, there follows a round or circuit, which they call a *periodos*, whose clauses are held in suspense by the voice of the speaker, until it ends with the last of them. Thus the first of the clauses that precede the period, is *that tribulation results in patience*, the second is *patience in approbation*, the third *approbation in hope*. Then the period is joined on, consisting of three clauses, in which the first is *while hope does not confound*, the second *because the love of God is poured out in our hearts*, the third *through the Holy Spirit which has been given to us*.[39]

Saint Augustine ends by saying that all these things are well-known and "taught in courses on the art of eloquence."[40] As far as Saint Paul is concerned, then, while we cannot claim that he consciously observes the rules of eloquence, neither can we deny that his eloquence is due to his content, that is, wisdom.

In the Second Letter to the Corinthians Saint Paul rebukes certain pseudoapostles from Judaism, who had scolded him. When forced to defend himself he admits his own folly, but, observes Saint Augustine, with what wisdom and what eloquence he does so! The Bishop of Hippo turns again to the idea of wisdom as the guide of an eloquence that achieves beauties of thought and phrase through the use of antonomasia: Paul acts as "the

---

39. *Ibid.*
40. *Ibid.*

companion of wisdom, the leader of eloquence, following the former, going ahead of the latter, and not spurning her as she follows."[41]

As he cites this entire passage (2 Cor 11:16–30), Augustine is struck by the commatic style of what he is transcribing. Historical linguistics at that time, which meant formal rhetorical analysis, had not yet viewed this as a stylistic genre, but it had adverted to its passing presence in some stichometric units. In order to talk of the phenomenon, rhetoricians had to fall back on the division of the period into *kôla* and *kommata*, which the Latins called "clauses" and "phrases" (*membra et incisa*).

As we saw a little earlier, the word *incisum* (phrase) is also called *caesum* (also = phrase) by Augustine in *Teaching Christianity*.[42] In order that I may not have to repeat myself I refer the reader to a study of mine on the shift from sentence construction "by short phrases" (*incisim*) in the variety proper to classical pagan prose, to the commatic genre, in the true and proper sense, of Christian writers.[43] In fact, to designate a style, whether the grand, the moderate, or the plain, Saint Jerome uses the term "commatic genre." It is the biblical exegetes who have uncovered its presence in sacred scripture and tell us of all the times it is present. Saint Augustine notes that a literary form reflects a particular state of mind.

He is very attentive to the variety of the movements of the soul that are expressed (in 2 Cor 11:16–30) through the sequence of words, in an always lively eloquence that does not become monotonous. Saint Augustine seems to be saying that construction "by clauses" (*membratim*) is not the same construction "by short phrases" (*incisim*). He meticulously points out the various parts of the discourse and calls attention to the effort that must be made in repeating well-known and more than well-known ideas. Let us not forget that his intention is to teach a lesson to relapsed rhetoricians, both pagan and Christian, who are not convinced that there is a wisdom in the Bible that is conveyed through formal values. He knows that his effort is not a superfluous one, since the demonstration of principles must be convincing.

His intention is to single out the clauses and periods on which the commatic structure depends. After the verbs "follow" and "add" and the adverbs of time such as "then" and "already" and the adverbs of place such as "thence" and the adversative conjunction "however," he lists the lines (in a stichometric analysis) that signal the commatic form. We are here being given an analysis of rhetorical form that is important because it takes us into a world that eludes us. He identifies the clauses of the period in order to prevent confusion, and immediately gives an example. He states beforehand that a period cannot have only one clause but must have two, three, four, five, six or even more.[44]

---

41. *Ibid.* IV, 7, 12.
42. *Ibid.*, IV, 7, 11.
43. See my book, *Dagli incisi al sermo commaticus* (Bari, 1956) 22–28.
44. *Teaching Christianity* 4, 7, 13.

A two-clause period, "For you put up with it, if anyone reduces you to slavery," is followed by three phrases:

If anyone swallows you up,
if anyone takes you in,
if anyone pushes himself forward.[45]

In the commatic structure a question is not lost sight of when the answer follows immediately. A period of three clauses, "But in whatever respect anyone puts on a bold face—I speak in folly—I do so too," is followed by three question-and-answer phrases:

Are they Hebrews? I am too.
Are they Israelites? I am too.
Are they the seed of Abraham? I am too.[46]

But in the fourth line the commatic pace is broken: there is a counter-clause instead of a counter-phrase:

Are they ministers of Christ? I speak as a fool—
I am more so.[47]

Next come four phrases that seem to give form to the claim just made:

In labors endlessly,
in prisons more frequently,
in beatings beyond measure,
at the point of death more often.[48]

Then a short period is inserted that consists of two clauses, these being indicated by the use of the voice:

From the Jews five times — have I received forty strokes less one,[49]

And this is followed by three phrases:

Three times have I been beaten with rods,
once I have been stoned,
three times shipwrecked.[50]

After the clause, "I have been a night and day in the depth of the sea," comes "flowing out with a most becoming force":

45. *Ibid.*
46. *Ibid.*
47. *Ibid.*
48. *Ibid.*
49. *Ibid.*
50. *Ibid.*

Often on journeys,
in danger of rivers,
in danger of robbers,
in danger from my kin,
in danger from the nations,
in danger in the city,
in danger in the wild,
in danger in the sea,
in danger among false brethren;
in toil and distress,
too often going without sleep,
in hunger and thirst,
too often fasting,
in cold and nakedness.[51]

Finally, there is a three-clause period: "Apart from these outward matters, the daily assault on me, my anxiety for all the churches."[52]

Saint Augustine excuses himself from going through the rest of this passage or other passages of scripture, but says that if one were to deal with other passages in the same manner, one would find that the devices taught in the schools of rhetoric are the same as those already to be seen in Paul. If they are taught by professors, they are highly esteemed and bought at a high price because they are communicated with great pomp and show. It is this self-advertisement that Augustine fears seeming to engage in when he speaks of these matters. He could not fail to respond to poorly educated people who scorn the books of sacred scripture, not because they lack eloquence which these people so greatly extol, but because they do not parade it.[53]

Turning from Saint Paul, Saint Augustine decides to say something about the eloquence of the prophets, whose figurative language conceals a great many things. From among the prophets he chooses Amos,[54] who says that he is a shepherd and herdsman and that he was taken from that activity by God in order that he might speak to the people. But Saint Augustine will not analyze the text as found in the Septuagint because the text there seems to have undergone additions meant to encourage readers to search out a spiritual sense; this is why we must assign to the translators some passages that are overly obscure because overly figurative. Instead he will analyze the Hebrew text as translated into Latin by the presbyter Jerome, who is highly knowledgeable about both languages.[55]

---

51. *Ibid.*
52. *Ibid.*
53. *Ibid.*, IV, 7, 14.
54. *Ibid.*, IV, 7, 15.
55. *Ibid.*

The prophet's opening denunciation could not but rouse the drowsy senses:

> Woe to you who are opulent in Sion, and place your trust in the mountain of Samaria, aristocrats, heads of peoples, pompously pacing into the house of Israel![56]

The prophet next shows how ungrateful these people were for the blessings of God, who had given them an extensive kingdom. Why ungrateful? Because they were putting their trust in the mountain of Samaria where they were worshiping idols. Therefore he continues:

> Pass over to Calneh and see, and go from there to Hamath the great; and go down to Gath of the Philistines, and to each of their best kingdoms, if their boundaries are wider than your boundaries.

In Saint Augustine's eyes, the prophet's discourse is here adorned with place names as with "lights": Sion, Samaria, Hamath the great, Gath of the Philistines. Furthermore, through the "nice variety" of the words associated with the places the prophet wanted to make use of varied terms that might seem synonymous but with their slight nuances of meaning acquire special values; the play of long and short syllables provides another embellishment by making the prose rhythmic.[57]

Due to the punctuation which we introduce into modern editions we miss out on this "embellishment" which the ancients looked for. Our punctuation is logical, but has removed the rhythm. Saint Augustine has been careful to point out the key rhythmic words that make vivid to us the way in which the rich of Israel move within the closed circle of their self-centeredness.

> Opulenti estis [you are opulent] = choreic foot
> confiditis [you place your trust] = cretic foot
> transite [pass over] = trochaic foot
> ite [go] = trochaic foot
> descendite [go down] = cretic foot.[58]

These are key words that are placed in the various clauses as points of reference for the rhythm. As I noted earlier, Saint Augustine sees the length of the various feet in relation not to the senses but to reason. Syllables are long in relation to short syllables and short in relation to long syllables. The iambic meter (a short and a long), even when pronounced rather slowly, never loses its proportion of one to two. On the other hand, if the pronunciation of a pyrrhic foot (two shorts) is slowed down, the result is a spondee (two longs), and in this case we are relying no longer on grammar but on music.[59]

---

56. *Ibid.*, IV, 7, 16. The whole of Amos 6:1–6 is cited here.
57. *Ibid.*, IV, 7, 17.
58. *Ibid.*
59. See my essay, "Le scienze e la numerologia," 424–426.

The words cited by Saint Augustine all show the one-to-two proportion. Present here is the great mystery of "one." He sees many precepts
regarding delivery in this and other passages of the prophet Amos, which
he comments on word for word.

When he comes to the final words, "And they felt nothing for the grinding down of Joseph,"[60] he observes that there is a figure of speech here that
had not been classified by the rhetoricians. The figure of speech consists, of
course, in this, that "Joseph" stands for all the other brothers, each of whom
has his own proper name. Augustine does not call this "synecdoche," and
in any case he avoids attributing great importance to the definition of the
various tropes. He even says: "Whether indeed this trope... is propounded
in that art of rhetoric which I both learned and taught, I do not know."[61]

Chapter 4

The exactness of Christian doctrine has stripped its language of redun-
dancy and has limited its use to the areas of grave and moderate eloquence.
An example is the style of Cyprian, although even he at times displays an
excessively embellished eloquence that is not in keeping with the serious-
ness of the subject.[62]

But when the moment for speaking comes, let churchmen reflect that a
properly ordered mind should remember what the Lord himself said: *It is
not you who are speaking, but the Spirit of your Father who is speaking in
you* (Mt 10:19). The rules telling us how to teach are necessary, however, and
mastery requires more than that the Holy Spirit be guiding us. Otherwise,
everything would become useless, even prayer, since *Your Father knows
what you need even before you ask it of him* (Mt 6:8). Nor should Paul have
told Timothy and Titus what and how to teach others.[63]

The two Letters to Timothy and the Letter to Titus should be always
before the eyes of those who have the office of teaching in the Church.
Those who in their discourses seek to persuade people to do what is good
by teaching, delighting, and swaying them should pray and do their utmost
to have people listen to them gladly and with understanding and docility.
Such speakers will reflect in their discourse what Cicero said: "That man
therefore will be eloquent, who can talk about minor matters calmly, about
middling ones moderately, about great matters grandly."[64]

Echoing Cicero, Saint Augustine is saying that a speaker will be eloquent
who in his teaching knows how to speak of minor matters in an unassuming
way; in order to please, he knows how to speak of things requiring average
intelligence in a temperate tone; and in order to persuade, he knows how

---

60. *Teaching Christianity* IV, 7, 2-.
61. *Ibid.*
62. *Ibid.*, IV, 15, 32.
63. *Ibid.*, IV, 16, 33.
64. *Ibid.*, citing Cicero, *De oratore* 29, 101.

to speak of important matters with a solemn eloquence.[65] Here we have the three kinds of style: the low or plain, the moderate, and the grand. Cicero can show us how the three styles are used in legal cases, but not in ecclesiastical situations. For us, on the other hand, everything we say, especially from the pulpit (Augustine: "from our higher position"), is important because it has to do with eternal salvation. Here everything becomes important, even small things. The gospel itself tells us that *anyone who is faithful in a minimal amount is also faithful in a great amount* (Lk 16:10). In other words, it is important to be faithful in unimportant matters.

The model here is a circle. In this geometric figure "the essence of roundness, that is where the lines from the center to the edge are all equal, is the same in a large dish as in a small coin." Saint Augustine concludes: "In the same way, where minor matters are dealt with justly, this does not diminish the greatness of justice."[66]

Saint Paul uses the grand or solemn style when in the First Letter to the Corinthians (6:1–9) he criticizes the faithful who started proceedings before the civil tribunals instead of resolving financial disputes within the community, as if there were no one there wise enough to act as judge between brothers and sisters. He reprimands, scolds, and threatens. He is greatly troubled in mind, and his voice changes. He uses solemn words for things that might seem negligible. But he acts in this way because of justice, charity, and faith, in the eyes of which even little matters are as important as great matters.[67]

"If we were advising people how they should conduct their secular business…before ecclesiastical judges, we would rightly advise them to present it calmly, as a minor matter."[68] But when dealing with a subject that is in itself a lofty one, a speaker should speak calmly when teaching, in a moderate style when preaching, and in a solemn style with a soul that had debased itself.[69] Solemn expression is in place when speaking of the divinity, but here again a variety of styles is needed.

Saint Augustine finds an example of the low or plain style in Saint Paul's Letter to the Galatians (3:15–22), where the apostle speaks of Abraham having two sons, one by a slave woman, the other by a free woman. Abraham was told of the promises to himself and his offspring: not to his offsprings but to his offspring, namely, Christ. If the inheritance were to come from the law, it would no longer come from the promises, and yet God gave it to Abraham in virtue of the promises.

But the question arises: Why was the law given if the inheritance does not derive from it? The answer: The law was given because of transgressions, until the offspring should come to whom the inheritance had been

---

65. *Ibid.*, IV, 16, 34.
66. *Ibid.*, IV, 18, 35.
67. *Ibid.*, IV, 18, 36.
68. *Ibid.*, IV, 18, 37.
69. *Ibid.*, IV, 19, 38.

promised. If a law had been given that could bestow life, righteousness would come through the law. But scripture encloses everything in sin because the promise was given to believers through faith in Christ. According to Saint Augustine, the teacher must render plain what is hidden and answer every question, provided we are not upset by questions we cannot answer.[70]

For the moderate style Saint Augustine refers to 1 Timothy 3:1; Romans 6:15; 12:1, 16; 13:8, 12–14. He calls attention not only to the speech patterns and the positioning of the clauses and period but also the harmony of the words, although this is difficult to preserve in the Latin translation. He says that the translation is a literal one, in which the order of words in the original is preserved but without having the rhythm of the original.[71]

He does not lay great emphasis on "number" [= rhythm or cadence], which, he says "is wanting in our authors."[72] But he does not want to play down the importance of their profound divine statements by seeking to judge them according to their rhythmical cadence, which perhaps we are unable to appreciate in their original languages. The prophets were familiar with flowing, harmonious discourse, and Saint Jerome tells us that he saw them in the Hebrew text. Saint Augustine writes: "I do not neglect these concluding rhythms in my own speaking, as far as I consider can decently be done; still what gives me more pleasure in our authors is that I find them there so very infrequently."[73]

The solemn or grand style differs from the moderate due to "the impetuous expression of deep feelings." It can use formal embellishments but does not go looking for them. The words themselves express the ardor of the heart. Saint Paul uses the solemn style in 2 Corinthians 6:2–11, a passage that does not lack these "embellishments of speech."[74]

The same holds for the Letter to the Romans, when the apostle speaks of the persecutions of this world that can be overcome only by a charity based on the hope of help from God (Rom 8:28–39).[75] The Letter to the Galatians is written in the calm style, except in one of its last parts (4:10–20), which can only be described as written in the moderate style.[76] Nor is it a lukewarm feeling that lends ardor to the apostle's expression of his thoughts; his words to the Galatians are profound. They are to be committed to memory. In order to plumb their full meaning there is need not only of a reader but of an exegete, whom Saint Augustine calls an "expositor."[77]

He sees that through the reading of the biblical texts Christian writers have in the course of time made progress in religious knowledge and, by

---

70. *Ibid.*, IV, 20, 39.
71. *Ibid.*, IV, 20, 40.
72. *Ibid.*, IV, 20, 41.
73. *Ibid.*
74. *Ibid.*, IV, 20, 42.
75. *Ibid.*, IV, 20, 43.
76. *Ibid.*, IV, 20, 44.
77. *Ibid.*, IV, 21, 45.

expressing themselves in these various styles, have rendered a great service to the Church. The Bishop of Hippo, with his historical awareness, knows ancient Christian literature in its stages of development. Here he gives the example of Cyprian who used the plain style in speaking of the sacrament of the cup and settling the question of whether the Lord's cup should have only water in it or water mixed with wine.

In his exegesis of Genesis 8:20–23 Saint Cyprian sees the passion of Christ prefigured by Noah, who drank not water but wine. In like manner, he sees the sacrament of the Lord prefigured by Melchizedek (Gen 14:18 and Ps 110:3–4) who offered bread and wine and blessed Abraham. Saint Ambrose, too, when dealing with the very exalted subject of the Holy Spirit and demonstrating the equality of the Spirit with the Father and the Son, uses the plain style and relies on exegesis of the Bible (1 Cor 10:4; Num 11:4; Lk 12:49).[78]

Turning back to Cyprian: he uses the moderate style in his praise of virginity,[79] the same style that is used by Saint Ambrose[80] when proposing models for consecrated virgins to imitate in their way of life. To exemplify the solemn style, Saint Augustine recalls that both Cyprian and Ambrose used the solemn style in inveighing with fervent pointedness against women who color their faces with various cosmetics.[81]

After citing a passage of Saint Ambrose in which he speaks of this alteration of one's natural features as a sin against nature, Saint Augustine thinks that on reading such a piece of eloquence women feel urged no longer to alter their natural appearance but to grow in modesty.[82] It is a piece of writing that is to be regarded as unqualifiedly in the solemn style. In both figures of speech and styles Saint Augustine is for variety. If a discourse remains too long in one style it cannot hold the hearers' attention, but if it shifts to a different style, the discourse becomes more acceptable. Nevertheless the prolonged use of the plain style is more tolerable than the prolonged use of the solemn style.[83]

It is left to the author's discretion to speak in the plain style of matters that might be conveyed in the solemn style. In praise or rebuke the moderate style should be used and introduced. In a discourse in the solemn style there is a place for the other two genres, and the same is true of a discourse in the plain style. Not to be forgotten is the rule that the moderate style is used to delight the spirit, not to rouse it to action.[84]

It is not to be thought that an orator will be applauded more often and more warmly if he speaks in the solemn style. The same result can be

---

78. *Ibid.,* IV, 21, 46.
79. *Ibid.,* IV, 21, 47.
80. *Ibid.,* IV, 21, 48.
81. *Ibid.,* IV, 21, 49.
82. *Ibid.,* IV, 21, 50.
83. *Ibid.,* IV, 22, 51.
84. *Ibid.,* IV, 23, 52.

obtained from the plain style and from the embellishments of the moderate style. The solemn genre should hush outcries and make the tears flow. In this context, Saint Augustine tells of his experience with "the mob" in Caesarea of Mauritania. He is referring to a fierce battle in which not only fellow citizens, but relatives, friends, brothers, parents and sons fought one another.

These people were divided into two factions and fought each other for two straight days, even to the point of killing one another. Augustine decided to have recourse to the solemn style in order to root out this cruel and inveterate practice from the hearts of the citizens of Mauritanian Caesarea. He did not think he had succeeded in his undertaking until he saw tears pour from their eyes. Applause may signify understanding, but tears reflect something deeper, namely, that the hearers are moved and fully convinced.[85] For eight or more years now nothing of that sort has been attempted again. Saint Augustine ends his vivid story of the incident with an aposiopesis: "There are many other experiences which have taught me that people have shown by their groans rather than their shouts, sometimes also by their tears, and finally by the change in their lives, what the grandeur of a wise man's speech has achieved in them."[86]

Saint Augustine continues to speak of the three styles and the shifts from one to the other, but on the level of formal rhetorical analysis.[87] As far as he can, he points out the motifs that interiorize the results desired. He sees, however, that questions are not really answered on the level of formal rhetoric. Even the use of the plain style changed people who were rather intellectually inclined. They may have been led to accept what they had thought unbelievable, but they were not moved to put it into practice.[88] Perhaps the solemn style was needed for this?

The task of all three genres of discourse is to persuade. If a speaker does not persuade, he does not achieve the goal he has set for himself, that is, the goal of eloquence itself. In the plain style he persuades people that what he says is true; in the solemn style he persuades them to put into practice what they know they ought to do but do not in fact do; in the moderate style he persuades them to admire the beauty of his speech. With a certain intolerance, Saint Augustine asks in regard to this last goal: "What need do we have of an aim like that?" Let those have this aim who glory in being mere men of letters; in their panegyrics let them speak so as to delight their hearers. We use the moderate or the solemn style for the purpose of having our hearers love what is good and avoid what is evil.

---

85. *Ibid.*, IV, 24, 53.
86. *Ibid.*
87. *Ibid.*, IV, 24, 54.
88. *Ibid.*, IV, 25, 55.

Chapter 5

In sections 21–30 of the fourth book Saint Augustine seems to dwell on general principles of eloquence, but in fact his intention is to stress the point that exegetes must explain the subject matter of the Bible to others. Eloquence is also related to wisdom.[89] The biblical writings are both wise and eloquent. Exegetes must not speak as though they possessed the same authority as the books which they are explaining, but must endeavor to make themselves understood. They must not concern themselves with being eloquent teachers but with the clarity of what they say.[90] They must set aside any affected language and use everyday words in order to avoid ambiguity and obscurity, thus practicing a kind of "diligent negligence."

Of what value is scrupulosity in the choice of words if the hearers are unable to understand the discourse? The listeners are to hear the truth and understand what they have heard.[91] Exegetes should not strive to teach with great fullness but rather so that the points are fixed in the minds of the hearers.[92] Good minds love what is true in words, not the sound of words themselves. Of what use is a golden key if it cannot open what we want?[93]

Saint Augustine borrows from oratory the principles that help exegetes to move the spirits of listeners, not to know what should be done but to do what they already know should be done.[94] This accounts for the exchanges between exegesis and ecclesiastical oratory, both of which have the same goal.

Great importance is given to the incantatory power of words; words can persuade people to do not only what ought not to be done but even very base and evil things. "May God spare his Church from experiencing what the prophet Jeremiah states about the synagogue of the Jews, when he says, *Amazement and horrid things have come upon the land; prophets were prophesying iniquity, and priests clapped their hands in applause, and my people loves it thus. And what will you do in the future?* (Jer 5:30–31)."

Saint Augustine sees this rebuke of Jeremiah as an axe that splits rocks. "Far be it from us that priests should applaud those who utter iniquity, and that the people of God should love it thus." Listen to what is just and not to what is iniquitous, even if this be said in an elegant discourse.[95]

The three genres (the plain, the moderate, and the grand) point to various circumstances, but they need some clarification. Our discourse falls within these three styles. Saint Augustine never moves beyond the bounds of formal rhetoric. For this reason he often returns to the details of each

---

89. See Marin, "Retorica ed esegesi," 215–223.
90. *Teaching Christianity* IV, 8, 22–23.
91. *Ibid.,* IV, 10, 25.
92. *Ibid.*
93. *Ibid.,* IV, 11, 26.
94. *Ibid.,* IV, 12, 27.
95. *Ibid.,* IV, 14, 30.

style. He notes that in using the solemn style we must not be boring if we expect to be heard willingly.[96]

In citing the testimonies of God, a situation in which we must use the plain style, we must speak so as to be heard with docility, as Psalm 92:5 desires: *Your testimonies have come to be exceedingly believed.* Many questions may be resolved using the plain style, and universal propositions, such as judgments, may be conveyed.[97] It is the aim of all three styles—the plain, the moderate, and the grand—to be heard with obedience compliance.[98] But if we are to be heard with obedient compliance, we must be fully understood.

In the matter of compliance, the speaker's manner of life carries greater weight than the grandeur of his discourse.[99] On the other hand, one who speaks learnedly and eloquently but lives an unworthy life may instruct many but will not profit his own soul, as Saint Paul says (Phil 1:18). Saint Augustine likes brevity and therefore he says things quickly. He tries to bring out even the smallest nuances in his exegesis of Paul. Christ must always be preached. But the truth can be preached even by a twisted and deceitful heart, by those who are seeking their own advantage, not that of Christ.

The faithful who listen obey not any human being but the Lord who says: *Do what they say; what they do, however, do not do, for they say and do not do* (Mt 23:3). For this reason it is possible to listen with profit to those who play an important part in the Church, a part established by sound doctrine, and do not dare to teach some views of their own. Of these scripture says: *They sit on the chair of Moses* (Mt 23:2). It is not their own chair, but the chair of Moses, and it compels them to say what is right even while doing what is wrong. In their personal lives they act in their own interest, but the chair prevents them from teaching their own views.[100]

Many people who are trying to defend their own bad behavior invoke their teachers.[101] They reproach them: "Why do you not do what you wish to teach me?" The pupils even reach the point of scorning the word of God.

Saint Paul speaks of this to Timothy: *Let nobody despise your youth* because of the qualities it must certainly show. *Be a model for the faithful in word, in behavior, in love, in faith, in charity* (1 Tm 4:12). In seeking to be heard with docile obedience, such a teacher may freely use the plain, the moderate, or the solemn style, because he does not live a disordered life.

He has chosen a good life and a good reputation before God and human beings (see 2 Cor 8:21). In speaking he keeps an eye on the truth and desires to be accepted for what he says. The teacher should not be the servant of his words, but the words the servant of the teacher, lest the power of Christ's

---

96. *Ibid.,* IV, 26, 56.
97. *Ibid.*
98. *Ibid.*
99. *Ibid.,* IV, 27, 59.
100. *Ibid.,* IV, 27, 60.
101. *Ibid.,* IV, 28, 61.

cross be frustrated. It is pointless to argue about words. Arguments over words only ruin those who are listening. Arguments should serve only to render clear and pleasing the truth that spurs to action. Even charity can never be rightly ordered if the things to be loved are not true but false.

Expression in which form and content are in harmony is a spontaneous application of one or other of the three styles: the plain, the moderate, or the grand. Such eloquence comes naturally if the speaker always has the truth before his mind and lives according to the Christian principles which he professes; such a life becomes a continual and effective catechesis: "a manner of life" that is itself "a kind of eloquent sermon."[102]

Those who steal take the belongings of others, but the word of God does not belong to others if the one who takes it is subject to him.[103] It becomes the possession of others in the case of those who, while communicating it well, live evil lives. Such is Saint Augustine's exegesis of Jeremiah 23:30. The ones who are stealing the words of God are those who want to appear good but are in fact wicked and act according to their own views. Saint Paul says of such people: *They claim that they know God, but they contradict it with their deeds* (Tit 1:16).

In another place scripture says: *Hypocrites, how can you say good things, since you are bad?* (Mt 12:34). An eloquent but bad person can compose a discourse in which he speaks the truth, but only provided it be delivered by another who is good, though not eloquent. Then the former hands over what is not his to another, while the latter receives what is his from the former.

In Saint Augustine's view, good Christians of orthodox faith communicate to one another, through the ordered lives they lead, the divine patrimony that belongs to all. He writes in his unmistakable prose: "When good men who are believers do this service for good men who are believers, both parties are saying what is their own, because God too is theirs and the things they are saying are his. And those who are unable to compose these good sermons make them their own, when they compose themselves to live according to what they contain."[104]

The holy bishop of Hippo believed that he could use his own experience to form those who set out to speak to the people. But, he says, anyone who must speak of things having to do not with temporal safety but with eternal salvation must pray even more fervently than Esther did before speaking to Ahasuerus.[105] The whole of *Teaching Christianity* is taken up with exegesis of the Bible; the fourth book is no different, but is in fact the culmination. Its intention is that the teaching of the faith should permeate

---

102. *Ibid.*
103. *Ibid.*, IV, 29, 62.
104. *Ibid.*
105. *Ibid.*, IV, 30, 63. See my essay, "Esth. 14, 13: 'Tribue sermonem compositum in ore meo,'" *Saggi patristici* (Quaderni de *Vetera Christianorum* 5; Bari, 1971) 245–262.

the thought and activity of anyone who wants to explain the word of God, which is never abstract but is meant to be translated into everyday life.

Close attention must be paid to the terms "teaching" and "Christianity," which Augustine uses. The work in its entirety brings together the word of God, the Church, and the duty of each believer to receive and pass on, with the single aim of salvation, what they themselves have assimilated and put into practice. At the end of the work the author admits that it has turned out to be longer than he expected. But he thinks it will not be long when the reader thinks of the other things left unsaid. What he has said is enough to awaken in the minds of others ideas and sentiments to be developed through images.

This is a work that should be read piecemeal and meditated on, because it can be fatiguing. The author thanks our God that with his limited abilities he has been able to set down in four books "what sort the pastor should be who is eager to toil away, not only for his own sake but for others, in the teaching of sound, that is of Christian, doctrine."[106]

A reading of the fourth book of *Teaching Christianity* has shown that in addition to grasping the tropological techniques used in the language of the Bible and to making a formal analysis of it, the exegete needs to conform his life to the principles which he intends to present to others as capable of implementation in everyday life. That is, Saint Augustine is raising the question of faith as a principle of knowledge for a greater understanding and better communication of biblical values.

Book IV of *Teaching Christianity* forms a natural conclusion to the first three, and its subject matter could not but have been taken up separately.

Antonio Quacquarelli

---

106. *Teaching Christianity* IV, 31, 64.

Hermeneutical Principles of Saint Augustine in *Teaching Christianity*

I do not intend, in this introduction, to discuss the whole of Augustinian exegesis. In Books II and III of *Teaching Christianity*[1] Saint Augustine expounds a series of hermeneutical principles for use in the explanation of scripture. My purpose is to review these rules of interpretation and to ask what value they may still have today for both the exegete and the practitioner of biblical theology. In his prologue Augustine says: "There are some rules for dealing with the scriptures, which I consider can be not inappropriately passed on to students; enabling them to make progress not only by reading others who have opened up the hidden secrets of the divine literature, but also by themselves opening them up to yet others again."[2]

Moving on, he anticipates three objections from those who maintain that such rules for interpretation will either not be understood or that, in the case of some who do understand them, they will be found to be inapplicable or that there are some who are able to understand the scriptures even without these rules. Augustine answers that he would not be at fault if he were to point to the new moon but the other either did not see his finger or did see it but could not find the heavenly body to which it pointed. They must pray that the Lord will open their eyes.[3] To the third objection he gives a modest answer: his purpose is simply to teach the alphabet to those who are unable to read, so that they can then read on their own.

The first book of *Teaching Christianity*, which together with Books II and III was probably written in 397 and revised in 427,[4] at which time Book IV was added, contains a summary of Christian doctrine that is based on the distinction between "using" (*uti*) and "enjoying" (*frui*). Only the Trinity and the mysteries of faith are to be enjoyed for their own sake; everything else, including the scriptures, are to be used in order to obtain faith, hope, and love:

---

1. PL 34:15–122; CSEL 80:3–169. This essay is a revision of an earlier article, "I principi ermeneutici di Sant'Agostino: una valutazione," *Lateranum*, n.s. 48 (1982) 209–223.
2. *Teaching Christianity*, prologue 1.
3. *Ibid.*, prologue 2–3.
4. *Revisions* II, 4, 30.

So what all that has been said amounts to, while we have been dealing with things, is that *the fulfillment and the end of the law* and of all the divine scriptures *is love.*[5]

So if it seems to you that you have understood the divine scriptures, or any part of them, in such a way that by this understanding you do not build up this twin love of God and neighbor, then you have not yet understood them.[6]

It is this principle of love as the ultimate goal of understanding of the Bible that relativizes, in Augustine's view, the efforts of a hypercritical exegesis that has knowledge as its sole aim. This does not mean that use should not be made of a "scientific" methodology, because if people who while misinterpreting the literal meaning nonetheless arrive at charity, they are like people who go astray from the right road but then by wandering across a field nonetheless accidentally reach their destination. Such persons should be corrected so that this sort of thing may not happen again.[7] It must be acknowledged, however, that many have reached the perfection of the three theological virtues even without books. For such persons the scriptures serve solely for the instruction of others.[8]

Fundamental to Augustinian hermeneutics is the distinction between thing and sign (although signs, too, are things which, in addition to the image of themselves which they transmit to the senses, by their presence bring something else to mind).[9] Signs can be natural or given (intentional, conventional),[10] and the latter in turn can be proper or metaphorical.[11] This confused multiplicity of signs is the source of the obscurity of the scriptures: "This is all due, I have no doubt at all, to divine providence, in order to break in pride with hard labor, and to save the intelligence from boredom, since it readily forms a low opinion of things that are too easy to work out."[12] At the same time, there are very many clear passages that rouse a hunger for further knowledge; in fact, there is almost nothing in obscure passages that is not also to be found in those that are clearer.[13]

Certain moral dispositions are essential if these obscurities are to be mastered, above all fear of God and humility, especially when scripture is rebuking us for our vices, lest we think we know better than what is written, even if obscurely.[14] Given these two stages in achieving wisdom through

---

5. *Teaching Christianity* I, 35, 39.
6. *Ibid.*, I, 36, 40.
7. *Ibid.*, I, 30, 41.
8. *Ibid.*, I, 39, 43.
9. *Ibid.*, II, 1, 1.
10. *Ibid.*, II, 1, 2.
11. *Ibid.*, II, 10, 15.
12. *Ibid.*, II, 6, 7.
13. *Ibid.*, II, 6, 8.
14. *Ibid.*, II, 7, 9.

the reading of the sacred text, we must persevere in knowledge, fortitude, counsel, the interior purification of the heart and, finally, in wisdom itself.[15]

Given the intermingling of clear and obscure passages, we must, logically, read "all" the scriptures, but only those that are "canonical." The apocrypha are useful only to those who are better instructed. In Augustine's time there was still some uncertainty as to what the canon included.[16] In Book II, 8, 13, he lists all the books which he considers canonical; his list will be defined, unchanged, at the Council of Trent.[17] What is of interest to us is the criterion which Augustine uses in determining the canonicity of a book:

> They will hold, therefore, to this standard with the canonical scriptures, that they will put those accepted by all the Catholic Churches before those which some do not accept; among these which are not accepted by all they will prefer those accepted by most of them, and by the greater ones among them, to those which fewer Churches and ones of lesser authority regard as canonical. Should they, however, discover that different ones are held to be canonical by the majority of Churches from those so regarded by the greater Churches—though this would be very unlikely—I consider that both should be regarded as having equal authority.[18]

This means that recognition of canonicity depends on their apostolic antiquity or else the number of Churches in which the books are publicly read. Augustine accepts the long canon, which includes the deuterocanonical books; this is not surprising in view of his attachment to the Septuagint version.

Those who read the whole of the scripture with the proper dispositions will find in the clear passages "everything that touches on faith, and good morals, that is to say hope and charity, which we dealt with in the previous book."[19] Therefore the rules of interpretation that follow will help in explaining the more difficult passages.

Difficulties can arise even from proper signs, that is, from words taken in their literal meaning. The first rule to be followed in shedding light on such doubtful words is to refer to the original languages, Hebrew and Greek. Even in the Latin manuscripts words can be found that are transcribed in their original Hebrew form, for example, amen, alleluia, raca, and hosanna;

---

15. *Ibid.*, II, 7, 10.
16. See I. Ruwet, *Institutiones Biblicae* (Rome, 1951) 132–141.
17. See H. Denzinger and A. Schönmetzer (eds.), *Enchiridion symbolorum* (32nd ed.; Freiburg, 1963) 1502–1503; J. Neuner and J. Dupuis (eds.), *The Christian Faith in the Doctrinal Documents of the Catholic Church* (rev. ed.; Staten Island, NY, 1983) nos. 211–212, or N. P. Tanner (ed.), *Decrees of the Ecumenical Councils* (2 vols.; London and Washington, D.C., 1990) II, 663–664.
18. *Teaching Christianity* II, 8, 12.
19. *Ibid.*, II, 9, 14.

these are not translated either out of respect for their antiquity or because they are untranslatable. To understand these words one must know Hebrew, but not only for the sake of these few words: "But it is not because of these few words, which can very easily be noted and asked about, that knowledge of these languages is necessary."[20]

In fact, Augustine complains that ever since the early days of the Church people who thought they understood Greek began to make translations into Latin, with the result that there were now so many conflicting translations. He complains that while those who have translated the Bible from Hebrew into Greek can be counted (he is referring to the Septuagint, the "Seventy"), translators from Greek into Latin are countless. Therefore the need of going back to the original languages.[21] He reviews some examples of conflicting translations to which he attempts to give an interpretation that fits both meanings. He adds that certain translations of idiomatic phrases have no meaning in Latin and give rise to barbarisms.[22]

Readers can find difficulty not only with ambiguous words but also with words or phrases unknown to them. When this happens, readers should either question those who speak the languages involved or learn these languages themselves, but if this is impossible they should consult the various translations, as long as the manuscripts of these are correct: "The first thing, in fact, to which those who wish to know the divine scriptures should devote their careful attention and their skill is the correction of their copies, so that the uncorrected ones give way to the corrected ones, which they derive, that is, from one and the same type of translation."[23] Augustine did not have the copyist's skill of a Jerome[24] so as to draw up rules for textual criticism, but he did know that preference should be given to more faithful manuscripts and to translations that followed the original more closely.

Among the various translations preference should be given to the "Itala," because it sticks more closely to the words and has a clearer grasp of the thought.[25] Scholars know the difficulty of identifying this "Itala," the only mention of which occurs in this passage. In the books which the Benedictines of Beuron already examined for their critical edition of the Vetus Latina, they have identified a certain number of passages which differ from those current in Africa, but they have not been willing to classify them under any of the titles thought up by earlier scholars, such as the "European Version" or the "Itala."[26]

From 400 on, Augustine used Jerome's revision (the Vulgate) of the four gospels in his church at Hippo, but he did not adopt Jerome's translation

---

20. *Ibid.*, II, 11, 16.
21. *Ibid.*
22. *Ibid.*, II, 12, 17—13, 20.
23. *Ibid.*, II, 14, 21.
24. See, for example, Jerome, *Comment. in Hier.* 31, 2, 15.
25. *Teaching Christianity* II, 15, 22.
26. For a modern discussion see *The Cambridge History of the Bible* I, 370–374.

of the Old Testament from the Hebrew, either because some other bishops had had negative reactions to it from their congregations[27] or because he himself had theological reasons for preferring the Septuagint.

In fact, "for correcting any Latin versions at all, Greek ones should be employed, among which, as regards the Old Testament, that of the Seventy Translators has the greatest authority."[28] From the *City of God* we know that Augustine was familiar with the other Greek translations, those of Aquila, Symmachus, Theodotion, and "the Fifth Edition."[29] His preference for the Septuagint was based on the story told by "Aristeas," that seventy translators had been closed up in separate rooms and had produced translations that were identical down to the least details. He interprets this as the work of the Holy Spirit who made use of an order from King Ptolemy to impel the translators to produce a version, suitable for the Gentiles among whom the gospel would later be preached, of the very scriptures that had so jealously been kept secret by the Jews:

> For this reason, even if things are found in Hebrew codices that differ from what the Seventy have put, in my judgment they should give way to what divine providence has achieved through these men; and that is that the books which the Jewish people were unwilling to share with others, whether out of a religious sense or out of envy, were made available by the Lord, using the royal authority of Ptolemy, to the nations that were going to believe. And so it can well be the case that these translated the Hebrew in such a way as the Holy Spirit, who was guiding them and gave them all one mouth, judged would be most suitable for the Gentiles.... As for the books of the New Testament, if there are any hesitations about the text due to the variety of Latin translations, nobody doubts that one should bow to the authority of the Greek texts, and of those especially which are to be found in the more learned and careful Churches.[30]

There is no difficulty with Augustine's approach to the New Testament. But when it comes to his preference for the Septuagint over the Hebrew text of the Old Testament, history has not gone along with him, although some critics are having second thoughts today.[31] The supremacy of the Vulgate in later centuries and its "canonization" by the Council of Trent[32] have proved Jerome right. Pius XII, for his part, prescribed the use of the original texts, while excusing Augustine on the grounds that Hebrew was

---

27. See Letter 71, 3, 5.
28. *Teaching Christianity* II, 15, 22.
29. *City of God* XVIII, 43.
30. *Teaching Christianity* II, 15, 22.
31. There is no doubt, of course, about the criticial vaue of the Septuagint for emending the Hebrew text; it is thought that the Septuagint reflects the Alexandrian tradition of the Hebrew text.
32. Denzinger-Schönmetzer, 1506; Neuner and Dupuis, no. 214; Tanner, II, 664.

not very well-known in his day.[33] In fact, nowadays all translations of the Old Testament into the vernacular are made from the Hebrew, but with an eye on the Septuagint. Today, however, some critics are taking more seriously the view that the Septuagint was inspired, even if no one believes anymore in the story told by Aristeas. It is a fact that the majority of the citations of the Old Testament in the New are taken from the Septuagint, even where this differs from the original and that some theological teachings, such as the virginity of Our Lord in Isaiah 7:14 (Mt 1:23), are based on the Septuagint.

Perhaps the "divine providence" of which Augustine speaks can be explained in a more scientific way, in accord with contemporary research, without appealing to a direct inspiration. Several centuries had passed between the composition of the old books in Hebrew and their translation into Greek; during these centuries the people were maturing religiously and theologically under the guidance of the Spirit of God. In the last centuries before the Christian era, then, certain doctrines had reached their mature form—especially doctrines on the resurrection, immortality, the angels, and the Bible itself—and are reflected in the Greek translation, which at times not only translated but interpreted the Hebrew. Thus, for example, in Job 42:17, Isaiah 26:19, and Daniel 12:2, which speak of resurrection, and in Deuteronomy 32:8, where it is said that "the children of Israel" become "the angels of the nations." The anthropomorphisms of the scriptures are toned down, and the books are given a different order. All this does not amount to the extensive reinterpretation that we find in the targums, but it does point to a type of interpretation that "updates" the thought of Israel in keeping with the final stages of divine revelation and makes it easier for Christians to use this translation when the right time comes.

The reason why Augustine went into the question of the necessity of knowing the original languages was to show the importance of "proper meanings" in the practice of interpretation. But the original languages play no less necessary a part in the interpretation of "metaphorical signs," especially when it comes to unlocking for us the meaning of certain proper names that have an exegetical interest (for example, the name "Siloam" in John 9:7[34]). But to this end there is also utility in all the human sciences and arts that help us understand a work like the Bible, which is at once historical and literary and belongs to a different environment. Augustine mentions in particular the natural sciences, music, the numerical sciences, astronomy (not astrology), art, history, the crafts, dialectic, logic, eloquence, and mathematics. All these sciences should be learned, not to make us proud but to serve the understanding of scripture, which increases love. They belong now by right no longer to the pagans who invented them but

---

33. Pius XII, Encyclical Letter *Divino afflante Spiritu*.
34. *Teaching Christianity* II, 16, 23.

to Christians. Thus is fulfilled what was written about the Hebrews: "And they shall despoil the Egyptians!"[35]

The third book of *Teaching Christianity* begins with a recapitulation of what has been said about the value of all this information in the understanding of scripture. It is evident that this insight of Augustine is, with the necessary adjustments, a surprisingly modern one. It shows a mind open to the contemporary culture that would later serve Boethius in laying the foundations of the medieval trivium and quadrivium. If Augustine values all these forms of knowledge in relation to charity, it is because he is speaking of them in the context of the understanding of scripture; he is speaking of them, that is, as what we today call "the auxiliary sciences to be used in the study of the Bible." The sciences are no longer the ones listed by Augustine, but the idea is inspired by the same purpose, namely, to shed light on the proper and metaphorical language of the text. When we speak today of identifying the literary genres of the Bible through study of the contemporary literatures, we are only extending the application of Augustine's method to explain this particular "metaphorical language."

In the third book Augustine speaks of the ambiguities that can arise in the reading and interpretation of scripture, and he begins with the ambiguities connected with ambiguities in words used in their proper sense. In this context he sets down some basic hermeneutical principles.

The first ambiguity can arise from the division of words or of the period, or else from pronunciation and intonation—a type of ambiguity that is explicable from the lack of punctuation and of the separation of words in the codices. The Doctor from Hippo writes in this connection:

> When, on paying closer attention you still see that it is uncertain how something is to be phrased, or how to be pronounced, you should refer it to the rule of faith, which you have received from the plainer passages of scripture and from the authority of the Church, about which we dealt sufficiently when we were talking in the first book about *things*. But if both possibilities, or all of them, if it is a multiple ambiguity, are consonant with the faith, it remains to refer to the whole context, to the sections that precede and that follow the ambiguous passage, holding it in the middle between them, so that we may see which of the several meanings that present themselves the context will vote for and allow to fit in with itself.[36]

This passage sets down some extremely valuable principles. In modern terms Augustine is saying that to resolve a difficulty met in reading we must have recourse first to the "analogy of scripture," then to the "analogy of faith," and thirdly to the immediate context. Since he deals in the second and third books with signs, the author gives us the key to his lengthy treatment

---

35. *Ibid.,* II, 16, 24—42, 63.
36. *Ibid.,* III, 2, 2.

of the principles of faith in the first book. There (he says) he was dealing with the "things" that will serve as the contextual criterion for interpreting ambiguous signs. Here, in section 3, he gives a very clear example: were we to read "In the beginning was the Word and the Word was with God and God was. This Word was in the beginning with God," it would be an Arian reading and to be excluded a priori.[37] This priority given to the analogy of scripture and the analogy of faith is a patristic datum that goes back to Irenaeus and Origen. It is a purely negative principle, that is, it excludes readings that are philologically possible but theologically erroneous, and has to do with discovering the literal (not the spiritual) sense of the text in itself. It presupposes, of course, that God is the sole author both of all the scriptures and of ecclesial traditions, a point not to be contradicted.

This method of interpreting the scriptures has always annoyed those who want philology to be the sole criterion. These critics do not realize that the criterion which they regard as unacceptable was already used by those, whether Jewish or Christian, who accepted a book into the canon, in which different points of view, such as those of Paul and John, can coexist, without any of them, in the mind of the Church, contradicting the rule of faith. "Where, however, an ambiguity can be resolved neither by the standard of faith nor by the actual context of the passage, there is no objection to your phrasing it in any of the ways that are open to you."[38]

Augustine is too easily satisfied here and finds ingenious explanations for two possible readings. The reason is that for him "context" means only the proximate context. He seems to neglect the remote context, whether historical or theological, in the thinking of the biblical writer he is discussing, even though in practice he sometimes appeals to this remote context. His introduction to his commentary on the Letter to the Galatians is like that of any modern handbook, and it is to be expected that this initial viewpoint would condition the entire commentary.

Up to this point in the third book Augustine has spoken of the method for resolving ambiguities arising from proper language. From Chapter 5, section 9, onward, he deals with metaphorical language. This part of the work is important because it raises the question not only of how to distinguish metaphors but also of how to recognize the spiritual and allegorical meaning of a passage.

The letter kills, but the spirit gives life (2 Cor 3:6). This is the principle that guides Augustine through this entire discussion: "When something that is said figuratively, you see, is taken as though it were meant in its proper literal sense, we are being carnal in our way of thinking."[39]

The distinction between metaphor and spiritual sense is based on another, that between useful signs and useless signs. The metaphors found

---

37. *Ibid.*, III, 2, 3.
38. *Ibid.*, III, 2, 5.
39. *Ibid.*, III, 5, 9.

in, for example, pagan literature are useless, and anyone who feeds on them feeds, like the prodigal son, on acorns, which are good only for pigs. Useful signs, on the other hand, are those which signify the new dispensation that has been inaugurated by the resurrection of Christ. Those who use useless signs or who use useful signs but without knowing that they are signs are living in slavery, enslavement to the flesh (*carnaliter*). Meanwhile, God has destroyed everything to which useless signs referred and has freed the Gentiles so completely that they will not serve even under useful signs but will "exercise their minds in the spiritual understanding of them."[40]

The Jews, on the contrary, served under useful signs, that is, signs that did not point simply to themselves, but what happened was this:

> Those, you see, who practice or venerate some kind of thing which is a significant sign, unaware of what it signifies, are enslaved under signs; while those who either carry out or venerate useful signs established by God, fully understanding their force and significance, are not in fact venerating what can be seen and passes away, but rather that reality to which all such things are to be referred. Such people are spiritual and free even during the time of slavery, in which it is not yet opportune for carnal spirits to have those signs openly explained to them, because they still need to be broken in under their yoke. Such spiritual people, however, were the patriarchs and prophets.[41]

In other words, freedom and spirituality depend on two things: the usefulness of the sign used, which refers to a future higher value, and the awareness of this reference. Even those who do not know what the sign signifies but do understand it to be a sign are free. "But it is better even to be oppressed by signs that are useful though not understood, than by interpreting them in a useless manner to withdraw one's neck from the yoke of slavery, only to insert it in the noose of error."[42] It is better to use a useful sign without knowing its meaning than to go astray by misinterpreting it. Augustine includes the Christian sacraments of baptism and the Eucharist in the category of useful signs instituted by Christ as a compendium of eschatological values.

According to the Bishop of Hippo. the opposite error is to interpret proper language as figurative. The method for discovering which of the two kinds of language is before us is to see whether the text inspires faith and charity; if it does not, it is to be interpreted figuratively.[43] It is easy for people who judge their own morals by relation to their time and place to give a figurative interpretation to everything in the scriptures that does not fit in with current custom. Scripture, however, gives us an unchanging standard:

---

40. *Ibid.*, III, 8, 12.
41. *Ibid.*, III, 9, 13.
42. *Ibid.*
43. *Ibid.*, III, 10, 14.

Scripture, though, commands nothing but charity, or love, and censures nothing but cupidity, or greed, and that is the way it gives shape and form to human morals.

Again, if people's minds are already in thrall to some erroneous opinion, whatever scripture asserts that differs from it will be reckoned by them to be said in a figurative way. The only thing, though, it ever asserts is Catholic faith, with reference to things in the past and in the future and in the present. It tells the story of things past, foretells things future, points out things present; but all these things are of value for nourishing and fortifying charity or love, and overcoming and extinguishing cupidity or greed.[44]

On the contrary, if certain ways of acting that are described in the scriptures are unseemly for holy persons, they are to be interpreted figuratively. It is to this category that Augustine's comment on Jacob's "lie" belongs: "It is not a lie but a mystery."[45] Here he gives a spiritual interpretation of the passage in John 12:3 on the woman who anoints the feet of Jesus with a precious ointment, because such a gesture cannot be put in the category of secular gestures: "The good odor, after all, stands for the good reputation...."[46]

Those not well disposed toward Augustine would call the first example a muddle rather than an explanation, and would say of the second that it is not a reason but the manifestation of a complex. The Bishop of Hippo is speaking here as a pastor rather than as a scholarly lecturer; his concern is not to scandalize his hearers rather than to look for the objective truth. In any case, apart from these last remarks, the criteria given for distinguishing the figurative sense from the proper come very close to the *theoria* of the Antiochene school, although there is lacking in Augustine the extensive application of it to prophecy, such as is found in the writings of the Antiochene school.[47]

Augustine's pastoral concern emerges clearly in the following summary:

So then, all the things, or practically all of them, which are contained in the books of the Old Testament, are to be taken not only in their literal sense, but also as having a figurative sense. All the same, when the people in the narratives, which the reader takes in the proper literal sense, were praised for doing things that are abhorrent to the manners of good men and women who keep God's commandments after the Lord's coming, the reader should not take the actual deeds as models for moral behavior, but should try to understand their figurative meaning. There are many things, after all,

---

44. *Ibid.*, III, 10, 15.
45. *Against Lying* 10, 24.
46. *Teaching Christianity* III, 12, 18.
47. See B. de Margerie, *Introduction à l'histoire de l'exégèse* I, 188–214.

which at that time were done out of duty that now can be only done out of lust.[48]

From this is it clear that Augustine accepts a literal sense everywhere, and, almost everywhere, a spiritual sense as well, that is, a scriptural sense that may help Christian faith and morals; but in the New Testament these morals have reached a point of maturity at which certain actions permitted under the old dispensation may not be done any longer. The term "figurative" can be applied to all those interpretations that Augustine gave in his sermons on the Old Testament, which he read with a Christian preunderstanding. This does not prevent his being aware that a word or phrase interpreted figuratively in one passage is not always to be so interpreted, and that the symbolism is not always the same; he gives as an example the word "leaven."[49]

We come now to two sections of Augustine's work that are very close to what Catholic exegetes call the "fuller sense" (*sensus plenior*). Because of its great importance I give the passage in its entirety.

> When from the same words of scripture not just one, but two or more meanings may be extracted, even if you cannot tell which of them the writer intended, there is no risk if they can all be shown from other places of the holy scriptures to correspond with the truth. However, those who are engaged in searching the divine utterances must make every effort to arrive at the intention of the author through whom the Holy Spirit produced that portion of scripture. But as I say, there is nothing risky about it, whether they do get at this, or whether they carve out another meaning from those words which does not clash with right faith, and is supported by any other passage of the divine utterances. That author, in fact, possibly even saw this very meaning in the same words which we wish to understand; and certainly the Spirit of God who produced these texts through him foresaw without a shadow of doubt that it would occur to some reader or listener; or rather he actually provided that it should occur to him, because it is upheld by the truth. How, after all, could the divine scriptures make more abundant and generous provision than by ensuring that the same words could be understood in several ways, which are underwritten by other no less divine testimonies?
>
> But where a possible meaning emerges which cannot be made entirely clear by other certain testimonies of the holy scriptures, it remains to elucidate it with arguments from reason, even if the writer whose words we are trying to understand did not perhaps intend that meaning. But this habit is risky; it is really much safer to walk along with the divine scriptures; when we wish to examine passages ren-

---

48. *Teaching Christianity* III, 22, 32.
49. *Ibid.*, III, 24, 35.

dered obscure with words used metaphorically, either let something
emerge from our scrutiny that is not controversial, or else if it is so,
let the matter be settled from the same scripture by finding and applying testimonies from anywhere else in the sacred books.[50]

This is the passage in which Augustine speaks most clearly of the
various senses of scripture. First of all, the true meaning of the Bible is
the "meaning intended by the author," because it is properly this which
is inspired by the Holy Spirit, and it is through the conscious intention of
the author that God speaks. If due to difficulty in uncovering the original
meaning of the author we are left with two or more different interpretations,
we ought not to be dismayed, because it is not impossible that as he wrote
the human author foresaw them. In any case, the divine author certainly
foresaw them and may also have foreseen that the reader would see them.
But there are criteria for deciding on the admissibility of these various
senses. They are admissible only if they are justifiable by the analogy of
scripture or the analogy of faith. We know that Augustine made use of the
Neoplatonists to explain certain difficult passages, but he never recommends this as a regular practice; he always prefers that the meaning of a
passage of scripture be confirmed by another passage of scripture, so as
to remain safely within the thought of the author.

The very great usefulness of this principle is evident, for, while leaving
open the possibility of an interpretation, or interpretations, that go beyond
the exact meaning of the words, it closes the door to fanciful or arbitrary
interpretations that depart from the language of the scriptures or the Church.
Who will not be reminded, in this context, of the interpretations of the Old
Testament that we find in the New (I am thinking of some obscure passages
in Zechariah) or of the reinterpretation of other passages that has become
quasi-official or even simply official in the Church? There can be a "sense
of the author" and a "sense of the text" that are equally valid.

Augustine is also familiar with the use of tropes, or figures of speech,
in scripture; he mentions allegory, enigma, and parable.[51] These are our
"literary genres," but Augustine knew only those of the Latins and Greeks.
If he had known those of the Semites he would have offered more "modern" interpretations, but, after all, we ourselves are hardly beginning to
be familiar with them.

The third book of *Teaching Christianity* ends with the hermeneutical
rules of Tychonius. This man, who died around 400 A.D., was a Donatist
layman and the author of several books, among them a commentary on the
Apocalypse; he was excommunicated by his sect because of his Catholic
views, but he did not go over to Catholicism. Around 380 he had published

---

50. *Ibid.*, III, 27, 38—28, 39.
51. *Ibid.*, III, 39, 41.

a *Book of Rules*[52] for which Augustine had a high esteem, although he did not accept it blindly. Tychonius gives seven rules for the interpretation of scripture. Augustine accepts the number seven with a grain of salt, either because in his introduction Tychonius claims that these seven rules will help resolve all difficulties (a little more modesty would have done no harm!), or because Tychonius himself in, for example, his commentary on the Apocalypse makes use of other exegetical rules not included in these seven.[53] Here are the seven rules with Augustine's commentary.

1) "About the Lord and his body," that is, since Christ and his Church form a single person, it is perfectly legitimate to pass from the head to the body.[54] Augustine qualifies this by saying that we must understand what is proper to the one and the other. This Tychonian principle has been extended in modern hermeneutics to what is now called the "corporate personality," a term coined by Wheeler Robinson. It says that in Semitic thought what is said of the founder of a family is also being said of his descendants, and that there are also certain figures, for example, the Servant of Yahweh or the Son of Man, which are both an individual and a collectivity. For this reason we often find in messianic prophecies passages which in their original meaning apply to Israel but which are understood as Christological (Hos 6:2), while Psalm 22, which is applied first to Christ, is also applicable to Christians in their own persecutions.

2) "About the twofold body of the Lord": this title does not please Augustine, who says: "It should not have been called that, because that which will not remain with him for ever in eternity is not really the body of the Lord.... It is not only in eternity, but even now that hypocrites should not be said to be with him, even though they appear to be in his Church."[55] He would prefer to say: "About the Church as a mixture." The point of Tychonius' rule is that many scriptural statements that praise or berate "Israel" (that is, the Church) are to be applied only to those categories that they have in view, whether the good or the bad, and not to all without distinction.

3) "About the promises and the law" or, in Augustinian terms, "about the spirit and the letter" or "about grace and commandments." He knows that this teaching is in itself a problem rather than a rule for resolving other problems, as the Pelagian controversy shows. Tychonius "did some good work in his treatment of it, but still left something to be desired,"[56] insofar as he interpreted it in a Semipelagian manner, that is, he said that the beginning of faith comes from us and is something we merit; this, of course, Augustine refutes.

---

52. See *Liber Regularum*, ed. F. C. Burkitt (Texts and Studies III/1; Cambridge, 1894).
53. *Teaching Christianity* III, 30, 43.
54. *Ibid.*, III, 31, 44.
55. *Ibid.*, III, 32, 45.
56. *Ibid.*, III, 33, 46.

4) "About species and genus." Augustine prefers to say "about the part and the whole." In other words, everything scripture says about a part, for example, about a city such as Babylon, applies to the entire country; or about a person, "as when things said about Solomon exceed his limitations, and becomes luminously clear when referred to Christ or to the Church, of which Solomon is a part."[57] Note the phrase "transcend his limitations" (*eius modum excedunt*), which is a principle of Origen but is broadly applied by all of Augustine's predecessors. It is precisely in accord with this rule of Tychonius that Augustine attributes to the universal Church what is said of the true Israel (for example, in Ez 36:17–29).

5) "About times": this is the rule about the part and the whole as applied to time; for example, the three days before Christ's resurrection, where a part of a day is regarded as an entire day. A number can, then, also be a figure, as when "seven" is used for "many."

6) "Recapitulation": when the scriptures do not carefully observe the temporal order of events but confuse the before and the after, it is up to the reader to restore the missing order.[58]

7) "About the devil and his body": This is Tychonius' first rule, but applied now to the wicked, who form the body of the devil.

Augustine ends his treatise on interpretation with an exhortation to expositors who are at a loss: "They should pray for understanding."[59]

What the holy Doctor says of Tychonius' rules for interpretation can be said of his own: they are not comprehensive. He himself makes use of still others in his own exegesis. A complete treatise on Augustinian exegesis would have to start from his exegetical practice rather than from his rules for interpretation. However, what he does offer us by way of theory is very useful for a better understanding not only of his own exegesis but of ours as well. It is of basic importance in dealing with Augustine to distinguish between his exposition of the scriptures in his preaching, in which he goes in extensively for the spiritual meaning, and his strictly theological exegesis, especially in controversy, in which his adversaries are perhaps better exegetes from a philological point of view but not from a theological.[60]

---

57. *Ibid.*, III, 34, 47.
58. *Ibid.*, III, 36, 52–54.
59. *Ibid.*, III, 37, 56.
60. In Letter 93, 8, he says, in fact, that a valid theological argument can be derived only from the literal sense.

What saved him from the errors into which his adversaries constantly fell is his constant appeal to the rule of faith, which makes him, if not always a very good philologist, one of the greatest biblical theologians in the history of Christian literature.[61]

Prosper Grech, O.S.A.

---

61. To be added here is what Augustine says in *The Advantage of Believing* 3 (PL 42:68) and Saint Thomas cites in *Summa theologica* i, q. 1, a. 10, as follows: "Scripture which is entitled the Old Testament has a fourfold meaning, namely according to history, to etiology, to analogy, to allegory." Saint Thomas does not regard this as a valid objection to his own fourfold division into the literal, allegorical, tropological, and anagogical senses, and he comments as follows on Augustine: "These three, history, etiology, and analogy, are grouped under the one general heading of the literal sense. For as Saint Augustine explains in the same place, you have history when any matter is straightforwardly recorded; etiology when its cause is indicated, as when our Lord pointed to men's hardness of heart as the reason why Moses allowed them to set aside their wives; analogy when the truth of one scriptural passage is shown not to clash with the truth of another. Of the four senses enumerated in the argument, analogy stands alone for the three spiritual senses of our exposition" (*Summa theologiae* I. *Christian Theology* [Ia, I], trans. T. Gilby [New York, 1964] 37, 39).

Translator's Note

I had better begin by explaining why I translate *De Doctrina Christiana* as *Teaching Christianity*. The one thing the work is not about is Christian doctrine. The word *doctrina* is not to be taken in the passive sense, which is the only one it has in English, of the matter taught, but in the active sense of the business of teaching. Professor H. I. Marrou, of happy memory, was of the opinion that the work is a kind of sketch of a Christian culture, that it presents us with a scheme for a Christian education, with what we might call Augustine's *Idea of a University.* I myself, while not denying l hat the elements of such a scheme can be drawn from the work, cannot believe that Augustine's purpose in writing it was to provide them. Unlike Newman, after all, Augustine never had an occasion for writing a treatise on the principles of Christian education. But that the *De Doctrina Christiana* was written for a particular occasion, to meet a particular pastoral need, I think we may take for granted. Augustine was far too busy a bishop to write books "in the air."

My suggestion is that the *De Doctrina Christiana* was undertaken, not only in response to a particular situation, but in response to a particular request from a particular person, Aurelius, bishop of Carthage. This is, of course, no more than a guess, but one which I hope to show is not over-fanciful.

In Letter 41, which the Maurists assign reasonably enough to the first years of his episcopate, Augustine writes to congratulate Aurelius on having achieved his *sancta cogitatio* "about all our ordained brethren, and especially about the priests preaching to the people in you r presence." What was the nature of Aurelius' achievement, which drew from Augustine the paean of rhetoric with which he continues the letter? I think we might say that it was nothing less that the official inauguration of the Catholic Church's renewal in North Africa. We know from Possidius' biography of Augustine that it had not been customary in Africa for priests to preach and expound the gospel, this task, or privilege, being reserved for the bishops, many of whom for one reason or another neglected it. We know from various remarks of Aurelius and other bishops recorded in the *Acts* of African Councils that there was an alarming shortage of trained and educated clergy in major orders. The fortunes of the Catholic Church, compared with those of its Donatisi rival, were at a very low ebb when Augustine was forcibly conscripted into the ranks of the clergy by the shrewd congregation of Hippo Regius. Here was an exceptional man indeed, and his bishop Valerius made quite exceptional use of him by making him do all his preaching far him.

Now it seems to me that it was the great virtue of Aurelius, as primate of all Africa, that he harnessed Augustine's widely recognized abilities to the fundamental task of raising the normal standard of clerical competence. The fact of Augustine's preaching while still only a priest had been an exception; Aurelius was determined to make it the beginning of a rule. Augustine had no sooner been ordained priest than he had asked Valerius for leave of absence to fit himself far his duties by studying the scriptures.[1] Aurelius was determined, one may suppose, that all clergy should be thus prepared for their duties before being raised to major orders. I suggest that his *sancta cogitatio,* his "holy plan about our ordained brethren," was the provision for them of some sort of course of ecclesiastical study. Augustine's self-given ecclesiastical education remained an exception, but Aurelius' great design was to make it as far as possible a model.

After an elaborate encomium of Aurelius' achievement—in so conservative and insular a society as that of Christian Africa there had almost certainly been some stubborn opposition to his measures—Augustine goes on in Letter 41, "We beg you ... to order such of their sermons [the priests'] as you wish, written up and corrected, to be sent to us. For I too am not neglecting what you commanded me, and I am still waiting to hear what your opinion is about the seven rules or keys of Tychonius, which I have often written to you about already." What was it that Aurelius had commissioned Augustine to do, something he was already getting on with, in connection with which he both wanted to know Aurelius' opinion about the rules of Tychonius, and to have copies sent him of the maiden sermons preached by priests?

I suggest he was engaged, at Aurelius' request, in writing a textbook or manual for use in training the clergy to teach and preach; in other words he was in the middle of *De Doctrina Christiana.* I think we can go even further, and say that when he wrote this letter, he had gotten as far as the point al which he abandoned the work, until he found it unfinished and completed it about thirty years later.[2] He was well on in the third book, which was dealing with the interpretation of the *signs* contained in scripture. He would soon be getting on to the fourth k, which would deal with the actual art of preaching, and for this he would find copies of the trial sermons of Aurelius' priests useful material. Before he started on that section, however, he wanted to complete his third book by discussing Tychonius' seven rules of interpretation. But Tychonius had been a Donatisi scholar; could his rules be incorporated into a Catholic textbook for training clergy, one of whose principal tasks of the moment would be conducting a polemic

---

1.   See Letter 21.
2.   see *Revisions* TI, 4, 1-2, which are included in this volume after this Translator's Note.

against the Donatists? Augustine was personally in favor, but junior bishop as he was, he would not take such a bold step without first consulting the primate of all Africa.

Perhaps Aurelius never answered, or perhaps he decided against Tychonius for the time being. And so Augustine laid the *De Doctrina Christiana* aside, and then forgot about it in the pressure of business, until he was writing his *Revisions* all those years later in 427 or 428. By that time the Donatisi controversy was practically dead; Augustine was an old man of worldwide prestige, who could make use of Tychonius the Donatisi on his own authority without asking Aurelius' permission. So he set to,and finished the work he had begun thirty years previously at Aurelius' request as a handbook for training the clergy in lheir pastoral and homiletic duties.

With respect, then, against Professor Marrou I would say that the *De Doctrina Christiana* is not so much concerned with Christian education, as with education in Christianity. More specifically, it is intended to help the teachers of Christianity, the clergy, "whom we long to have well trained for the service of the Church," *utilitari ecclesiasticae erudiri*. And so, *Teaching Christianity* is how I think the title of the work should be translated. Christianity is, or ought to be, pre-eminently taught by preaching; so the work leads up to the fourth book as to its goal. But Christian preaching is, or ought to be, in terms of scripture; so the would-be preacher must first be taught how to interpret the Bible. And since some, if not most, of the clergy are always going to find interpreting the Bible a fearfully bewildering business, however many guides to it they are provided with, it is as well to begin this textbook by telling them beforehand what the substance, the *res,* is of what they are going to find in the Bible. And then, if necessary, if they find scripture too hard for them altogether, lhey can preach about these *res,* these substantive things, God and Christ, and faith, hope, and love, without opening their Bibles at all.

If then there is any educational establishment which the *De Doctrina Christiana* prophetically envisages, I would say it is the seminary or ecclesiastical college, not the university. And seminaries could do very much worse than use it as a textbook, even today.

Revisions II, 4

When I found the books on *Teaching Christianity* incomplete, I preferred to complete them, rather than to leave them as they were and pass on to revising other works. So I finished the third book, which had been written as far as the place where I referred to the passage from the gospel, about the woman who hid the yeast in three measures of meal, until the whole was leavened.[1] I also added the last book, and thus completed this work in four books, of which the first three help in the understanding of the scriptures, while the fourth suggests how what we have understood is to be passed on to others.[2]

In Book II, what was said by me about the book most people call the Wisdom of Solomon, that Jesus son of Sirach also wrote it as he did Ecclesiasticus,[3] is not the general opinion, so I afterward learned; and I have been informed that it is altogether more probable that he is not the author of this work. But where I said, "It is to these forty-four books that the authority of the Old Testament is confined,"[4] I used the expression "Old Testament" in the way the Church is now in the habit of using it; the apostle, however, only seems to mean by "Old Testament" the covenant given on Mount Sinai.[5] And where I said that Saint Ambrose had solved a historical problem about times by suggesting that Plato and Jeremiah were contemporaries, my memory deceived me. In fact, what this bishop said about that matter can be read in his book which he wrote about the sacraments, or about philosophy.[6]

This work begins, "There are some rules" *(Sunt praecepta quaedam)*.

---

1. Book III, 35; see Lk 13:21. It is in section 42 of the third book that he starts explaining the rules of Tychonius. My impression is, that while he completed the work he did not in fact revise what he had already written. There are a number of roughnesses in the style, and a few incoherences in the treatment of his subjects, which he would have surely ironed out if he had revised it.
2. See the opening sentence of Book I.
3. Book II, 13.
4. The same section.
5. See Gal 4:24.
6. Book II, 43. The work of Ambrose he is referring to is not the one known as *De Sacramentis,* now universally recognized as not being by Ambrose; in any case no mention is made in it of Plato or Jeremiah. The work referred to is presumably lost. Jeremiah in fact, who lived about 500 B.C., was some 200 years Plato's senior. Perhaps what Ambrose said, and Augustine now verified, was that when Plato went to Egypt he found the book of Jeremiah, and borrowed much of his philosophy from it. But Ambrose does refer to Plato visiting Egypt, in order to study the wisdom of the Israelites among others, in his treatment of Psalm 119 (118), *Sermon* 18, 4. He also suggests that Plato borrowed from Prv 17:6, in his *Flight from the World,* 8:51 and in *On Abraham* II, 7, 37.

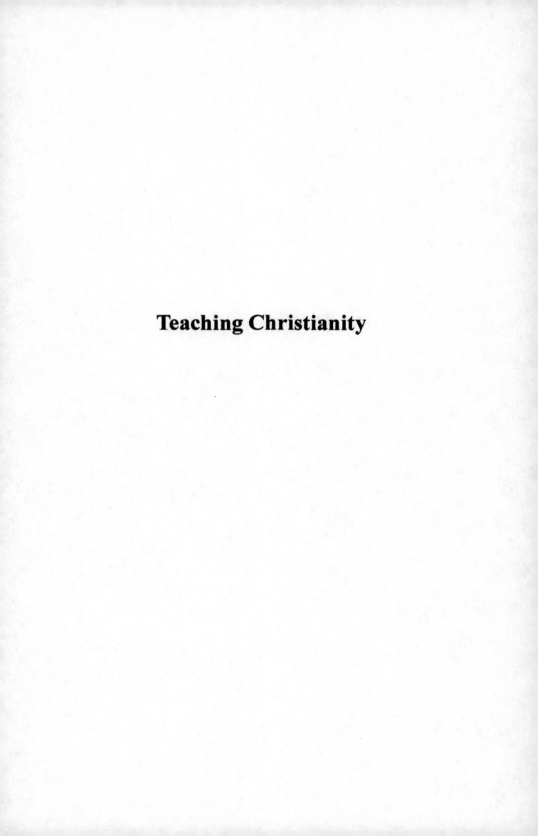

Teaching Christianity

Prologue

1. There are some rules for dealing with the scriptures, which I consider can be not inappropriately passed on to students, enabling them to make progress not only by reading others who have opened up the hidden secrets of the divine literature, but also by themselves opening them up to yet others again. I have undertaken to pass these rules on to those who are both willing and well qualified to learn, if our Lord and God does not deny me, as I write, the ideas he usually suggests to me in my reflections on the subject.

Before I embark on the task, however, it seems to me that I should first reply to those who are going to find fault with what I say, or who would do so if I did not satisfy them first. But if some people do find fault with me even after this, at least they will not be upsetting others, or luring back from useful study into idle ignorance those whom they might easily upset unless they found them forewarned and forearmed.

2. Some people, you see, are going to find fault with this work, when they fail to understand the rules I will be laying down. Some, on the other hand, when they wish to make use of what they have understood, and attempt to deal with the divine scriptures according to these rules, and find they lack the skill to open up and explain what they would like to, will reckon that I have labored in vain; and because they have not found this work any help, they will conclude that nobody else will either.

The third group of fault-finders consists of those who either do indeed interpret the scriptures very well, or who think that they do. They see, or imagine, that they have acquired the ability to expound the holy books without reading any of the observations I have undertaken to offer to the public; and therefore they will declare that nobody needs these rules, but that it is simply a divine gift which makes possible the praiseworthy opening up of the obscurities of this sacred literature.

3. Let me reply briefly to them all; what I can say to those who do not understand what I write is this: I am not the one to be blamed because they do not understand. It's as though they wished to see the old or the new moon, or some very dim star, which I would be pointing to with my outstretched finger; but if their eyesight was not good enough for them even to see my finger, that would be no reason why they should get indignant with me. As for those who have learned these rules and grasped their import, and even so have been unable to fathom the dark depths of the divine scriptures, they

should count themselves as indeed being able to see my finger, but unable to see the heavenly bodies to which it is pointing. So both these and those others should please stop blaming me, and should rather pray that God may grant them light to see with. After all, while I am able, no doubt, to use my finger to point to something, I am not also able to sharpen people's eyes so that they can see either me pointing or the objects I am wishing to point out.

4. And now, finally, for those who rejoice in having received a divine gift, and are proud of understanding and commenting on the holy books without the aid of such rules as I have undertaken to pass on here, and who therefore reckon that what I have wished to write is quite superfluous; this is how their objection is to be met: they should recollect that, though they are quite right to rejoice in a splendid gift from God, it was still from human beings that they learned, at the very least, how to read and write. Nor is that any reason why they should be crowed over by that holy and perfect man Antony, the Egyptian monk,[1] who is said to have known the divine scriptures by heart simply through hearing them, though he himself didn't know how to read, and to have understood their meaning through intelligent reflection on them; or for that matter by that barbarian slave, a Christian, about whom we have recently been informed by the most serious and trustworthy men.[2] No human being had taught him how to read, but he prayed that the secret of it might be fully revealed to him, and after three days of prayer he obtained his request, so that he was able to read out loud from a volume that was handed him, to the amazement of those who were present.

5. Or if anyone should think this is untrue, I am not going to quarrel about it. After all, I am clearly dealing with Christians, who rejoice over their knowing the holy scriptures without human guidance; and if that is the case, it is a genuine good they are rejoicing over, one quite out of the ordinary. So let them grant me that each one of us, from earliest childhood, has had to learn our own language by constantly hearing it spoken, and has acquired a knowledge of any other language, whether Hebrew or Greek, or any of the rest, either in the same way by hearing it spoken, or from a human teacher. So now then, if you agree, let us advise all our brothers and sisters not to teach their small children these things, because after all it was in a single instant of time, with the coming of the Holy Spirit, that the apostles were filled and spoke in the tongues of all nations;[3] or else none of us who have not experienced such things should consider ourselves to be Christians, or to have received the Holy Spirit.

---

1.   1. Antony was the first, or almost the first, hermit in the Egyptian desert. He died in 356 at the age of 105, two years after Augustine was born. Saint Athanasius, whom he had supported with his immense prestige in his life-long battle against the Arians, wrote his life.
2.   Two manuscripts give his name as Macarius. Augustine, like almost all his contemporaries, could sometimes be very credulous.
3.   See Acts 2:1–4. It is as well, perhaps, to point out that he is being sarcastic.

But no, on the contrary, let us not be too proud to learn what has to be learned with the help of other people, and let those of us by whom others are taught pass on what we have received without pride and without jealousy.[4] We must never tempt the one we have come to believe,[5] or we may be deceived by the cunning and crooked wiles of the enemy into refusing to go to church in order to hear and learn from the gospel, or to read the Bible, or to listen to anybody reading it out and preaching it; and into expecting to be snatched up to the third heaven, *whether in the body or out of the body*, as the apostle says, *and there hear unutterable words which it is not lawful for man to speak* (2 Cor 12:2–4), or there see the Lord Jesus Christ and listen to the gospel directly from his mouth rather than from other people.

6. Let us be on our guard against all such dangerous temptations to pride, and let us rather reflect on how the same apostle Paul, although he had been struck down and instructed by the divine voice from heaven, was still sent to a man to receive the sacraments and be joined to the Church;[6] and how the centurion Cornelius, although it was an angel who told him his prayers had been heard and his almsgiving acknowledged, was still handed over to Peter to be instructed and baptized.[7] And it could all, of course, have been done by the angel; but then no respect would have been shown to our human status, if God appeared to be unwilling to have his word administered to us by other human beings.

How, after all, could the saying be true, *For the temple of God, which is what you are, is holy* (1 Cor 3:17), if God never gave any answers from his human temple,[8] but only thundered out his revelation from the sky and by means of angels? Then again charity itself, which binds people together with the knot of unity, would have no scope for pouring minds and hearts in together, as it were, and blending them with one another, if human beings were never to learn anything from each other.

7. And certainly the apostle Philip did not send on that eunuch, who was reading the prophet Isaiah without understanding him, to an angel; nor was the point he did not understand explained to him by an angel, or revealed to him in his mind by God without any human ministry. What happened in fact was that Philip, who knew the prophet Isaiah, was sent to him by a prompting from God, and sat with him, and in human words and human language opened up to him what was hidden in that passage.[9]

---

4. For the linking of these two vices in a pair, see Sermon 399, 7 (Vol III/10 in this series), where he calls pride the mother of envy. See note 13 there for other references.
5. See Mt 4:7; Dt 16:16.
6. See Acts 9:3–19.
7. See Acts 10:1–6.
8. Temples very commonly housed oracles in the pagan world; and the same had been true of Israelite shrines, including the temple in Jerusalem.
9. See Acts 8:27–35.

Did God not speak with Moses face to face? And yet, being extremely prudent and not in the least proud, he accepted advice on how to direct and govern such a great people from his father-in-law, that is to say from a man who was a foreigner.[10] Moses knew, of course, that from whatever soul good advice had issued, it was to be attributed not to that person, but to the one who is truth itself,[11] the unchanging, unchangeable God.

8. Finally, those who can boast of understanding whatever is obscure in the scriptures by a gift from God, without being furnished with any rules, are right indeed to believe, and it is in fact true, that this ability of theirs does not derive from themselves, but has been granted them by God. This shows that they are seeking God's glory and not their own. But since they themselves read the Bible, and understand it without any other human being explaining it to them, why are they so eager to explain it to others, instead of referring them back to God, so that they too may come to understand it through his teaching them inwardly, and not through the teaching of other men? But of course, they are afraid they might hear from the Lord, *Wicked servant, you should have given my money to the bankers* (Mt 25:26.27).

So these people too make known to others what they understand, either by lecturing or by writing; and if I, in the same way, publish things not only for them to understand but also for them to put into practice when understood, they certainly have no right to blame me for this. None of us, though, should claim our understanding of anything as our very own, except possibly of falsehood. Because everything that is true comes from the one who said, *I am the truth* (Jn 14:6). What do we have, after all, that we have not received? But if we have received it, why should we boast as though we had not?[12]

9. The person who reads some writing out loud to other listeners obviously knows what he is pronouncing, while the one who teaches people in literacy classes does this so that they too may know how to read. Each of them, all the same, is handing on what he has received. In the same sort of way those too who explain to an audience what they understand in the scriptures are, as it were, performing the office of reader and pronouncing letters they know, while those who lay down rules about how they are to be understood are like the person who teaches literacy, who gives out the rules, that is, on how to read. So just as the person who knows how to read does not require another reader, when he gets hold of a volume, to tell him what is written in it, in the same way, those who have grasped the rules we are endeavoring to pass on will retain a knowledge of these rules, like letters, when they come across anything obscure in the holy books, and will not require another person who understands to uncover for them what is shrouded in obscurity. Instead, by following up certain

---

10. See Ex 18:13–26.
11. See Jn 14:6.
12. See 1 Cor 4:7.

clues, they will be able themselves to get the hidden meaning of a passage without any error—or at the very least to avoid falling into any absurdly wrongheaded opinion.

Accordingly, while this very work should make it abundantly clear that nobody can rightly object to my dutifully undertaking this laborious task, still this preface provides, I think, a sufficient answer to any such critics. This, then, is how it has seemed right to me to embark upon the road I wish to travel in this book.

Book I

The purpose of scripture study is both to discover its meaning and to pass it on to others; both tasks to be undertaken with God's help

1, 1. There are two things which all treatment of the scriptures is aiming at: a way to discover what needs to be understood, and a way to put across to others what has been understood. Let us first discuss the way of discovery, and after that the way of putting our discoveries across.[1] A great and arduous work, and if it is difficult to keep up, I am afraid it may be thought rash to have undertaken it. And so it certainly would have been, had I been relying solely on my own powers; but as it is, my hopes of carrying this work through rest in the one from whom, in my reflections, I have already received many ideas on this matter; and so there need be no fear that he will refrain from giving me the rest, when I begin spending on others what I have already been given. Every kind of thing, you see, which does not decrease when it is given away, is not yet possessed as it ought to be, while it is held onto without also being given out to others. Now he said himself, *Whoever has shall be given more* (Mk 4:25). So he will give to those who have; that is, for those who make generous use of what they have received he will complete what he has given, and heap even more upon them.

Those loaves were five and seven in number, before they started being given to the hungry crowds; but when that began to happen, they filled hampers and baskets after satisfying so many thousands of people.[2] So just as that bread increased in quantity when it was broken, in the same way all the things the Lord has already granted me for setting about this work will be multiplied under his inspiration, when I start passing them on to others. And thus not only will I not experience any lack of means in this ministry of mine, but on the contrary I shall even rejoice in a marvelous surplus.

---

1. The way of discovery in Books I—III; the way of putting our discoveries across—that is to say, the art of preaching—in Book IV. This makes it clear from the start that when he completed the work thirty years later, he did not depart in the least from his original plan.
2. See Mk 6:34–44; 8:1–9.

The difference between things and signs

2, 2. All teaching is either about things or signs; but things are learned about through signs. What I have now called things, though, in the strict sense, are those that are not mentioned in order to signify something, such as wood, a stone, an animal, and other things like that. Not, however, that piece of wood which we read of Moses throwing into the bitter water to remove its bitterness; nor that stone which Jacob placed under his head; nor that animal which Abraham sacrificed instead of his son.[3] All these, in fact, are things in such a way as also to be signs of other things. There are, however, other signs which are only used for signifying, such as words. Nobody, after all, uses words except for the sake of signifying something.

From this it will be easy to understand what I am calling signs; those things, that is, which are used in order to signify something else. Thus every sign is also a thing, because if it is not a thing at all then it is simply nothing. But not every single thing is also a sign. And therefore, in this distinction between things and signs, when we are speaking of things let us so speak that even if some of them can be employed to signify, this will not prevent us from dividing up the work in such a way, that we first discuss things, later on signs; and let us bear in mind all the time that what has to be considered about things is that they are, not that they signify something else besides themselves.

The division of things; what is meant by enjoying and using

3, 3. So then, there are some things which are meant to be enjoyed, others which are meant to be used, yet others which do both the enjoying and the using. Things that are to be enjoyed make us happy; things which are to be used help us on our way to happiness, providing us, so to say, with crutches and props for reaching the things that will make us happy, and enabling us to keep them.

We ourselves, however, both enjoy and use things, and find ourselves in the middle, in a position to choose which to do. So if we wish to enjoy things that are meant to be used, we are impeding our own progress, and sometimes are also deflected from our course, because we are thereby delayed in obtaining what we should be enjoying, or turned back from it altogether, blocked by our love for inferior things.

4, 4. Enjoyment, after all, consists in clinging to something lovingly for its own sake, while use consists in referring what has come your way to what your love aims at obtaining, provided, that is, it deserves to be loved. Because unlawful use, surely, should rather be termed abuse or misuse.

---

3.   See Ex 15:23–25; Gn 28:11–19; 22:9–14. The wood thrown into the water was a sign of the cross healing the world; the stone Jacob rested on, and set up and anointed, was a sign of Christ the cornerstone; the ram Abraham saw caught in the thorn bush and sacrificed in place of Isaac was, like Isaac, a sign of Christ sacrificed on the cross.

Supposing then we were exiles in a foreign land, and could only live happily in our own country, and that being unhappy in exile we longed to put an end to our unhappiness and to return to our own country, we would of course need land vehicles or sea-going vessels, which we would have to make use of in order to be able to reach our own country, where we could find true enjoyment. And then suppose we were delighted with the pleasures of the journey, and with the very experience of being conveyed in carriages or ships, and that we were converted to enjoying what we ought to have been using, and were unwilling to finish the journey quickly, and that by being perversely captivated by such agreeable experiences we lost interest in our own country, where alone we could find real happiness in its agreeable familiarity. Well that's how it is in this mortal life in which we are exiles *away from the Lord* (2 Cor 5:6); if we wish to return to our home country, where alone we can be truly happy, we have to use this world, not enjoy it,[4] so that we may behold *the invisible things of God, brought to our knowledge through the things that have been made* (Rom 1:20); that is, so that we may proceed from temporal and bodily things to grasp those that are eternal and spiritual.

God, Father, Son and Holy Spirit, is the ultimate thing to be enjoyed; but he is inexpressible

5, 5. The things therefore that are to be enjoyed are the Father and the Son and the Holy Spirit, in fact the Trinity, one supreme thing, and one which is shared in common by all who enjoy it; if, that is to say, it is a thing, and not the cause of all things; if indeed it is a cause.[5] It is not easy, after all, to find any name that will really fit such transcendent majesty. In fact it is better just to say that this Trinity is the one God *from whom are all things, through whom all things, in whom all things* (Rom 11:36). Thus Father and Son and Holy Spirit are both each one of them singly God and all together one God; and each one of them singly is the complete divine substance, and all together are one substance.

---

4. We must be on our guard against taking Augustine's stark antitheses too literally. He spent a very large part of his life traveling; and while he undoubtedly felt immense relief whenever he reached his destination, Carthage, or back home in Hippo Regius, or wherever it was, I am sure he did not refuse to enjoy whatever distractions the journeys offered, if only the conversation of his companions. But he did not make such enjoyments his goal. So here, in telling us only to use the world and not to enjoy it, he is telling us not to make enjoyment of it our goal, our one aim in life. We have to use it in order to reach the perfect joys of our true home country. But he would agree that there is no harm in making the best of our use of the world, and enjoying it when we can.

5. In the ordinary, human sense of cause, or of thing. He is simply adverting to the total inadequacy of all human language when applied to the divine mystery, or at least of all language that is not purely and simply scriptural. But if pressed, he would have agreed that the scriptural terms he goes on to deploy are not adequate either, though they cannot be improved upon.

The Father is neither the Son nor the Holy Spirit; the Son is neither the Father nor the Holy Spirit; the Holy Spirit is neither the Father nor the Son; but the Father is only the Father, and the Son is only the Son, and the Holy Spirit is only the Holy Spirit. The three possess the same eternity, the same unchangeableness, the same greatness, the same power. In the Father unity, in the Son equality, in the Holy Spirit the harmony of unity and equality; and these three are all one because of the Father, are all equal because of the Son, are all linked together because of the Holy Spirit.[6]

6, 6. Have I said anything, solemnly uttered anything that is worthy of God? On the contrary, all I feel I have done is to wish to say something; but if I have said anything, it is not what I wished to say. How do I know this? I know it because God is inexpressible; and if what has been said by me were inexpressible, it would not have been said. And from this it follows that God is not to be called inexpressible, because when even this is said about him, something is being expressed. And we are involved in heaven knows what kind of battle of words, since on the one hand what cannot be said is inexpressible, and on the other what can even be called inexpressible is thereby shown to be not inexpressible. This battle of words should be avoided by keeping silent, rather than resolved by the use of speech.

And yet, while nothing really worthy of God can be said about him, he has accepted the homage of human voices, and has wished us to rejoice in praising him with our words. That in fact is what is meant by calling him God. Not, of course, that with the sound made by this one syllable any knowledge of him is achieved; but still, all those who know the English language[7] are moved, when this sound reaches their ears, to reflecting upon some most exalted and immortal nature.

7, 7. When that one God of gods is thought about, after all, even by those people who assume there are other gods whether in heaven or on earth, and who invoke and worship them, he is thought about in such a way that our thoughts strive to attain to something, than which there is nothing better or more sublime.[8] People are, of course, moved by a whole variety of goods, some by those which are available to the bodily senses, some by those which the intelligent spirit can attain to. Those who are given over to the senses of the body consider that either the sky, or what they can see shining brightly in the sky, or the universe itself, is God. Or if they exert themselves to go outside the universe, they imagine something full of light, and either make it infinite, or vainly suppose it to have the shape they think

---

6. An interesting formula, this last sentence. There is nothing quite like it in his *The Trinity*, attributing specifically distinct but still shared attributes to each of the three persons. It is, we could say, a poetically pleasing formula, but lacking in theological rigor.

7. Of course, Augustine says the Latin language, and talks of the two syllables of the word *Deus*.

8. Is this where Saint Anselm was to get his quasi-definition of God as that than which nothing greater can be thought of?

best—or even endow it with a human form, if that is the one they prefer to others. But if they do not think there is one God of gods, and assume rather that there are many, indeed countless gods of equal rank, even these they represent to themselves in imagination as being whatever they consider superlative in bodies.

Those on the other hand, who proceed by using their minds to conclude that God is, place him above all visible and bodily natures, also over all intelligible and spiritual ones—over everything in fact that is subject to change. All of them,[9] however, put up a strenuous and zealous fight for God's excelling everything else there is; nor can any be found who suppose that God is something than which anything else is better. And so all agree that God is whatever they put above all other things.

God as unchangeable Wisdom

8, 8. Now all who think about God think about him as something alive; so those alone can avoid absurdity in their reflections about God who give some thought to life as such, and take as axiomatic that whatever physical form may occur to them, it only lives, or does not live, with life; and hence they understand that the living bodily form, however brilliantly it may shine, however superlatively great it may be in size, however beautiful its proportions, is itself one thing, and the life that quickens it another; and this they acknowledge to be of incomparably greater worth than that mass which it quickens and animates.

Next, they proceed to examine this life, and if they find it simply of a vegetative kind, without sensation, like the life of trees, they put sentient or sensitive life above it, such as the life of animals; and again above this they place intelligent life, such as the life of human beings. When they observe that even this is still subject to change, they are obliged to put above it some kind of unchangeable life, namely that kind which is not sometimes wise, sometimes unwise, but is rather Wisdom itself. The wise mind, after all, the one namely that has acquired wisdom, was not wise before it acquired it, while Wisdom itself, on the contrary, never was unwise, and never can be. If they did not see this, in no way would they confidently prefer life that is unchangingly wise to life that is subject to change. They can see, after all, that the very rule of truth, by which they declare it to be better, is itself unchanging; nor can they see this anywhere, except above their own nature, considering that they observe themselves to be subject to change.

9, 9. Nobody, surely, can be so shamelessly fatuous as to say, "How do you know that the unchangeably wise life is to be preferred to the changeable variety?" The very thing they are querying, after all, how I know, is

---

9.   He has in mind, in general, all the old Greek philosophers, from the early pre-Socratics up to the Stoics and Neoplatonists.

universally and unchangeably present to all for their contemplation.[10] And anyone who does not see this is like a blind man in the light of the sun, whom that clear, bright light, presently pouring into the place where his eyes should be, benefits not at all. Those, however, who do see it and run away from it, have had the sharpness of their minds blunted by growing accustomed to the dark shadows of the flesh. So people are beaten back from their home country, as it were, by the contrary winds of crooked habits, going in pursuit of things that are inferior and secondary to what they admit is better and more worthwhile.

To see God, the mind must be purified; the example given us by Wisdom incarnate

10, 10. That is why, since we are meant to enjoy that truth which is unchangeably alive, and since it is in its light that God the Trinity, author and maker of the universe, provides for all the things he has made, our minds have to be purified, to enable them to perceive that light, and to cling to it once perceived. We should think of this purification process as being a kind of walk, a kind of voyage toward our home country. We do not draw near, after all, by movement in place to the one who is present everywhere, but by honest commitment and good behavior.

11, 11. Of this we would be quite incapable, unless Wisdom herself had seen fit to adapt herself even to such infirmity as ours, and had given us an example of how to live, in no other mode than the human one, because we too are human. But we, of course, when we come close to her, are acting wisely; so when she came to us, she was thought by proud men to have acted rather foolishly. And when we come close to her, we grow strong; so when she came to us she was reckoned to have been made weak. But *the foolishness of God is wiser than men, and the weakness of God is stronger than men* (1 Cor 1:25). So since she herself is our home, she also made herself for us into the way home.[11]

How God's Wisdom came to us and healed us

12, She is present everywhere, indeed, to inner eyes that are healthy and pure; but to those whose inner eyes are weak and unclean, she was prepared to be seen by their eyes of flesh as well. *For because in the wisdom of God the world was unable to come to know God through wisdom, it was God's pleasure through the folly of the preaching to save those who believe* (1 Cor 1:21).

---

10. Here we have the basic tenet of Augustine's illuminationist epistemology: that we know whatever we do know in the light of unchanging—that is, divine—truth, which is always illuminating our minds.
11. See Jn 14:6.

12. So it was not by locomotion through space that she is said to have come to us, but by appearing to mortals in mortal flesh. So she came where she already was, because she was in the world, and the world was made through her.[12] But human beings, greedy to enjoy the creature instead of the creator, had taken on the coloring of this world—and so were most aptly called by the name of "the world"; that is why they did not recognize her, and why the evangelist said, *And the world did not know him* (Jn 1:10). And so it was in the Wisdom of God that the world was unable to come to know God through wisdom. So why did she come, when she was already here, if not because it was God's pleasure through the folly of the preaching to save those who believe?

13, How did she come, if not by the Word becoming flesh and dwelling amongst us?[13] It is something like when we talk; in order for what we have in mind to reach the minds of our hearers through their ears of flesh, the word which we have in our thoughts becomes a sound, and is called speech. And yet this does not mean that our thought is turned into that sound, but while remaining undiminished in itself, it takes on the form of a spoken utterance by which to insert itself into their ears, without bearing the stigma of any change in itself. That is how the Word of God was not changed in the least, and yet became flesh, in order to dwell amongst us.

14, 13. Any treatment, of course, is a way to health; so this treatment undertook to restore sinners to complete health. And just as when doctors bind up wounds, they do not do it untidily, but neatly, so that the bandage, as well as being useful, can also to some extent have its proper beauty, in the same sort of way Wisdom adapted her healing art to our wounds by taking on a human being, curing some of our ills by their contraries, others by homeopathic treatment. It is the kind of way a doctor treating the body's wounds sometimes applies contraries, like something cold to a hot inflammation, or something moist to a dry condition, or other things of that kind; and he also applies like to like, as for example a round plaster to a round wound, or an oblong to an oblong one, and does not apply the same sort of bandage to all the limbs, but fits like to like. That is how the Wisdom of God treats the ills of humanity, presenting herself for our healing, herself the physician, herself the physic.

So because man had fallen through pride, she applied humility to his cure. We were deceived by the wisdom of the serpent; we are set free by the folly of God. On the one hand, while her true name was Wisdom, she was folly to those who took no notice of God; on the other hand while this is called folly, it is in fact Wisdom to those who overcome the devil. We made bad use of immortality, and so ended up dying; Christ made good use of mortality, so that we might end up living. When a woman's mind

---

12. See Jn 1:10. Augustine is indeed in complete accord with the mind of the writer of this text in identifying the Word of God with the Wisdom of God.
13. See Jn 1:14.

was corrupted, the disease entered in; from a woman's body preserved intact, health and salvation issued forth. That our vices are cured by the example of his virtues belongs to the same list of contraries. Now as regards homeopathic remedies being applied to our limbs and wounds, examples are that those led astray through a woman were set free by one born of a woman, human beings by a human being, mortals by a mortal, the dead by a death. Those who are not held back, by the necessity of completing a work just begun, from reflecting on many other instances of the sort, will appreciate how well furnished the Christian medicine cupboard is with both contrary and homeopathic remedies.

The death, resurrection and ascension of Christ are models for our spiritual death and resurrection in his body the Church, and also for our bodily death and resurrection at the end of the world

15, 14. Now indeed, the Lord's resurrection from the dead and his ascension into heaven, once believed, supports our faith with a very great hope. After all he very effectively demonstrated how willingly he had laid down his life for us, by having the power in this way to take it up again.[14] So what confidence and comfort must it give the hope of believers, when they consider how great the sufferer was, and how much he suffered for those who did not yet believe! Since, on the other hand, his coming is awaited from heaven as judge of the living and the dead, it strikes real fear in the hearts of the careless, to prompt their conversion to a more diligent practice of the faith, so that by living good lives they may be in a position to desire his coming, rather than to dread it because they are living bad ones.

What words, though, can express, or what thoughts can grasp the reward he is going to give us at the end, seeing that for our comfort and consolation on this journey he has given us so much of his Spirit? In the Spirit we already possess, amid the adversities of this life, that great confidence and love of the one whom we cannot yet see, as well as gifts proper to each one of us for the building up of his Church,[15] so that whatever he has shown us is to be done, we may do not only without grumbling, but even with positive delight.

16, 15. The Church, after all is his body, as the teaching of the apostle confirms, and it is also called his wife.[16] So while his body consists of many parts, having different functions, he binds it tightly together with the knot of unity and love, as its proper kind of health.[17] But during this age he trains and purges it with various kinds of salutary vexation and distress, so that once it has been snatched from this world, he may bind his wife the

---

14. See Jn 10:17–18.
15. See 1 Cor 12—14.
16. See Eph 1:22–23; 5:28–33.
17. See Rom 12:4–5; Eph 4:3; Col 3:14.

Church to himself for ever, *not having any stain or wrinkle, or any such thing* (Eph 5:27).

17, 16. Furthermore, we are still on the way, a way however not from place to place, but one traveled by the affections. And it was being blocked, as by a barricade of thorn bushes, by the malice of our past sins. So what greater generosity and compassion could he show, after deliberately making himself the pavement under our feet along which we could return home,[18] than to forgive us all our sins once we had turned back to him, and by being crucified for us to root out the ban blocking our return that had been so firmly fixed in place?[19]

18, 17. These then were the keys that he gave to his Church, so that whatever it loosed on earth would be loosed in heaven, and whatever it bound on earth would be bound in heaven;[20] which means that any who did not believe they were forgiven their sins in the Church would not be forgiven them, while those who did so believe and by amending their lives turned away from their sins, finding themselves in the bosom of the Church, would be healed by that very faith and amendment. Those on the other hand, who do not believe their sins can be forgiven them, become even worse through despair, as though nothing better remains for them than to be evil, seeing that they have no trust in the fruits of their conversion.

19, 18. Now, however, there is a certain death of the spirit, consisting in the abandonment of previous habits and way of life, which comes about by repentance; and in the same sort of way the death of the body consists in its ceasing to be animated by the soul as formerly. And just as the spirit is refashioned for the better after the repentance which has abolished its old habits of depravity, so too we are to believe and hope that the body, after this death which we all owe to the chains of sin, is going to be changed for the better at the time of the resurrection. Thus it will not be flesh and blood taking possession of the kingdom of God, which cannot be; but *this perishable thing will put on imperishability, and this mortal thing will put on immortality* (1 Cor 15:50.53), and will cause the spirit no trouble, because it will not experience any need, but will be quickened in perfect peace by a perfect and blissful soul.

20, 19. Those, however, whose spirits do not die to this world and this age, and do not even begin to be remodeled on the truth, are dragged down by the death of the body into a more grievous death still. Nor will they come to life again to be changed into a heavenly condition, but to pay the ultimate penalty for their sins.

21, And so this is the conviction of faith, and this is how we must believe that things stand: that neither the human spirit nor the human

---

18. See Jn 14:6.
19. See Col 2:13–14.
20. See Mt 16:19.

body will experience total extinction, but that the godless will rise again
to unimaginable punishments, the godly on the other hand to eternal life.

God alone is to be enjoyed

22, 20. Among all the things there are, therefore, those alone are to
be enjoyed which we have noted as being eternal and unchanging, while
the rest are to be used, in order that we may come at last to the enjoyment
of the former sort. And so we, who both enjoy and use other things, are
ourselves also things. Yes, a great thing indeed is man, made *to the image
and likeness of God* (Gn 1:26–27), not insofar as he is enclosed in a mortal
body, but insofar as he takes precedence over the animals in the dignity of
a rational soul. And so the great question is whether human beings ought
to regard themselves as things to be enjoyed, or to be used, or both.

We have been commanded, after all, to love one another; but the question is whether people are to be loved by others for their own sake, or for
the sake of something else. If it is for their own sake, then they are things
for us to enjoy; if for the sake of something else, they are for us to use.
Now it seems to me that they are to be loved for the sake of something else,
because if a thing is to be loved for its own sake, it means that it constitutes
the life of bliss, which consoles us in this present time with the hope of it,
even though not yet with its reality. *Cursed*, however, *is the one who places
his hopes in man* (Jer 17:5).

21. But none of us ought either to find enjoyment in ourselves, if you
consider the matter straightforwardly, because we ought not either to love
ourselves for our own sakes, but for the sake of the one whom we are to
enjoy. Then indeed are people as good as can be, when they aim all their
lives long at that unchanging life,[21] and cling to it with all their hearts. But
if they love themselves for their own sakes, they are not relating themselves
to God; rather, in turning to themselves, they are not turning to anything
unchangeable. And that is why their enjoyment of themselves is to some
extent defective, because they are better when they cleave to the unchangeable good and are tightly bound to it, than when they release themselves
from it to cling even to themselves.

So if you ought not to love yourself for your own sake, but for the
sake of the one to whom your love is most rightly directed as its end, other
people must not take offense if you also love them for God's sake and not
their own.[22] This, after all, is the rule of love that God has set for us: *You*

---

21. This is just another name, here, for God.
22. This is where Augustine's sticking so uncompromisingly to his guns can appear
    to us rather dauntingly inhuman, even inhumane. But we need to make an effort
    of sympathetic imagination or, in older phraseology, of pious interpretation, and
    see that while by loving you for your own sake or loving myself for my own sake,
    he means doing it without reference to God; by loving you or myself for God's
    sake he does *not* mean "and not also for your or my sake." When I love you for
    God's sake, I thereby (in Augustine's use of the term) necessarily love you for

shall love, he says, *your neighbor as yourself; God*, however, *with your whole heart and your whole soul and your whole mind* (Mk 12:31.30; Lv 19:18; Dt 6:5). Thus all your thoughts and your whole life and all your intelligence should be focused on him from whom you have received the very things you devote to him. Now when he said *with your whole heart, your whole soul, your whole mind*, he did not leave out any part of our life, which could be left vacant, so to speak, and leave room for wanting to enjoy something else. Instead, whatever else occurs to you as fit to be loved must be whisked along toward that point to which the whole impetus of your love is hastening.

So all who love their neighbors in the right way ought so to deal with them that they too love God with all their heart, all their soul, all their mind. By loving them, you see, in this way as themselves, they are relating all their love of themselves and of the others to that love of God, which allows no channel to be led off from itself that will diminish its own flow.

We had no need of a commandment to love ourselves and our bodies

23, 22. Not all things, however, which are to be used are also to be loved, but only those which can be related to God together with ourselves in a kind of social companionship, such as human beings or angels or which being related to ourselves are in need of God's benefits through us, such as our bodies. Because of course the martyrs did not love the crimes their persecutors were committing against them, but still they made use of them in order to deserve well of God. So now, as there are four kinds of things to be loved: one which is above us, the second which we are ourselves, the third which is on a level with us, the fourth which is beneath us, about the second and the fourth there was no need to give any commandments. However far, after all, people may fall away from the truth, there remains in them love of self and love of one's own body. When the spirit, you see, takes to flight from the unchanging light that regulates all things, it does so in order independently to regulate itself and its own body; and that is why it is impossible for it not to love itself and its own body.

23. Now the human spirit thinks it has something great if it can lord it over its fellows, that is over other human beings. It is ingrained, you see, in the vitiated spirit to be striving more than anything else for what it claims as if it were its due, but what is in fact due to the one God alone. Such love of self, though, it is better to call hatred. It is, after all, a simple case of iniquity, because such a spirit is wanting to be served by what is beneath it, while refusing to serve what is above it; and it is very properly said, *Whoever loves iniquity hates his own soul* (Ps 11:5, LXX). And as a result

your own sake, for your truest, deepest sake, because it means I am loving you, and hence "enjoying" you, in God, where you properly belong, and am wanting you to join me in enjoying God for ever.

the spirit sickens, and begins to be tormented by means of the mortal body. It cannot help loving it, after all, and yet must needs find itself overburdened by its perishable nature.[23] For the immortality and imperishability of the body results from the health of the spirit; and the health of the spirit consists in clinging unshakably to the one who is more powerful, that is to the unchanging God. But when it aspires also to lord it over those who are its natural equals, that is over other human beings, this is a case of altogether intolerable pride.

24, 24. So hating oneself is something nobody does. And on this point there has never been any dispute with any school of thought. But neither do any people hate their own bodies; what the apostle said is certainly true: *Nobody has ever hated his own flesh* (Eph 5:29). And as for what some people say, that they would much prefer to do without a body altogether, they are completely mistaken; it is not in fact their bodies that they really hate, but the weight of them and their liability to decay. And so it is not that they do not wish to have a body at all, but that they would like to have a body that does not decay and that is as fleet and swift as a bird. But they assume that if anything is like that, it is not a body, because they think that is what the soul is like.[24]

As for their apparently harrying their bodies with self-restraint and hard toil, if they are doing this in the right manner, they are not doing it in order not to have bodies at all, but in order to have them broken in and ready for any necessary work. They are aiming, you see, by subjecting the body to a kind of arduous drill, at extinguishing the lusts that make bad use of the body, that is to say the habits and tendencies of the soul to seek enjoyment in inferior things. They are not, after all, doing away with themselves, but taking care of their true health of mind and body.

25. As for those who do this in the wrong manner, they are waging war against their bodies as if they were their natural enemies. Here they are being misled by their reading of the text, *The flesh lusts against the spirit, and the spirit against the flesh; for these are opposed to each other* (Gal 5:17). Now this was said with an eye to the undisciplined habits of the flesh, against which the spirit is lusting, not in order to do away with the body, but in order to break in its lusts, that is its bad habits, and thereby make it subject to the spirit, as the natural order of things requires. This, after all, is how it will be after the resurrection, that the body, being in every possible way quietly and supremely peacefully subject to the spirit, will enjoy a flourishing immortality; so thought has to be given even in this life to making changes for the better in the habits of the flesh, and not letting

---

23. See Wis 9:15.
24. Does he have in mind here some philosophical school, or more vaguely different groups of Christian ascetics? He goes on, at least, to present briefly a picture of true and false asceticism, the latter in section 25 possibly being that of the "perfect" among the Manichees; also perhaps of some orthodox Christians influenced by Manichee extremism.

them put up a resistance to the spirit with their disordered impulses. But until this happens, *the flesh lusts against the spirit, and the spirit against the flesh.* This does not mean that the spirit resists the flesh out of hatred, but out of principle, because it wishes what it loves all the more to be subordinate to the better. Nor does it mean that the flesh resists the spirit out of hatred, but only because it is being dragged along by the chains of habit, which have grown into a kind of law of nature, being rooted in the inheritance derived from our first parents.[25] So what the spirit is doing in taming the flesh is canceling as it were the perverse agreements made with bad habits, and making peace with good habits.

All the same, not even those who have been seduced by false ideas into loathing their bodies would be prepared to lose one eye, even if they felt no pain, and even if the sense of sight left in the other was as acute as it had been in both, unless they were constrained to it by some cause or thing that was clearly to be preferred. And so it is by such evidences as this that people who are seeking the truth without obstinately sticking to their opinions can be shown how definitive the apostle's judgment is, where he says, *For nobody has ever hated his own flesh.* He also added, *but he nourishes and cherishes it, as Christ does the Church* (Eph 5:29).

25, 26. So what human beings have to be instructed in is precisely the way in which we are to love ourselves so as to benefit from it. But to doubt whether we do love ourselves and wish to benefit from doing so is simply crazy. We also need to be instructed how to love our bodies, so as to care for them in an orderly and prudent manner. Because again, it is equally obvious that we do also love our bodies, and wish to have them hale and hearty. So then, you can, of course, love something more than the health and well-being of your body. We find, after all, that many people have willingly submitted to pain and the loss of some of their organs or limbs—but in order to obtain other benefits which they valued more highly. So it is no reason to say that people do not value the health and safety of their bodies, just because there is something they love more. Take the case of a miser, for instance; even though he loves money, he still buys himself bread, and when he does this he gives away money that he loves so much and wants to get more of. But this is because he places a higher value on the welfare of his body, which is maintained by that bread. It would be a waste of time to discuss such a totally obvious point any further, though for all that the error of godless people[26] so often obliges us to do so.

---

25. Augustine tended to identify disordered lust, or concupiscence, with original sin, instead of seeing it, as a more refined theology will do, as the primary effect and sign of original sin, which in itself is simply the lack of God's integrating grace.
26. Here he almost certainly means the Manichees.

The right order of love

26, 27. So there is no need, then, for a commandment that we should love ourselves and our bodies, because it is by an unalterable law of nature that we do love what we are and what is below us but still part of us. The same law has been enacted for animals—I mean, animals too love themselves and their bodies. But the need remained for us to receive commandments about what is above us, and what is next to us. *You shall love*, he says, *the Lord your God with your whole heart, and with your whole soul, and with your whole mind; and you shall love your neighbor as yourself. On these two commandments depends the whole law, as well as the prophets* (Mt 22:37.39–40). And so *the end of the commandment is love* (1 Tm 1:5), and this is twofold—love, that is to say, of God and neighbor.

But if you understand yourself as the whole of you, that is your spirit and body, and your neighbor as the whole of him, namely his spirit and body—man, after all, consists of spirit and body;[27] then no kind of things that are to be loved has been overlooked by these two commandments. When indeed love of God is put first, and the manner of that love is clearly prescribed, indicating that everything else is to converge on it, nothing seems to be said about love of yourself. But when it says, *You shall love your neighbor as yourself,* love of yourself by yourself is being simultaneously included.

27, 28. But living a just and holy life requires one to be capable of an objective and impartial evaluation of things; to love things, that is to say, in the right order, so that you do not love what is not to be loved, or fail to love what is to be loved, or have a greater love for what should be loved less, or an equal love for things that should be loved less or more, or a lesser or greater love for things that should be loved equally. No sinner, precisely as sinner, is to be loved; and every human being, precisely as human, is to be loved on God's account, God though on his own. And if God is to be loved more than any human being, we all ought to love God more than ourselves. Again, other people are to be loved more than our own bodies, because all these things are to be loved for God's sake, and other people are capable of enjoying God together with us, which our bodies cannot do, because what gives life to our bodies is our souls, and it is with these that we enjoy God.

28, 29. All people are to be loved equally; but since you cannot be of service to everyone, you have to take greater care of those who are more closely joined to you by a turn, so to say, of fortune's wheel, whether by occasion of place or time, or any other such circumstance. Say, for example, that you had a surplus of something, which ought properly to be given to

---

27. To us this looks like laboring the obvious. But it was not so to Augustine. This marks his authentically Christian or biblical awareness of what constitutes humanity, over against the dominant Neoplatonist *zeitgeist*, which so deeply affected all his thinking, and which identified the human self exclusively with the spirit or mind.

anyone who had none of it, but there was not enough to give to two people. If you came across two people of whom neither was more obviously in need, or more closely related to you than the other, there is nothing more just that you could do than to toss for it, to decide which of them should be given what could not be given to both. In the same way, as you are unable to take care of all your fellow men, treat it as the luck of the draw when time and circumstance brings some into closer contact with you than others.[28]

29, 30. Now of all those who are able to enjoy God together with us, some we love as people we can help, some as people we can be helped by, some as ones both whose help we need, and whose needs we help to meet, while there are some on whom we ourselves confer no benefits, and from whom we do not expect any either. Still, we ought to want all of them to love God together with us, and all our helping them or being helped by them is to be referred to that one single end.

If, for example, in the theaters of godlessness someone has a favorite actor, and enjoys his art as a great, not to say the greatest good, he also loves all those who share his love for this actor, not loving them for their own sakes, but on account of the man they all love together; and the more ardent his love for him is, the more he tries in whatever way he can to get him loved by more people, and the more he longs to show him off to as many others as he can. And if he notices someone is rather cool about him, he tries to stir him up by singing the actor's praises, while if he finds someone who takes an opposite view of his favorite actor, he hates and detests that person's dislike of his favorite, and sets about trying to eradicate it in whatever way he can.

So what in comparison ought we, in the fellowship of the love of God, to be doing, seeing that enjoying him means living in bliss, and that from him all those who love him derive both their very existence and their love for him, and that about him it is impossible to fear that anyone who knows him should dislike him, and that it is his will that he should be loved, not to gain anything from it himself, but in order to confer on those who love him an eternal reward, which is in fact himself, the very one they love? The consequence of this is that we should love our enemies; after all, we have nothing to fear from them, because they cannot possibly deprive us of what we love; instead we feel sorry for them, because the more they hate us, the more it shows how far they are cut off from the one whom we

---

28. This rather casual way of leaving the order of charity to chance will not satisfy the scholastic mind, certainly not that of Saint Thomas. He devotes thirteen articles to the subject in his *Summa Theologiae*, IIa IIae, q.26 (English translation, volume 34), going into great detail. He decides, for instance, that love of parents takes precedence over love of one's children and love of one's father over love of one's mother—other things, of course, such as their goodness and holiness, being equal. All the quotations from Augustine in this question come from this part of *Teaching Christianity*. Augustine, I suggest, is to be congratulated on not being so meticulous in the matter.

love. If, however, they are converted and turn back to him, they must needs love both him as their bliss-conferring good, and us as their companions in enjoying such an unimaginable good.

Whether we are also commanded to love the angels

30, 31. Here, however, quite a considerable question arises about the angels. They, after all, are in bliss by enjoying the one we too are eager to enjoy; and the more we enjoy him in this life, at least *in a mirror* or *in a riddle* (1 Cor 13:12), the more tolerable we find it to put up with our wanderings away from him, and the more ardently we long for them to come to an end. But the question can be asked, not unreasonably, whether love for the angels is included in those two commandments. That the one who commanded us to love our neighbor made no exception of any human being is something the Lord himself showed us in the gospel, as well as the apostle Paul. You remember that when the man to whom he quoted those two commandments, saying that the whole law and the prophets depended on them, went on to ask him, *And who is my neighbor?* (Lk 10:29),[29] he presented him with the case of a certain man going down from Jerusalem to Jericho, who fell among thieves and was badly wounded by them, and left seriously hurt and half dead. The lesson he taught was that the only one who acted as neighbor to this man was the one who took pity on him to the extent of reviving him and treating his wounds, as the man who had asked him the question was obliged to admit when questioned in his turn. To him the Lord said, *Go and do likewise yourself* (Lk 10:37).

In this way we are given to understand that anyone is our neighbor to whom the duty of compassion is to be extended when needed.[30] From which it now follows that anyone by whom such a kindness in turn should be shown to us is also our neighbor. But anybody can see that no exception is made of any to whom the duty of compassion can be denied, when the command is extended even to enemies, with the Lord also telling us, *Love your enemies; do good to those who hate you* (Mt 5:44).

32. The apostle Paul also teaches the same lesson, when he says, *For, you shall not commit adultery, you shall not commit murder, you shall not steal, you shall not covet, and any other commandment there may be, is summed up in this saying: You shall love your neighbor as yourself. Love does no wrong to your neighbor*[31] (Rom 13:9–10). So if you assume the

---

29. In fact, in Luke's account of the episode it was the lawyer who quoted the two commandments when Jesus asked him how he read the law. Augustine is mixing up Luke's account with Matthew's—or very possibly using a translation of Tatian's harmony of the gospels, the *Diatessaron*.
30. He repeats the same phrase in the subjunctive, "or to whom it would have to be extended, were it needed," which is so superfluous as to be merely mystifying in English. So I leave it out of the text.
31. The Latin has *Dilectio proximi malum non operatur*, which is the Vulgate reading, and which is most naturally translated, "Love of neighbor does no wrong."

apostle did not state this commandment with reference to everybody, you
will be obliged to admit, which is utterly absurd, not to say criminal, that
in the apostle's view it is not a sin if someone defiles the wife of a man who
is not a Christian, or is an enemy, or kills him or covets his property. So if
saying such a thing is sheer lunacy, it is clear that every single human being
is to be counted as a neighbor, because wrong is not to be done to anybody.

33. So now then, if anyone is rightly to be called neighbor, either to
whom the duty of compassion is to be extended, or by whom it is to be
extended to us, it clearly follows that the holy angels are included as well
in this commandment bidding us to love our neighbors. They do, after all,
show us so many courtesies and kindnesses, as it is easy to note from so
many places in the divine scriptures. For the same reason our Lord and
God himself wished to be called our neighbor, because it is himself that
the Lord Jesus Christ is indicating as the one who came to the help of that
man lying half dead on the road, beaten up and left there by robbers;[32] and
the prophet says in prayer, *As for a neighbor, as for our brother, so I sought
to please*[33] (Ps 35:14).

But because the divine substance is altogether more excellent than our
nature and high above it, the commandment bidding us to love God was
distinguished from the one about love of neighbor.[34] He, after all, takes pity
on us because of his own goodness, while we take pity on each other, not
because of our goodness but again because of his. In other words, he takes
pity on us, so that we may enjoy him, while we take pity on each other,
again so that we may all enjoy him, not one another.

How God does not enjoy us, but makes use of us

31, 34. For that reason there still seems to be some uncertainty about
what we have been saying: that we enjoy that thing which we love for its

---

But the Greek has "neighbor" in the dative case, not the genitive—"Love does no
wrong to the neighbor"; and the end of this section strongly suggests that is how
Augustine understood the text; either because his Old Latin version correctly
had *Dilectio proximo...*, and it was later copyists who here "vulgatized" the text,
as often happened; or else because he shrewdly construed the genitive *proximi*
with the noun *malum* that follows it, rendering, literally, "Love does not work
neighbor's wrong." This was as peculiar in Latin as it is odd in English, but was
getting the right meaning from a faulty text.
32. The almost unanimous patristic interpretation, in addition to the obvious moral
lesson, of the parable of the good Samaritan, Lk 10:30–37.
33. The prophet, that is the psalmist, is assumed to be speaking in the person of Christ.
Augustine is probably thinking more of the second half of the verse, which he
does not actually quote: *As mourning and grieving for him, so I was humbled*,
as alluding to Christ's passion.
34. Here two manuscripts add the following sentence: "But because we are all equal
by nature, and when all boasting is set aside we are all nothing else but human
beings, the commandment bidding us love our neighbor was not distinguished
from loving ourselves."

own sake, and that only that thing is to be enjoyed by us which makes us perfectly happy, or blissful, while everything else is simply to be used. God, after all, loves us, and the divine scriptures draw our attention to his love for us again and again. So the question is: how does he love us? So as to use us, or to enjoy us? But if he enjoys us, it means he is in need of some good of ours, which nobody in his right mind could possibly say. Every good of ours, after all, is either God himself, or derived from him. And can anyone doubt, or find it an obscure statement, that the light is in no need of the brightness of those things which it has itself illuminated? The prophet, anyway, says as plainly as could be, *I said to the Lord, my God are you, since you have no need of my good things* (Ps 16:2). So he does not enjoy us, but makes use of us; because if he neither enjoys us nor makes use of us, I cannot find any way in which he can love us.

32, 35. But he does not make use of us, either, in the same way as we use things; because our making use of things is directed to the end of enjoying God's goodness, while God's making use of us is directed to his goodness.[35] Because he is good, after all, we simply are; and insofar as we are, we are good. Furthermore, because he is also just, we cannot be bad with impunity; and insofar as we are bad, to that extent our very being is diminished. For he is the one who supremely and primordially is, being absolutely unchanging; and so he was able to say in the fullest possible sense, *I am who I am*; and, *You shall say, He who is has sent me to you* (Ex 3:14), which means that everything else that is, not only could not be unless it came from him, but also can only be good insofar as it has received its being so from him.

The use, therefore, by which God is said to make use of us is directed to our benefit and not to his, but only to his goodness. But when we, on the other hand, feel sorry for people and care about them, we do it for their benefit, and that is what we have in mind. But in some way or other we also benefit ourselves, because God does not leave unrewarded the compassion we show to those in need. And the supreme reward is that we should enjoy him and that all of us who enjoy him should also enjoy one another in him.

33, 36. Because if we do that in ourselves, we are standing still on the road, and placing all our hopes of bliss in human beings, or angels. This is a position proud people and proud angels arrogate to themselves, and they are delighted when others place all their hopes in them. But holy people and holy angels, even when we are longing out of weariness to stay still and find our rest in them, prefer rather to provide us simply with refreshment, whether from the fare for the journey they have received for us, or even from what they have received for themselves—but "received" is the word.

---

35. But not as a *means* toward his enjoyment of his goodness. It will emerge shortly that God "uses" us for our own good, as means indeed toward our enjoyment of his goodness.

And so they urge us, thus refreshed, to continue on the way toward the one by enjoying whom we will share their bliss on equal terms.

After all, the apostle also exclaims, *Was Paul crucified for you? Or were you baptized in the name of Paul?* (1 Cor 1:13); and again, *Neither the one who plants nor the one who waters is anything, but the one who gives the growth, namely God* (1 Cor 3:7). And the angel warns the man who is on the point of worshiping him to worship rather the Lord under whom he himself is also a fellow servant.[36]

37. But when you enjoy a human being in God, you are really enjoying God rather than the human being. You will be enjoying the one, after all, in whom you find your bliss, and you will be delighted to have reached the one in whom you now hope, in order to come to him at last. It is in this sense that Paul writes to Philemon. *In this way, brother,* he says, *let me enjoy you in the Lord* (Phlm 20). But if he had not added *in the Lord,* and had merely said *let me enjoy you,* he would have been placing his hopes of bliss in Philemon.

Although, as a matter of fact, there is a closely related sense of "enjoy," meaning "to use with delight."[37] When something that is loved, after all, is available to you, delight is also bound to accompany it; but if you pass through this and refer it to that end where you are to remain permanently, you are really using it, and are said by a figure of speech, and not in the proper sense of the word, to enjoy it.[38] If, however, you cling to it and remain fixed in it, placing in it the end of all your joys, then you can be said really and truly to enjoy it. But this should not be done except with that divine Trinity, that is with the supreme and unchangeable good.

34, 38. Notice how Truth itself, and the Word through whom all things were made, became flesh in order to dwell amongst us;[39] and yet the apostle can say, *Even if we once knew Christ according to the flesh, we know him so no longer* (2 Cor 5:16). Christ, of course, is the one who wished to offer himself not only to be possessed by those who have arrived, but also to be the way there for those who have come to the beginning of the ways; that is, he wished to take flesh to himself. That is the meaning of the text, *The Lord created me in the beginning of his ways* (Prv 8:22); that is where those who wish to arrive must begin from. So then the apostle, though he was still walking along the way and following God who was calling him to the prize of the call up above, all the same *forgetting what lay behind and stretching out to what lay ahead* (Phil 3:12–14) had already passed through the beginning of the ways; that is to say, he no longer needed it,

36. See Rv 19:10; 22:8–9.
37. *Cum delectatione*; two venerable manuscripts have *cum dilectione*, to use with love.
38. Here at last we have Augustine's way of explaining all the obvious pleasures and joys of this life and this world—a somewhat grudging acceptance of them, one may feel!
39. See Jn 1:3.14.

even though it is the point from which all those who desire to attain to the truth and to abide in eternal life must commence their undertaking of the arduous journey thither.[40]

That, after all, is what the Lord meant by saying, *I am the way, and the truth, and the life* (Jn 14:6); that is, "It is along me that you come, at me that you arrive, in me that you abide." For when you reach him, you also reach the Father, because it is through his equality that the one to whom he is equal can be recognized, with the Holy Spirit binding and so to say gluing us in there, so that we may abide for ever in that supreme and unchangeable good. From this it can readily be understood how nothing must be allowed to hold us back on the way, when even the Lord himself, insofar as he was prepared to be the way for us, did not wish us to hold onto him, but to pass along him. He did not wish us to cling feebly to any temporal things, even those he took to himself and carried for our salvation, but rather to run eagerly along and through them, and so deserve to be swiftly and finally conveyed to him himself, where he has deposited our nature, freed from all temporal conditions, at the right hand of the Father.[41]

Love of God and neighbor is the sum of what scripture teaches

35, 39. So what all that has been said amounts to, while we have been dealing with things, is that *the fulfillment and the end of the law* and of all the divine scriptures *is love* (Rom 13:8; 1 Tm 1:5); love of the thing which is to be enjoyed, and of the thing which is able to enjoy that thing together with us, because there is no need for a commandment that we should love ourselves. So in order that we might know how to do this and be able to, the whole ordering of time was arranged by divine providence for our salvation. This we should be making use of with a certain love and delight that is not, so to say, permanently settled in, but transitory, rather, and casual, like love and delight in a road, or in vehicles, or any other tools and gadgets you like, or if you can think of any better way of putting it, so that we love

---

40. This passage rather shows up the weakness of Augustine's exclusively Johannine, Word-centered christology. He assumes that by saying he no longer knows Christ according to the flesh, Paul means he is no longer interested in his humanity, which, when one considers the emphasis placed by Paul on the cross and on the blood of Christ, is preposterous.

What does Paul mean, then? In the first place he did not, as the later patristic theology would do and as we have done ever since, "analyze" Christ, so to say, into the two components of his divine and his human natures. His view of Christ, to adopt a fashionable "in" word, was holistic. So by "Christ according to the flesh," he possibly meant what is now called the Jesus of history, or Jesus as he appeared to his contemporaries; and that is how Paul knew him—and persecuted him—before his conversion. But since then he has known only Christ, *the Lord of glory*, (1 Cor 2:8).

41. Here he does, finally, acknowledge the significance of Christ's glorified humanity as well as of his divinity.

the means by which we are being carried along, on account of the goal to which we are being carried.⌐

36, 40. So if it seems to you that you have understood the divine scriptures, or any part of them, in such a way that by this understanding you do not build up this twin love of God and neighbor, then you have not yet understood them. If on the other hand you have made judgments about them that are helpful for building up this love, but for all that have not said what the author you have been reading actually meant in that place, then your mistake is not pernicious, and you certainly cannot be accused of lying. Being a liar, of course, means having the intention of saying what is false; and that is why we find many people intending to lie, but intending to be mistaken, none.

So since a person does the one thing knowingly, experiences the other thing unwittingly, it is abundantly obvious that over one and the same thing the person who is mistaken or deceived is better than the person who tells a lie. Everyone who tells a lie, after all, is committing iniquity; and if it seems to anyone that a lie may sometimes be useful, then it can also seem to him that iniquity is sometimes useful. No liar, after all, in the very act of telling a lie is keeping faith; but what he wants, of course, is that the person he tells it to should have faith in him, faith which by lying he is for all that failing to keep. But every violation of faith, or trust, is iniquitous. Either, therefore, iniquity is sometimes useful, which cannot be, or lying is never useful.[42]

41. But any who understand a passage in the scriptures to mean something which the writer did not mean are mistaken, though the scriptures are not deceiving them. But all the same, as I had started to say, if they are mistaken in a judgment which is intended to build up charity, which is *the end of the law* (1 Tm 1:5), they are mistaken in the same sort of way as people who go astray off the road, but still proceed by rough paths to the same place as the road was taking them to. Still, they must be put right, and shown how much more useful it is not to leave the road, in case they get into the habit of deviating from it, and are eventually driven to take the wrong direction altogether.

37, But by rashly asserting something that the writer they are reading did not mean, people frequently hit upon other opinions which it is impossible to square with the author's meaning, such that if they are convinced these opinions are true and certain, what the writer meant cannot be true. Then it can happen with them, how I cannot tell, that they start being angrier with scripture than with themselves—a bad attitude which will be

---

42. Saint Thomas Aquinas will follow Saint Augustine in this severe view about the wrongness of all lying without exception; later moral theologians will be more lenient about what is popularly known as the white lie, and the lie told as a joke. See Augustine's works, *Lying*, and *Against Lying*, in which occurs his famous explanation, and exculpation, of Jacob's far from white lie in Gn 27:19–29, *Non est mendacium sed mysterium*, it is not a lie but a mystery (*Against Lying* 24).

totally destructive if they allow it to spread. *For we walk by faith, not by sight* (2 Cor 5:7); but faith will start tottering if the authority of scripture is undermined; then with faith tottering, charity itself also begins to sicken. Because if you fall from faith, you are bound also to fall from charity; it is impossible, after all, to love what you do not believe exists. On the other hand, if you both believe and love, then by doing good and complying with the requirements of good morals, you ensure that you also hope to come eventually to what you love. And so we have these three things, for whose sake all knowledge and all prophecy are pressed into service, faith, hope, charity.[43]

38, 42. But faith gives way to sight, which we shall see, and hope gives way to bliss itself, which we are going to arrive at, while charity will actually grow when these other two fade out. After all, if we love by believing what we cannot yet see, how much more will we do so when we have begun to see it? And if we love, by hoping for it, what we have not yet attained to, how much more when we have attained to it? This, indeed, is the difference between temporal and eternal things, that something temporal is loved more before it is possessed, but loses its appeal when it comes along; this is because it cannot satisfy the soul, whose true and certain abode is eternity. But anything eternal is loved more fervently when acquired than when just desired. This is because while you are desiring it, you cannot possibly think better of it than it really is, so that it disappoints you when you find it does not come up to your expectations; on the contrary, however great your estimate of it while you are on the way to it, you will find it exceeded when you eventually attain to it.

39, 43. And so people supported by faith, hope and charity, and retaining a firm grip on them, have no need of the scriptures except for instructing others. And so there are many who live by these three even in the desert without books. This leads me to think that the text has already been fulfilled in them, *As for prophecies, they shall be done away with, as for tongues, they shall cease, as for knowledge, it shall be done away with* (1 Cor 13:8). But with them as a kind of scaffolding, such an impressive structure of faith and hope and charity has arisen, that these people, holding on to something perfect, do not seek that which is in part—perfect, of course, insofar as that is possible in this life; because compared with the future life not even the lives of holy and just people here below are perfect. That is why *there abide* he says, *faith, hope, charity; but the greatest of these is charity* (1 Cor 13:13), because when anyone attains to the things of eternity, while the first two fade away, charity will abide, more vigorous and certain than ever.

40, 44. For that reason, when you come to realize that *the end of the law is love, from a pure heart, and a good conscience, and faith without pretense* (1 Tm 1:5), you will relate all the understanding of the divine scriptures to these three, and so be able to approach the study of those

---

43. See 1 Cor 13:8–13.

books without the least anxiety. When he said *love*, you see, he added *from a pure heart*, meaning that nothing else is loved except what should be loved. He brought in *a good conscience*, though, because of hope; it is those, after all, whose bad consciences trouble them like grit in their shoes, who despair of attaining to what they believe and love. Thirdly, *and faith*, he says, *without pretense*. If our faith lacks any falsity, then we do not love what ought not to be loved, and by living upright lives we hope for what we do love in such a way that our hope cannot possibly be disappointed. That is why I have wished to talk about things to do with faith, as much as I judged sufficient for the moment; because much has already been said on the matter in other volumes, whether by other people or by myself.

And so let that be the limit of this book. In the rest we shall discuss signs, as the Lord may grant us the ability to do so.

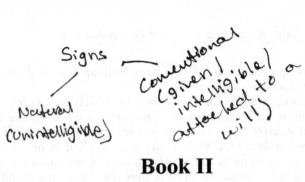

Signs

Natural
(unintelligible)

Conventional
(given /
intelligible /
attached to a
will)

Book II

What signs are, and how many kinds there are

1, 1. While I was writing about *things*, I put in a warning at the beginning that one should only consider in them that they are, and what they are, and not also whether they signify anything besides themselves. So now, being about to treat of *signs*, I have this to say, that we are not particularly interested in the fact that they are, but rather that they are precisely signs, that is that they signify. A sign, after all, is a thing, which besides the impression it conveys to the senses, also has the effect of making something else come to mind; as when we see a spoor, we think of the animal whose spoor it is; or when we see smoke, we know there is fire underneath; and when we hear the cry of a living creature, we can tell what its mood is; and when the trumpet sounds, soldiers know that they must advance or retreat, or whatever else the battle requires.

2. Among signs, then, some are natural, some conventional. Natural ones are those which have the effect of making something else known, without there being any desire or intention of signifying, as for example smoke signifying fire. It does not do this, after all, because it wishes to signify; but through our experience of things and our observation and memory, we know that fire is there, even if only smoke can be seen. And again, the spoor of a passing animal is this kind of sign; and the expression of an angry or sad person signifies his mood, even without the angry or sad person wishing it to do so. And any other stirring of the spirit can be betrayed by our expressions, even if we are not deliberately revealing it.

But it is not now my purpose to discuss this whole sub-category of signs. Still, as it falls within the division of our subject, it could not be passed over completely; but let it suffice to have taken note of it to this extent.

2, 3. Conventional or given signs, on the other hand, are those which living creatures give one another in order to show, as far as they can, their moods and feelings, or to indicate whatever it may be they have sensed or understood. Nor have we any purpose in signifying, that is in giving a sign, other than to bring out and transfer to someone else's mind what we, the givers of the sign, have in mind ourselves. It is this category of signs, therefore, insofar as it concerns human beings, that we have undertaken to consider and treat of, because even the signs given by God, which are contained in the holy scriptures, have been indicated to us through the human beings who wrote them down.

Animals too have signs for each other, by which they express their desires and intentions. Thus when the farmyard cock finds some food it gives the sign of its crowing to the hen to come running up; and by its cooing the male dove calls the female or is in his turn called by her; and there are many other such instances commonly noticed. Whether, however, like the expression or cry of someone in pain, they just follow the mood of the spirit, without any intention of signifying, or are really and truly given in order to signify, is another question, and does not concern the business we have in hand; so let us eliminate it from this work, as not being at all needed or relevant.

3, 4. Of the signs, therefore, with which human beings communicate their thoughts among themselves, some are directed to the sense of sight, most of them to the sense of hearing, very few to the other senses. Thus when we beckon, we are only giving a sign to the eyes of the person whom we are wishing by this sign to acquaint with our will. And some people do indeed signify a great many things with the gestures they make with their hands. And vaudeville artists are able to give signs to the *cognoscenti* by the movements of every part of their bodies, and to carry on a kind of conversation with the eyes of their audiences. And military flags and banners signal the will of commanders to the eyes of their men; and all these things are rather like visible words.

But as I said, there are many more signs that are directed to the ears, above all with words. Trumpets, of course, and flutes and guitars also frequently give out tunes that have a significant meaning as well as a pleasant sound. But compared with words, all such signs are few indeed. Words, after all, are far and away the principal means used by human beings to signify the thoughts they have in their minds, whenever anyone wishes to express them. Yes, it is true that the Lord gave some sign through the odor of the ointment which was poured over his feet.[1] And in the sacrament of his body and blood the Lord signified what he wished to through the sense of taste.[2] And when the woman was healed by touching the hem of his cloak,

---

1. See Jn 12:3–7; the trigger phrase here is "and the house was filled with the odor of the ointment." This is a sign directed to the sense of smell. Jesus explains its meaning in words—that it was done for his burial. But see also Sg 1:3, Latin: "Attract me; we will run after you in the odor of your ointments."

   Instead of The Maurists' "the odor of the ointment," CCL rather oddly reads, "the anointing odor," *odore ungenti.*

2. Reading with CCL and several manuscripts, *per gustatum.* The Maurists follow earlier editors in reading *praegustato,* giving the sense, "and by first tasting the sacrament, the Lord signified…" But there is very little manuscript support for this; and in Luke's account of the last supper, at least, Jesus deliberately refrained then from eating the passover; and finally, Augustine is clearly wishing to give an instance of a sign directed to the sense of taste. He was no doubt prompted by Wis 16:20, the versicle sung at Benediction.

The human conciousness is irreducible

it certainly signified something.[3] But the verbal signs with which human beings express their thoughts are almost infinite in number. Because of all these other kinds of sign which I have touched on briefly, I have been able to give an account in words, while in no way at all could I give an account of words with these other kinds of sign.

4, 5. But because words immediately pass away once they have agitated the air waves, and last no longer than the sound they make, letters were invented as signs of words. Thus spoken utterances can be shown to the eyes, not in themselves, but through what are signs of them. It has not been possible, therefore, for these signs to be common to all nations, as a result of a kind of sin of human dissension, when everyone grabbed at the first place for himself. A sign of this pride was the building of that tower to reach heaven, when humanity was rewarded for its impiety by discord in its speech as well as in its thoughts and its ambitions.[4]

5, 6. As a result of this it came about that divine scripture too, which provides treatment for so many diseases of the human will, starting out from language, was able when the time came to be disseminated throughout the world, spreading far and wide through translation into a variety of other languages, and thus came to the knowledge of the nations for their salvation. In reading it their one intention is to discover the thoughts and will of the authors it was written by, and through them to discover the will of God, which we believe directed what such human writers had to say.

What the scriptures are; in what way they are written; what is required in order to understand them

6, 7. But those who read them in a light-minded spirit are liable to be misled by innumerable obscurities and ambiguities, and to mistake the meaning entirely, while in some places they cannot even guess at a wrong meaning, so dense and dark is the fog that some passages are wrapped in. This is all due, I have no doubt at all, to divine providence, in order to break in pride with hard labor, and to save the intelligence from boredom, since it readily forms a low opinion of things that are too easy to work out.

I mean, why is it, I would like to know, that if anybody says that there are holy and perfect people, by the example of whose life and behavior the Church of Christ cuts off from all kinds of superstition those who come to her, and in some way or other incorporates them into herself by their

---

3. See Mk 5:27–34; a sign given through the sense of touch. The act of touching signified for Augustine the act of faith. See Sermons 243, 21; 244, 3; 245, 3. He also says somewhere that the hem of the Lord's garment represents Saint Paul, the last and least of the apostles (1 Cor 15:8–9); and thus the episode of this woman and her cure represents the conversion of the Gentiles. See Sermons 63A, 3; 63B, 3.

4. See Gn 11:1–9. Augustine also possibly had in mind, as hinting at dissension and ambition, Gn 10:9–10.

imitating her good members; and that these faithful and true servants of God, on laying aside the burdens of the world,[5] came to the holy bath of baptism, and stepping up from it, conceived by the Holy Spirit and gave birth to the twin fruit of charity, that is to love of God and neighbor—why is it that if anybody says that, it gives less pleasure to the hearer than if he expounds in that sense the passage from the Song of Songs, where the Church is told, when she is being praised as a beautiful woman, *Your teeth are like a flock of shorn ewes coming up from the washing, which all give birth to twins, and there is not one among them that is barren* (Sg 4:2)? Are you learning anything different than when you hear this in plain words, without the help of this comparison? And yet I don't know how it is, but I find it more delightful to contemplate the saints when I see them as the Church's teeth that cut people off from their errors, and after softening up their hardness by biting them off and chewing them transfer them into its body. I also get enormous pleasure from recognizing who the shorn ewes are, the burdens of the world laid aside like their fleeces, as they come up from the wash, that is from baptism, and all give birth to twins, that is to the two commandments of love, and from seeing that none of them is barren and lacking this holy fertility.

8. But why I should see this with greater pleasure than if no such comparison were forthcoming from the divine books, it is hard to say, since the subject is the same, and the knowledge is the same; in any case, that is another question. What is not in dispute, all the same, is both that one gets to know things more enjoyably through such comparisons, and also that discovering things is much more gratifying if there has been some difficulty in the search for them. Those, after all, who never discover what they are looking for suffer from starvation, while those who do not have to look, because everything is ready to hand, often start wilting out of sheer boredom; in either case a malady to be avoided.

Magnificent and salutary, therefore, is the way the Holy Spirit has so adjusted the holy scriptures, that they ward off starvation with the clearer passages, while driving away boredom with the obscurer ones. There is almost nothing, in fact, that can be extracted from their obscurities, which cannot be found very plainly said somewhere else.

7, 9. What is needed above all else, therefore, is to be converted by the fear of God[6] to wishing to know his will, what he bids us seek and shun. Now this fear of necessity shakes us with thoughts of our mortality and of our death to come, and so to say nails our flesh and fixes all the stirrings of pride to the wood of the cross. What is needed next is to grow modest with piety, and not to contradict the divine scripture, whether we have

---

5. As those about to be baptized laid aside all their clothes.
6. He is here running through the gifts of the Holy Spirit, Is 11:2–3, LXX, backward from the last, the fear of the Lord, to the first, the spirit of wisdom. He does this because the fear of the Lord is the beginning of wisdom, Ps 111:10. He also interweaves the beatitudes into the gifts.

understood it when it lashes our vices, or whether we have not understood it, as though we could have better ideas and make better rules ourselves. Instead, we should rather think and believe that what is written there is better and truer, even if its meaning is hidden, than any good ideas we can think up for ourselves.

10. After these two stages of fear and piety, we come to the third stage of knowledge, which I have undertaken to deal with here and now. Because it is with this stage that every serious student of the scriptures has to occupy himself; and he is not going to find anything else in them but that God is to be loved on God's account, and one's neighbor on God's account; to love God, indeed, with one's whole heart, with one's whole soul, with one's whole mind, but one's neighbor as oneself,[7] that is to say, that one must refer all the love of one's neighbor, as of oneself, to God. We discussed these two commandments in the previous book, when we were dealing with things.

So one first has to discover oneself, in the scriptures, as tied up in love of this world, that is of temporal things, and far removed from such love of God and such love of neighbor as scripture itself prescribes. Then, however, that fear by which one reflects on the judgment of God, and that piety by which one cannot help believing in and yielding to[8] the authority of the sacred books, oblige one to mourn for oneself. Because this knowledge, filled with good hope, leads one to bewail oneself, not to vaunt oneself; and in this frame of mind one begs with assiduous prayer for the consolation of divine help, to prevent one from being crushed with despair, and one begins to reach the fourth stage, that of fortitude or courage, in which one is hungry and thirsty for justice.[9] For in this frame of mind one extricates oneself from all deadly delight in passing things, and turning away from that, one turns instead to love of eternal things, namely to the unchanging unity which is at the same time a trinity.

11. On fixing your gaze, to the extent that you are able, on this light as it sheds its rays from afar, and on perceiving that with your weak sight you cannot bear its brightness, you come to the fifth stage, that is to the stage of counsel which goes with mercy,[10] and you purge your restless and ill-behaved soul of its appetite for inferior things and the dirt it has picked up from them. Here, though, you drill yourself diligently in love of your neighbor, and come to perfection in it; and filled now with hope and having all your powers unimpaired, you climb up to the sixth stage,[11] at which you purge and clean those eyes with which God can be seen, insofar as he can

---

7.   See Mk 12:30–31.
8.   An untranslatable little piece of wordplay: *qua non potest nisi credere et cedere auctoritati.*
9.   See Mt 5:6. We have just had the previous beatitude, those that mourn, connected with the gift of knowledge. The first one, the poor in spirit, was connected by implication with the two gifts (only one in the Hebrew text) of fear and piety.
10. See Mt 5:7.
11. That of understanding, which oddly enough he does not actually name.

be by those who die to this world, insofar as they can; because we see, to the extent that we do die to this world, while to the extent that we live for this world, we do not see.

And the reason that the beauty of this light is still said to be seen *in a riddle and through a mirror* (1 Cor 13:12), even though it is already beginning to be manifested to us more surely, already borne more easily and found to be more enjoyable, is that we are walking more by faith than by sight as long as we are on our journey through this life, though our true abode is in heaven.[12] But at this stage those who have died to this world so purge and clean the eyes of their hearts that they do not even put their neighbors before the truth, or on a level with it, nor themselves either, therefore, because not the ones whom they love as themselves. So these holy people will be so single-minded and pure in heart,[13] that they cannot be diverted from the truth either by any determination to please men, or by a concern to avoid any of those inconveniences that tend to spoil this life. Such children of God are now climbing up to wisdom, which is the last and seventh stage, which is to be enjoyed in peace and tranquillity.[14] Thus *the fear of the Lord*, you see, *is the beginning of wisdom* (Ps 111:10; Sir 1:16); and it is through these stages that one moves from that to this.

8, 12. But let us turn our attention back to that third stage,[15] about which we had undertaken to set out and discuss whatever the Lord might suggest. So then, the really accomplished investigators of the divine scriptures will be those who have begun by reading them all and becoming familiar with them at least by reading, if not yet by understanding them all—just those, that is, which are called canonical; because the others[16] are best left to be read by people who are well instructed in the truths of faith,[17] or else they may so enthrall the feebler spirits that they delude them with dangerous falsehoods and fancies to the prejudice of sound understanding. But for the canonical scriptures, they should follow the authority of the majority of the Catholic Churches, among which, of course, are those that have the privilege of being apostolic sees and having received letters from the apostles.

---

12. See 2 Cor 5:7.6; Phil 3:20.
13. See Mt 5:8.
14. See Mt 5:9.
15. That of knowledge, yoked to the beatitude of those who mourn.
16. That is, the apocryphal books. The African Church in Augustine's time was one of the first Latin-speaking regional Churches to publish a list of the books it accepted as canonical, in councils held at Hippo Regius in 393 and at Carthage in 397. Their list is exactly the same as the one put out over a thousand years later by the Council of Trent.
17. The Latin says, "in the faith of truth," *in fide veritatis*, an inversion of the genitive which occurs not infrequently in the sermons. A kind of explanation, or at least illustration, of it occurred to me one day in Lesotho, when a young friend of mine, whose English was rather elementary, introduced two women he had brought to see me as "my wife and my mother's wife."

They will hold, therefore, to this standard with the canonical scriptures, that they will put those accepted by all the Catholic Churches before those which some do not accept; among these which are not accepted by all they will prefer those accepted by most of them, and by the greater ones among them, to those which fewer Churches and ones of lesser authority regard as canonical. Should they, however, discover that different ones are held to be canonical by the majority of Churches from those so regarded by the greater Churches—though this would be very unlikely[18]—I consider that both should be regarded as having equal authority.

13. But the whole canon of the scriptures, which we are saying is to be the subject of our consideration,[19] consists of the following books: The five of Moses, that is, Genesis, Exodus, Leviticus, Numbers, Deuteronomy; and one book of Jesus son of Nave,[20] one of Judges, one little book which is called Ruth, which seems rather to belong to the beginning of the Kingdoms; then the four of Kingdoms,[21] and the two of the Paralipomenon,[22] which do not follow on, but run parallel beside them. This is all history, which contains the sequence of times and the order of events. There are other historical books, which are not connected to each other, nor to this order and sequence, such as Job and Tobit and Esther and Judith, and the two books of the Maccabees, and the two of Ezra,[23] which do seem more to follow the order of that history which ended with Kingdoms or Paralipomenon.

Next the prophets, among whom are David's one book of psalms, and three books of Solomon, Proverbs, the Song of Songs, and Ecclesiastes. The fact is, those two books, one of which is entitled Wisdom and the other Ecclesiasticus, are only said to be Solomon's from a certain resemblance to the others, because it is the constant tradition that Jesus son of Sirach wrote them;[24] but since they have been thought worthy of being accorded canonical authority, they are to be counted among the prophetic books. The rest are the books of those who are properly called prophets, each single book of the twelve prophets, which joined together, since they have never been separated, are treated as one book; the names of the prophets being these: Hosea, Joel, Amos, Obadiah, Jonah, Micah, Nahum, Habakkuk, Zephaniah, Haggai, Zechariah, Malachi; next the four prophets, each with

---

18. So the Maurists; *quamquam hoc facile inveniri non possit*. But CCL omits *facile*, giving the sense, in my paraphrase, "though this could not happen."
19. In the stage of the gift of knowledge.
20. Joshua, son of Nun; but I have to keep Augustine's Septuagint version of Joshua's name, because he and his contemporaries were very conscious of the identity of his name with that of our Lord, and hence of his prefiguring Jesus in a very special way.
21. Which we call Kings—or rather which we now call 1 and 2 Samuel, 1 and 2 Kings.
22. The Greek name for Chronicles, meaning something like "The left-overs."
23. That is, Ezra and Nehemiah.
24. See the extract from the *Revisions* at the beginning of this work.

his greater volume, Isaiah, Jeremiah, Daniel, Ezekiel.[25] To these forty-four books is confined the authority of the Old Testament.

But in the New Testament there are the four books of the gospel, according to Matthew, according to Mark, according to Luke, according to John; the fourteen letters of the apostle Paul, to the Romans, to the Corinthians two, to the Galatians, to the Ephesians, to the Philippians, to the Thessalonians two, to the Colossians, to Timothy two, to Titus, to Philemon, to the Hebrews; two letters of Peter, three of John, one of Jude and one of James; the one book of the Acts of the apostles,[26] and the one book of the Apocalypse of John.

What is required for a fruitful study of scripture

9, 14. What those who fear God and have a docile piety are looking for in all these books is the will of God. The first step in this laborious search, as I have said, is to know these books, and even if not yet so as to understand them, all the same by reading them to commit them to memory, or at least not to be totally unfamiliar with them. Next, those things that are put clearly in them, whether precepts about how to live or rules about what to believe, are to be studied with the utmost care and diligence; the greater your intellectual capacity, the more of these you will find. The fact is, after all, that in the passages that are put plainly in scripture is to be found everything that touches upon faith, and good morals, that is to say hope and charity, which we dealt with in the previous book.

Only then, however, after acquiring some familiarity with the actual style of the divine scriptures, should one proceed to try to open up and unravel their obscurities, in such a way that instances from the plainer passages are used to cast light on the more obscure utterances, and the testimony of some undoubted judgments is used to remove uncertainties from those that are more doubtful. In this matter what is of the greatest value is a good memory; if this is wanting, these instructions cannot be of any great assistance.[27]

10, 15. Now there are two reasons why texts are not understood: if they are veiled in signs that are either unknown or ambiguous. Signs, for their part, can be either proper or metaphorical. They are said to be proper when

---

25. It is curious that he reverses the order of the last two, departing from the order of the Septuagint.

26. There are several idiosyncratic changes of order in his New Testament list; the most striking being this placing of Acts after the epistles; and among them, the placing of Colossians after Thessalonians, and of James as the last instead of the first of the so-called "catholic" or general epistles.

27. A guess at the meaning of a very elliptical phrase: "if it is lacking, *non potest his praeceptis dari*"; literally, "it"—what? the memory?—"cannot be given to these precepts." Augustine himself clearly had a prodigious memory, and not only came as close as is possible to knowing the Bible by heart, but also had in his memory a marvelous system of cross-references.

they are introduced to signify the things they were originally intended for, as when we say "ox" to signify the animal which everyone who shares the English language[28] with us calls by this name. They are metaphorical when the very things which we signify with their proper words are made use of to signify something else, as when we say "ox," and by this syllable understand the animal which is usually so called, but again by that animal understand the evangelist,[29] whom scripture itself signified, according to the apostle's interpretation of *You shall not muzzle the ox that threshes the corn* (1 Cor 9:9; Dt 25:4).

11, 16. The best remedy for ignorance of proper signs is the knowledge of languages; and in addition to the English and Latin languages,[30] the people whom I have now undertaken to advise have need of the two other languages of the divine scriptures, namely Hebrew and Greek, so that they can have recourse to the earlier versions whenever doubt about the meaning of a text is raised by the infinite variety of Latin—and English—translations. Although we also often find Hebrew words untranslated in the books of the Bible, like Amen and Alleluia and Raca[31] and Hosanna, and any others there may be. Of these some, though they could have been translated, have been traditionally kept as they are because of their more sacred associations, like Amen and Alleluia;[32] while of others it is said that they could not be translated, like the other two I mentioned. There are some words, after all, in particular languages which defy translation into any other language. And this is above all the case with exclamations, which are words indicating some emotion of the spirit, rather than any part of a connected sentence.[33] These two, in fact, are generally considered to be such words; they tell us that Raca is a word expressing ill-natured contempt, while Hosanna expresses joy.

But it is not because of these few words, which can be very easily noted and asked about, that knowledge of these languages is necessary, but because of the variety of the translations, as has been said. Those who translated the scriptures from Hebrew into Greek can be counted;[34] this

---

28. The Latin language, of course, in the text.
29. Paul appears in this passage to have been referring rather to himself. Is the reason Augustine says the evangelist that the ox was already in his time accepted as the symbol of Luke's gospel, being one of the four living creatures supporting God's throne, Rv 4:6–7?
30. He just says the Latin language, of course. I retain it here, as well as transposing it as usual into "the English language."
31. See Mt 5:22.
32. It is surprising that he does not give the translation of these words, which he is always ready to do in his sermons, as occasion arises; telling us, correctly, that Amen means "It's true," and Alleluia means "Praise the Lord."
33. Reading *sententiae connexae* with three manuscripts, instead of *sententiae conceptae*, "of a thought out sentence," with CCL, the Maurists, and the rest of the manuscripts. CCL does not even mention this "variant" in its apparatus.
34. He presumably had in mind Origen's *Hexapla*, which besides the official Septuagint version included three others, those of Symmachus, Theodotion, and Aquila.

is certainly not true of Latin translators. The fact is that whenever in the early days of the faith a Greek codex came into anybody's hands, and he felt that he had the slightest familiarity with each language, he rushed in with a translation.

12, 17. In fact, this state of affairs has been more of a help than a hindrance to the understanding of the scriptures, provided only that readers are not casual and careless. The examination of several versions has often been able to throw light on obscurer passages, as with that text of the prophet Isaiah (58:7), where one translation has, *And do not despise the household of your seed*, and another has, *And do not despise your own flesh*. Each corroborates the other; that is, each can be explained by the other, because on the one hand flesh could be taken in the proper sense, so that the reader could suppose he was being warned not to despise his own body; while on the other the household of one's seed could be understood metaphorically as Christians, born spiritually from the same seed of the word as ourselves.[35]

But now, putting the minds of the translators together, we hit upon the more probable meaning that we are being commanded, according to the literal sense, not to despise our blood relations, because when you connect the household of your seed with your flesh, it is your blood relations that immediately occur to you. I am sure that is what the apostle meant when he said, *If I may by any means provoke my own flesh to jealousy, in order to save some of them* (Rom 11:14); that is, that by being jealous of those who had believed, they themselves might come to believe as well. By his flesh, clearly, he meant the Jews, because of their blood relationship.

Again, there is that text of the same prophet Isaiah, *Unless you believe, you shall not understand*, which another translator rendered, *Unless you believe, you shall not endure*[36] (Is 7:9). Which of these two, though, followed the original words one cannot tell, unless one reads copies of the original language. But all the same, for those who are shrewd readers, something important is being suggested by each version. It is difficult, after all, for translators to differ so much from each other, that they do not come close to some extent. So then, understanding refers to everlasting sight, while faith in temporal things as in a kind of cradle is, so to say, nourishing little ones on milk;[37] now, however, *we are walking by faith and not by sight* (2 Cor 5:7), but unless we walk by faith, we shall never be able to reach the sight which does not pass away but endures, when with our understanding purified we cleave to Truth. And that is why one translator says, *Unless*

---

35. See Jas 1:18; 1 Pt 1:23; Jn 1:13.
36. In its first, less correct form, one of Augustine's favorite quotations.
37. See 1 Cor 3:2; Heb 5:12; 1 Pt 2:2. The prime object of faith, for Augustine, is not the eternal truths and mystery of God, but the temporal mystery of the incarnation—more precisely, the flesh of the Word incarnate. See *The Trinity*, XIII, 25; XIV, 3.

you believe, you shall not endure, while the other has, *Unless you believe, you shall not understand.*

18. And translators are often misled by ambiguities in the original language, when they are insufficiently familiar with the context, and translate the meaning of a word which is clearly far from the author's mind. Thus some versions have, *Their feet are sharp to shed blood; oxys*, you see, in Greek can mean both "sharp" and "swift." So the one who got the author's meaning was the one who translated, *Their feet are swift to shed blood* (Rom 3:15[38]), while the other went wrong by following in the wrong direction a sign that points two ways. And in such cases we have to do, not with obscurity, but with falsehood; so here another condition has to be met, the requirement being to correct, rather than simply to understand, copies of such versions. Here too is another instance: because the Greek *moschos* means "calf," some translators failed to understand that *moscheumata* means "seedlings," and so they translated it as "calflings."[39] This mistake has indeed infected so many copies that you can scarcely find one with the other reading. And yet the meaning is as plain as can be, because the next words make it quite clear; after all, *Bastard seedlings will not strike deep roots* (Wis 4:3) makes better sense than *calflings*, which walk on the ground with four feet, and do not strike roots. The rest of the context in this place also confirms this translation.

13, 19. But the proper meaning of a passage, which several translators attempt to express, each according to his capacity and judgment, can only be definitely ascertained from an examination of it in the language they are translating from; and translators frequently deviate from the author's meaning, if they are not particularly learned. So one should either aim at a knowledge of those languages from which the scriptures have come to their Latin and English versions, or else get hold of translations which have been the most strictly literal, word for word, renderings of the original, not because they are sufficient in themselves, but because they can help one to control the freedom,[40] or even the mistakes, of those translators who have

---

38. Augustine probably thought he was quoting Ps 14:3, because Paul in Romans joins several other texts onto it—this particular verse comes from Prv 1:7—and as a result the whole of Paul's chain of quotations, Rom 3:10–18, got incorporated into Ps 14:3 in the Septuagint (where it is numbered Ps 13:3).

39. But when I look up *vitulamen* in Lewis & Short, they give as its meaning, "a shoot, sucker, sprig." They also derive it from the verb *vitulo*, to celebrate, and not from *vitulus*, a calf. However, the only text they refer to in support is from a letter of Saint Ambrose, 37, 57, and then this Vulgate text from Wisdom. So very possibly Augustine is right about the proper meaning of the word, and Ambrose is very sensibly interpreting its occurrence in Wis 4:3 to mean what it ought to mean.

40. Reading *libertas* with CCL and the older editors, instead of *veritas*, truth, which the Maurists prefer on the strength of eleven manuscripts. Augustine is clearly comparing here free with literal translation. The modern equivalent of the literal translation he favors as an aid would be the interlinear cribs of some old-fashioned school textbooks.

preferred to follow the meanings rather than the words of the authors. It is often the case, after all, that not only single words but also whole phrases are transposed which simply cannot go into correct Latin or English usage, if one wishes to stick to the standards of the old classical authors who spoke the languages. Sometimes this in no way prevents one from understanding a passage, but still it does offend those who find greater pleasure in the substance of the things said, if a certain propriety is preserved in the signs by which they are conveyed.

What are called solecisms, after all, are simply cases where words are put together without observing the rules followed by our predecessors, whose manner of writing and speaking was not without authority. I mean, whether you say in Latin *inter homines* or *inter hominibus*,[41] or in English *between you and me* or *between you and I*, makes no difference to our ability to get the meaning. Again, what else is a barbarism but the spelling or pronunciation of a word in a way which was not accepted by received authors of the past? I mean, whether you pronounce *ignoscere* with a long or short e in the third syllable, or *forgive* to rhyme with "hive" or "sieve," is of little concern to those who are begging God to forgive their sins, however they may manage to pronounce that word. What else then is correctness of speech but the observation of a manner that is foreign to one,[42] which has been established by the authority of past speakers?

20. But for all that, people are the more readily offended by such instances the less sense they have; and they show less sense the more they wish to be thought learned or well educated, not by knowledge of things which build up, but by knowledge of signs, which it is very hard to avoid being puffed up by,[43] since even knowledge of the substance of things can give us swollen heads and stiff necks, unless we submit them to the Lord's yoke.[44] After all, is one in the least prevented from understanding this passage, because it is written as follows: *What is the land in which these people reside upon it, whether it is good or bad; and what are the cities in which they dwell in them*[45] (Num 13:19)? I consider this is just a form of

---

41. The right and wrong way of saying "among men," with the accusative and the ablative cases respectively.
42. *Alienae consuetudinis*; thus most of the manuscripts, so the Maurists assure us. One sympathizes with the older editors, and perhaps some manuscripts, who substitute *latinae consuetudinis*. But Augustine probably did write *alienae*, and had in mind the equivalent of people in Britain speaking "BBC English," or "with an Oxford accent," when they would be much happier relaxing into their native Cockney, Geordie, or West Country burr; in other words, his ordinary Numidian countrymen who naturally spoke their local dialect, but were sometimes pressured into speaking "correct"—and "alien"—Latin.
43. See 1 Cor 8:1.
44. See Mt 11:29-30.
45. A pair of characteristic Hebraisms, Hebrew lacking any equivalent to relative pronouns, and having instead simply a relative particle. Sesotho and related African languages have a similar idiom.

expression derived from a foreign language, rather than any hint of some deeper meaning.[46] There is also that mistake we cannot now remove from the mouths of our psalm-singing congregations, *But on him my sanctification* floriet *(shall flourish)* (Ps 132:18), which in no way detracts from the sense; still, the better educated listener would prefer it to be corrected, and *florebit* substituted for *floriet*; and the only thing that stops such a correction being made is the habit the singers have got into. So these things can even be easily shrugged aside, if you are not fussy about avoiding little errors that do not get in the way of a proper understanding.

But as for this that the apostle says, *The folly of God is wiser than men, and the weakness of God is stronger than men* (1 Cor 1:25), if someone[47] had wished to preserve the Greek idiom, and instead of saying, *Quod stultum est Dei sapientius est hominibus, et quod infirmum est Dei fortius est hominibus,* had said *Quod stultum est Dei sapientius est hominum, et quod infirmum est Dei fortius est hominum,*[48] a sharp-eyed reader might have got the right sense, but the less quick-witted might either not have understood at all, or else have even got a back-to-front meaning out of it, because such an expression is not only bad Latin, it is also ambiguous, so that it could be taken to mean that the folly of men and the weakness of men seems to be wiser or stronger than the folly or weakness of God, though even the correct *sapientius hominibus* is not without the possibilities of ambiguity, because only the whole sentence can tell us whether *hominibus* is in the dative or the ablative case;[49] so it would be better to say, *Sapientius est quam homines* and *fortius est quam homines.*

14, 21. But we shall talk about ambiguous signs later on; for the time being we are dealing with unknown ones, of which there are two sorts, as far as words are concerned; because it is either an unknown word or an unknown expression that causes a reader to get stuck. If these come from foreign languages, their meaning can either be sought from people who speak those languages, or the languages can be learned, if you have the leisure or the knack, or several translations can be compared. But if it is some words or expressions of our own language that we are ignorant of, we can get to know them through the habit of reading or listening. None, certainly, are to be more carefully committed to memory than those words and expressions which we do not know; so that when we meet someone more learned whom we can ask about them, or when what goes before or what follows in such a reading can show what their force is, and what is

---

46. I wonder if someone like Origen, or his Latin disciple and admirer Rufinus, Augustine's contemporary and the victim of Jerome's merciless invective and vitriolic pen, had tried to extract some mystical meaning from this Hebraism.
47. From here to the end of the section I just paraphrase, for reasons that will be obvious.
48. The Greek genitive of comparison instead of the Latin ablative.
49. If it were the dative, I suppose it would mean, "... is wiser for men...is stronger for men."

signified by what we do not know, then with the aid of memory we can easily notice and learn.

Though such, as a matter of fact, is the power of habit even for learning, that people who have been as it were reared and brought up on the scriptures are more surprised at other non-scriptural forms of expression, and think they are less proper Latin or English than the ones they have learned in the scriptures, which are not found in authors of classical Latin or English. Here too the examination and discussion of a variety of versions that can be compared is of the greatest help—provided only that they are not full of mistakes. The first thing, in fact, to which those who wish to know the divine scriptures should devote their careful attention and their skill is the correction of their copies, so that the uncorrected ones give way to the corrected ones, when they derive, that is, from one and the same type of translation.

The special virtue of the old Itala Latin, and of the Greek Septuagint versions

15, 22. Among the versions themselves, however, the *Itala* is to be preferred to the rest, because it sticks more closely to the actual words, while at the same time having a clear perception of the meaning. And for correcting any Latin versions at all, Greek ones should be employed, among which, as regards the Old Testament, that of the Seventy Translators[50] has the greatest authority. These are said, throughout all the more learned Churches,[51] to have been so directed by the Holy Spirit in their translations, that while being so many they had but a single mouth. If, as the story goes, and many by no means unreliable authors declare, they were all kept apart from each other in separate rooms, and when they had finished their translations nothing was to be found in any of their copies whch was not there in exactly the same words and the same order as in all the others, who could possibly put any other version on a level with such an authority, let alone prefer one to it? If, on the other hand, they collaborated in order to speak with one voice by the common consideration and judgment of them all, even in that case no single individual, however well qualified, may decently aspire to correcting what was agreed to among so many venerable and learned scholars.

---

50. The Septuagint, or 70, LXX. The Maurists list some of the Fathers who retailed the story of the 70 separate cells. And they also say that Saint Jerome poured scorn on the story, and said that Aristeas, whose letter is at the base of it, only wrote that the 70 scholars were housed by King Ptolemy II Philadelphus, about 250 BC, in a "basilica, where they were collaborating, not prophesying"; and that this is how the Jewish historian Josephus also tells the story. See *City of God* XVIII, 42 and 43.

51. Not necessarily Greek-speaking Churches. He would have had primarily in mind the Churches of Carthage, Rome, and Milan—and would soon have won the right to include the Church of Hippo Regius among them.

For this reason, even if things are found in Hebrew codices that differ from what the Seventy have put, in my judgment they should give way to what divine providence has achieved through these men; and that is that the books which the Jewish people was unwilling to share with others, whether out of a religious sense or out of envy, were made available by the Lord, using the royal authority of Ptolemy, to the nations that were going to believe. And so it can well be the case that these translated the Hebrew in such a way as the Holy Spirit, who was guiding them and gave them all one mouth, judged would be most suitable for the Gentiles. But still, as I said above, comparing their text with that of translators who stuck more closely to the words of the original is often useful for explaining the meaning.

So then, Latin volumes of the Old Testament, as I had started to say, should be corrected where necessary according to the authority of the Greek ones, and particularly of the Seventy who are held to have translated in unanimous agreement. But as for the books of the New Testament, if there are any hesitations about the text due to the variety of Latin translations, nobody doubts that one should bow to the authority of the Greek texts, and of those especially which are to be found in the more learned and careful Churches.

What is required for understanding metaphorical signs

16, 23. As far as metaphorical signs, however, are concerned, wherever readers find themselves stuck because of their unfamiliarity, they need to investigate them partly by a knowledge of languages, partly by a knowledge of things. Take the pool of Siloam, for instance, where the Lord told the man to wash his face, after he had anointed his eyes with mud made from spittle; it certainly has some force as a comparison and undoubtedly suggests some hidden meaning; but unless the evangelist had translated that name of an unknown language, the understanding of such an important truth would have escaped us.[52] So also there can be no doubt that many Hebrew names, which were not translated by the authors of these books, will be of no little value and help in solving the riddles of the scriptures, if you can translate them. And several men, learned in that language, have conferred what is indeed no small benefit on posterity by collecting all such words from the scriptures and translating them, and telling us what Adam means, or Eve, or Abraham, or Moses; or with place names too, what Jerusalem means, or Zion, or Jericho, or Sinai, or Lebanon, or Jordan, or any other names in that language whose meaning is unknown to us. When these have been

---

52. See Jn 9:6–7. As the name means "Sent," the pool signifies Christ, in whom we wash in the sacrament of baptism, thereby having the eyes of our faith illuminated. This provides Augustine with the key by which to interpet the whole passage in terms of the salvation brought to humanity (born blind in original sin) through the Word becoming flesh (spittle mixed with soil).

translated and made plain, the meaning of many figurative expressions in the scriptures is revealed.

24. Ignorance of things, on the other hand, makes figurative expressions obscure, when we are ignorant of the natures of animals, or stones, or herbs, or other things which are frequently mentioned in scripture by way of similes and comparisons. Take what is known about serpents, for instance, that in order to protect their heads they present their whole bodies to those who are striking them; what a light it throws on the meaning of the Lord's bidding us to be as cunning as serpents,[53] namely that for the sake of our head, which is Christ, we should rather offer our bodies to the persecutors, lest our Christian faith should as it were be slain in us, if to spare our bodies we were to deny God! Or there's the way in which a snake is said to squeeze through a narrow cranny in a cave, in order to lay aside its old skin and so take on a new lease of life; how well it chimes in with imitating this cunning of the serpent by putting off the old self, as the apostle says, in order to put on the new;[54] and with putting it off by squeezing through narrow places, as the Lord says, *Enter by the narrow gate* (Mt 7:13)!

So just as knowledge of the nature of serpents throws light on many comparisons which scripture habitually made with this animal, in the same way ignorance of several other animals which it mentions no less frequently by way of comparison will be a very common hindrance to true understanding. So too with ignorance of stones, of herbs, or anything held in place by roots. Thus on the one hand knowledge of rubies, which shine in the dark, throws light on many obscure passages in the books which mention them for comparison; and ignorance of beryls and diamonds frequently closes the door to understanding. And the only reason it is easy to understand that perpetual peace is signified by the olive twig which the dove brought back to the ark on its return[55] is that we know that the soothing touch of oil is not easily spoiled by other harsher liquids, and that that tree is in leaf all the year round. Many people, on the other hand, because they are ignorant about hyssop, and do not know what virtue it has, either for clearing the lungs, or for splitting rocks with its roots even though it is such a small and lowly plant, are quite unable to discover why it says, *You will sprinkle me with hyssop, and I shall become clean* (Ps 51:7).

25. Unfamiliarity with numbers is also the cause of one's not understanding many things which are put down metaphorically and mystically

---

53. See Mt 10:16. It is indeed usually the fabulous knowledge of things that helped the Fathers, and great spiritual writers like Saint Francis de Sales, to extract profound mystical meanings from the figurative expressions of scripture.
54. See Eph 4:22–24; Col 3:9–10.
55. See Gn 8:11.

in scripture.[56] One's native wit, surely— if I may so put it[57]—cannot help wondering what it could mean, that both Moses and Elijah and the Lord himself fasted for forty days.[58] The knotty symbolism of this kind of action cannot be unraveled except by knowledge and consideration of this number. It contains, you see, four times ten, which is as much as to say knowledge of all things woven into the times. It is in terms of the number four, after all, that both the daily and the annual cycles run their course; the daily one through the morning, midday, evening and nocturnal hours; the annual one through the months of spring, summer, autumn and winter. Now we should be fasting and abstaining from the delights of the times while we are living in time, for the sake of the eternity in which we wish to live although the very course of time should be driving home to us how wise the teaching is that we should make light of temporal things and set our hearts upon those of eternity.

Furthermore, the number ten signifies knowledge of creator and of creature; there is, after all, the trinity of the creator, while the number seven indicates the creature, because of its life and body: because in its life there are three things, which is why God is to be loved *with one's whole heart, one's whole soul, one's whole mind* (Mt 22:37), while in the body the number four is as evident as could be, in the elements of which it consists.[59] So by this number ten, as it is being proposed to us in the context of time—being multiplied by four, that is—we are being advised to live in chaste abstinence from the delights of time, that is to fast for forty days. This is the advice of the law, represented by Moses, the advice of the prophets, represented by Elijah, the advice of the Lord himself. This is why, as if being vouched for by the law and the prophets, he appeared in glory on the mountain between those two, with the three disciples as astonished witnesses.[60]

Next one may ask in the same sort of way how from the number forty there arises the number fifty, which in our religion has no mean sacred significance because of Pentecost, and how being multiplied by three because of the three ages, before the law, under the law, under grace, and[61] because of the name of the Father and of the Son and of the Holy Spirit, having the Trinity itself added to complete the number, it can be referred to the mystery of the Church in its most purified state, and comes to the one hundred and fifty-three fishes, which the nets caught on being cast on the right hand side

---

56. He is not referring to ignorance of elementary arithmetic, but of what one may call theological or mystical arithmetic, the symbolism of numbers—let us call it arithmology.
57. He is lightly apologizing for a Latin pun which cannot be conveyed in translation: *Ingenium quippe, ut ita dixerim, ingenuum...*
58. See Ex 24:18; 1 Kgs 19:8; Lk 4:2.
59. The four elements of ancient chemistry, earth, water, air, and fire.
60. See Mk 9:2–8.
61. Reading *et* instead of the text's *vel*, or. He is not giving the Trinity as an alternative reason for multiplying 50 by 3, but as a reason for then adding 3, to get 153.

after the Lord's resurrection.[62] In the same sort of way hidden symbolic meanings are contained in several other numbers to be found in the sacred books, which are closed to readers unskilled in arithmology.[63]

26. Ignorance of various musical matters also closes off and veils understanding of not a few mysteries; thus one commentator[64] has not unsuitably derived some symbolic meanings from the difference between a psaltery and a guitar; and about *the ten-stringed psaltery* (Ps 33:2) the learned ask themselves reasonably enough whether it has any musical *rationale* which requires such a large number of strings, or whether, if it lacks this, the number is rather to be taken as having a sacred significance, either because of the ten commandments of the law, in which the number is again to be referred to creator and creature,[65] or because of the interpretation given above of the number ten.

And that number connected with the building of the temple which is mentioned in the gospel, namely *forty-six years* (Jn 2:20), has something or other musical about it,[66] and when referred to the structure of the Lord's body, on account of which mention is made of the temple, it obliges a number of heretics to confess that the Son of God clothed himself, not with a false, but a true body, and a human one. And in many, many passages in the holy scriptures we find numbers and music given an honorable place.

What use can be made of secular doctrines; the errors of pagan myths and superstitions

17, 27. So we should pay no attention to the errors of pagan superstition, which pretended that the nine Muses are daughters of Jupiter and Memory.[67] Varro himself refuted them, and I do not know if anyone more learned or

---

62. See Jn 21:11. The fish represent the Church of the blessed after the resurrection of the dead. This gives us Augustine's earliest way of interpreting this number 153. See Sermon 229M, 2–3 for his more mature preference in this matter, treating 153 as the "triangle" of 17; that is, $17+16+15...+1 = 153$. See also Sermons 250, 251, 252A, 270. In Sermon 252, on the other hand, an earlier sermon preached in 396, about the time he was writing this work, he treats the number as here in our text.

    To us it may all seem rather bizarre; and yet surely Augustine is right in assuming that the evangelist regarded the number 153 as significantly symbolic.

63. It is I who impose this word on Augustine; he just says unskilled in numbers; but we have seen what a very special "science of numbers" he has in mind.

64. *Quidam* in the singular. I suspect he means Tychonius. See Translator's Note.

65. With the first three commandments, as Augustine counted them, referring to our duties to God, and the next seven to our duties to our neighbor.

66. To explain how this number has something musical about it, and how knowledge of musical theory helps to unravel its mystery, would call for a rather long article. Instead of writing one here, I refer the reader to *The Trinity* in this series, Book IV, sections 1–10, and note 40 to that book.

67. Two manuscripts have *Minerva* instead of *Memory*. But in his work *on Order* II, 41, he mentions the same myth, and there too the Muses are daughters of Memory.

curious about such matters can be found among the pagan authors. He tells us, you see, that some city or other, I forget the name of it, placed an order with three sculptors for three images of the Muses each, to place as a gift in the temple of Apollo, on the understanding that whichever of them produced the most beautiful statues, it would choose them and buy them from him. And what happened in fact was that the work of all three sculptors turned out to be equally beautiful, and that all nine images delighted the city, and it bought all nine, to be dedicated in the temple of Apollo; and the poet Hesiod later on gave them their names. So it was not Jupiter who begot the nine Muses, but three sculptors who created three each.

That city, however, had placed an order for three Muses, not because someone had seen them in a dream, or because they had revealed themselves to the eyes of some citizen as being that many, but because it was easy to observe that every sound which songs are made of can naturally take three forms. It is either produced by the voice, as with those who sing with their mouths without any instrument; or by wind, as with trumpets and pipes; or by beat, as with guitars and drums, and any other instruments that produce melodious sounds on being struck.[68]

18, 28. But whether or not it all occurred as Varro recorded, still we for our part should certainly not allow such heathen superstitions to make us shun all knowledge of music, if we can snatch anything from it that we can use for the understanding of the holy scriptures; nor on the other hand should we let ourselves be converted to their fondness for theatrical trifles, if we happen to discuss some points about guitars and other instruments which may help us to a better grasp of spiritual things. After all, it is no reason for us not to learn our letters, just because they say Mercury is their patron god;[69] nor, just because they have dedicated temples to Justice and Virtue, and have preferred to worship in stone images what should carried in the heart, is that any reason for us to shun justice and virtue.

On the contrary indeed, all good and true Christians should understand that truth, wherever they may find it, belongs to their Lord; then, after weighing it up and acknowledging it also in the sacred books, they

---

68. Whether this "rational" explanation of the three original Muses, so to say, comes from Varro or Augustine himself, I cannot tell. Given the derivation of the word "music" from "muse," the explanation seems likely enough. Of the nine to whom Hesiod is said to have given names, Euterpe was conventionally the Muse of music, and Polyhymnia, presumably, of choral singing; Calliope possibly of instrumental music. But they do not seem to have been allotted the spheres of influence which Augustine suggests. The other six were Clio, the Muse of history, Thalia of comedy, Melpomene of tragedy, Terpsichore of dancing, Urania of astronomy, and Erato, presumably, of lyric poetry.

69. So the CCL text, with almost all the manuscripts. The Maurists, however, emend *deum* to *repertorem*, "their inventor," without giving its warrant for doing so. As a sheer emendation of the text it is certainly very bold.

should repudiate all superstitious fictions,[70] and grieve over and beware of people *who, while knowing God, have not glorified him as God, or given thanks, but have faded away in their thoughts, and their foolish hearts have been darkened; for while calling themselves wise they became fools, and changed the glory of the imperishable God into the likeness of the image of a perishable man, and of birds and of four-footed beasts, and of reptiles* (Rom 1:21–23).

19, 29. But it is of the utmost importance that we should go into this whole question much more thoroughly. So let us begin by saying that there are two kinds of teaching, which even govern the morals of the heathen. One is about those institutions which human beings have established, the other about things they have observed as having already occurred, or as having been established by God.[71] The kind concerning human institutions is partly superstitious, partly not.

20, 30. Superstition includes anything established by human beings which refers to the making and worshiping of idols, or the worshiping of creation or any part of creation as God; or to consultations and certain agreed codes of communication, settled in collusion with demons. This is the sort of thing the efforts of the magical arts are directed at, and these the pagan poets have been more in the habit of mentioning than of teaching. Of this sort too, but examples, so to say, of officially licensed futility, are the books of the soothsayers and augurs.[72] To this class also belong all amulets and remedial charms, which the medical profession frowns upon too; whether they consist of incantations, or certain signs which they call "characters," or of any objects to be hung or tied round the neck, or even to be danced[73] somehow or other, not for exercising the patients' bodies, but in order to signify certain hidden or even obvious meanings.

They call all these things by the milder name of "physic," to make it seem as if they proceed from nature, and do not involve any superstition, things like earrings in the tips of each ear, or rings made from ostrich bones

---

70. As the Maurists punctuate, this sentence would run: "... and acknowledging it, they should repudiate all superstitious fictions even in the sacred books." While Augustine could indeed allow that the scriptures contained superstitious fictions —for example, the brazen serpent (2 Kgs 18:4)—I do not think that that interpretation fits this context, and what he goes on immediately to say, which refers to idolatries universally condemned in the scriptures.
71. See section 41 onward.
72. They were of a *quasi licentiore vanitate*, because they were the official diviners employed by the Roman state, before it was formally converted to Christianity.
73. *Saltandis*; so CCL and almost all the manuscripts. The Maurists, on the strength of one manuscript, of which CCL does not even acknowledge the existence, substitutes *aptandi*, "or even to be applied somehow or other." But this is very feeble and flat.

The "dancing" of charms or spells is, I believe, a feature in some so-called voodoo rites of the Caribbean, or vodun of West Africa—dancing controlled by symbolic signs marked out in various colors on the dancing floor.

on the fingers, or your being told, when you hiccup, to hold your left thumb in your right hand.

31. To these can be added a thousand and one observances of the stupidest kind, if a limb twitches or jerks, if when two friends are walking along arm in arm a stone or a dog or a child comes in between them, and their kicking the stone as though it were breaching their friendship is less offensive than when they slap an innocent child hard, if he runs in between them as they walk together. But what is nice is that the children are sometimes avenged by the dogs, because such people are often so superstitious that they are even bold enough to kick a dog running in between them, and this they do not do with impunity, because occasionally the dog will very speedily send the man who kicks him straight from this futile remedy to the real medical man.

Here too we can fit in such practices as these: treading on your threshold when you go past your house; going back to bed if you sneeze when you are putting on your shoes; going back home if you stumble as you go out; when your clothes have been gnawed by shrew-mice, trembling at the prospect of some future evil more than lamenting your present loss. On this point there is Cato's witty retort, when he was consulted by someone who said his boots had been gnawed by shrews, replying that there was nothing of ill omen in that, but that it would indeed have been an ill omen if the shrews had been gnawed by the boots.

21, 32. Nor are those exempt from this kind of pernicious superstition who are called genethliacs because of their examination of birthdays,[74] but are now more commonly called astrologers. While they do indeed note and follow the true position of the stars when someone is born, and sometimes even prognosticate it,[75] still by claiming to predict from their observations either our actions or the consequences of our actions they wander very far from the truth, and sell uneducated people short with a wretched slavery. Because whenever a free man goes in to one of these astrologers, he pays him money in order to come out the slave of either Mars or Venus, or rather of all the constellations. These were given the names of animals because of

---

74. The casters of horoscopes. The Oxford English Dictionary does give "genethliac" as an English word; the Greek *genethlia* means first of all a birthday party—an important element of which, no doubt, was the casting of the host's horoscope. The Latin word translated "astrologers" is *mathematici*. The superstition he is here attacking is of course both very common and very lucrative today.

75. The text, both CCL and the Maurists, has *et aliquando etiam pervestigent*; but *pervestigent* adds nothing to the previous verb, *consectentur*; it simply means to investigate thoroughly. So I am guessing that Augustine wrote *praevestigent*—possibly inventing the word, as it does not figure in Lewis & Short. He would have been thinking, I assumed, of forecasts of eclipses and other such celestial phenomena made by astrologers.

a certain resemblance, or of human beings to do them honor, by those who were the first to fall into this error, and who then passed it on to posterity.[76]

This is hardly surprising, surely, when we consider that even in more recent times closer to our own the Romans attempted to dedicate what we call the morning star in honor of the name of Caesar. And perhaps this might have happened and become an ancient and accepted custom, had not Venus his forebear given her name to this property; and there was no legal way in which she could pass it on to her heirs, because she never actually possessed it during her life or asked to possess it.[77] But where a place was vacant, and not occupied in honor of someone who had died before, that happened which usually happens in such cases. Thus instead of Quintile and Sextile[78] we call those months July and August, named in honor of the human beings Julius Caesar and Augustus Caesar. So anyone who wishes to can readily understand that those stars as well previously wandered round the sky without any of those names; but that when important persons died whose memory people wished to honor, whether out of human vanity or forced to do so by royal authority, their names were attached to the stars, and people thought they were elevating the dead themselves to the heavens.

But whatever they may be called by human beings, they are still just stars, which God set in place and regulated as he wished; and they have their definite movements by which the seasons are distinguished and alternate. Noting these movements and their mutual relationships when anyone is born is easy enough to do by following the rules that have been worked out and written down by the people whom holy scripture condemns when it says, *For if they have been able to know so much that they could calculate the age of the universe, how is it that they did not all the more readily find its Lord?* (Wis 13:9).

22, 33. But wishing as a result of such observations to predict the morals, the actions and the future of those who are born is a great mistake and great nonsense. And those who have learned how to unlearn such things can refute this superstition without the slightest hesitation. For what these people call a person's stars[79] are the relationships observed between the stars when the person was born, about whom these unfortunates are consulted by people more unfortunate still. Now it can happen that some twins emerge from the womb so quickly one after the other that no interval of time can

---

76. He is referring to the names of the signs of the zodiac, as well as of certain con-stellations. The human beings would be Gemini, the twins Castor and Pollux, Virgo, Sagittarius, Aquarius, and constellations such as Orion.
77. Presumably what he means is that the goddess Venus never actually existed.
78. The old names for July and August, counting the months from March. As no other imperial worthies emerged to match the two founders of the Julian dynasty, the next months remained the seventh, eighth, ninth and tenth; September, October, November, December.
79. Literally, "constellations"; but the use of this word in its astrological sense is obsolete in English, while its nearest equivalent, "conjunctions," is a respectable term of scientific astronomy.

be perceived between them and marked against the numbers of their stars. So it must follow that many twins have the same stars, while they do not have the same history of things they do and things they undergo, but often ones so different from each other that one is very fortunate in life while the other is very unfortunate.

Thus we are informed that Esau and Jacob were born as twins, and that Jacob, who was born second, was found *to be grasping in his hand the foot of his brother* (Gn 25:25), who preceded him. Undoubtedly the day and time of birth of these two could only be noted down as giving them one and the same set of stars; but how different they were in their morals, their deeds, their trials and their fortunes, is evident from the scripture story that is already a commonplace among all nations.

34. Nor is it to the point when they say that the minimal, tiny moment of time which separates the birth of twins counts for much in nature, considering the speed at which the heavenly bodies rush along. For even were I to grant that it counts for ever so much, it still cannot be discerned by the astrologer in the stars, by inspecting which he claims to tell people's fate. So how is he helped by what he cannot find in the set of stars, which he is bound to inspect as a unit, whether he is consulted about Jacob or about his brother, if it is different in the sky which he has no qualms at all about blaming, and no different in his tables, which he is anxiously and pointlessly scrutinizing?

So it is that these opinions, by which human presumption has treated things as signs of this sort, should be put down to those same agreements and bargains made with demons that we mentioned before.

23, 35. For it will come about as a result of this, that by a mysterious divine judgment people who are greedy for bad things are handed over to be fooled and cheated as their evil wishes deserve, fooled and cheated by the apostate angels, to whom a ruling of divine providence has so neatly and fittingly subjected this lowest part of the universe.[80] The way they are made fools of and cheated is that many past and future events are declared by means of these superstitious and pernicious kinds of divination that occur, or have occurred, exactly as declared, and that to those who bother about such observances,[81] many things do happen such as the observances suggest. So they are caught like flies in a spider's web, and become more obsessed than ever with these things, getting themselves entangled more and more inextricably in this direst, most baneful of errors.

In their concern for our salvation the divine scriptures did not pass over in silence this kind of fornication of the soul; nor did they try to deter the soul from it by saying that the reason such things should not be indulged

---

80. See Eph 2:2. It was a common Jewish belief that the lower atmosphere was infested with evil spirits, just as it is a common contemporary belief that it is infested with germs. See also Lk 10:18, Rv 12:9.
81. Such as going back to bed if you sneeze when putting on your shoes.

in was that their practitioners always uttered falsehoods; but *even if what they say to you*, it says, *comes to pass, do not trust them* (Dt 13:2–3). Just because the shade of the dead Samuel, after all, foretold the truth to King Saul, that does not mean that such sacrilegious rites as were used to conjure up his shade are to be any the less abominated; or just because the ventriloquist woman in Acts bore witness to the Lord's apostles, that was no reason for the apostle Paul to spare that spirit, and not rather purge the woman by rebuking and expelling the demon.[82]

36. All such superstitious arts, therefore, whether of a trifling or harmful nature, which have been instituted through a pestilential association of human beings with demons, in a kind of pact of faithless and fickle friendship, are to be utterly repudiated and shunned by the Christian. *Not that an idol is anything*, says the apostle, *but because what they sacrifice they sacrifice to demons and not to God; I do not wish you to become the associates of demons* (1 Cor 10:19–20). And what the apostle said about idols and about the sacrifices which are offered in their honor is to be taken as applying to all the imaginary signs that either draw people to the worship of idols or of creation and its parts as though they were gods, or that have to do with remedial charms and other observances which have not been, so to say, publicly promulgated by God to promote love of God and neighbor, but which instead distract the hearts of wretched people in pursuit of their own private appetites for temporal goods.

So in all these teachings the close association of demons is to be dreaded and avoided, because with their prince the Devil they direct all their efforts to no other end than that of bolting and barring the way to our return.[83] But just as humanity has systematized its erroneous guesses about the stars, which God created and set in their places, so too in the same sort of way many people have committed many things to writing about certain monstrous births or any strange events that occur by decree of divine providence, giving mere human guesswork about their meaning the apparent force of logical conclusions, as when unusual things happen, like a mule giving birth, or something being struck by a thunderbolt.

24, 37. All such things only have the value that has been agreed upon by presumptuous spirits as forming a kind of common language with demons. Yet they are all fraught with pestilential curiosity, with agonizing anxiety, with deadly slavery. They have not, in fact, been noted down because they had any value, but they have been given a certain value by being noted down and treated as signs. And so it is that they signify different things to different people according to their assumptions and ways of thinking. For these evil spirits, whose sole desire is to deceive, procure for any particular

---

82. See 1 Sm 28:8–19, Acts 16:16–18.
83. The only return scripture mentions as being barred to us is the return to paradise, Gn 3:24, and that was barred by an angelic sentry placed there by God. Augustine is writing rather loosely here; but that seems to have been the image at the back of his mind.

person such things as they see his guesses and his cultural conventions have already ensnared him into expecting.

Take for example the single shape of the letter which indicates ten;[84] it has one value in Greek, another in Latin; and this not because of its nature, but because of some kind of decision and agreement about what it should signify. And that is why someone who knows both languages, if he wants to write to a Greek speaker, will not use this letter to mean what he uses it to mean when writing to a Latin speaker; and the word *beta*, with one and the same sound, is the name of a letter for the Greeks, and of a vegetable for the Latins;[85] and when I say *"lege,"* a Greek understands one thing by these two syllables, a Latin speaker another.[86] So all these various meanings strike people's minds according to what has been agreed by the language group each of them belongs to; and because each group has a different agreement they will strike each person differently. And people have not agreed about their meanings because they already had in themselves any particular signifying value; but the reason they have such value is that people have come to an agreement about them.

In the same sort of way, then, those signs by which a baleful association with demons is established are only effective according to the value attributed to them by anyone's pet observations. This is made abundantly clear by the rites of the augurs, who both before they make their observations and after they have recorded the signs they have observed take great care neither to look at the flights of birds nor to listen to their cries, because none of these things are signs except by the consensus of those who observe them.[87]

The value, or otherwise, of non-superstitious human arts

25, 38. Having pruned off and rooted out this kind of signs from the Christian mind, we must next take a look at those human institutions that are not superstitious, those that is which have not been established together with demons, but just among human beings. Because all those things that

---

84. The letter X—ten in Roman numerals, the letter *chi* in the Greek alphabet, the equivalent of the guttural German "ch" in *achtung*.
85. It means a beet root in Latin.
86. In Greek it means "say," in Latin "choose" or "read." For Augustine personally it would primarily have meant "read," recalling the dramatic incident of his conversion, when he heard a child's voice singing *Tolle, lege, tolle, lege*—"Pick up and read, pick up and read"—and he picked up the volume of Paul's letters, opened it at random, and read Rom 13:3–14 (*Confessions* VIII, 12).
87. Augury was the art of divination by bird watching. Augustine seems here to be assuming what he is setting out to prove, namely, that such things are only signs when they are being observed as such. The fact, if it was a fact, that augurs only observed them when divining, and not at other times, hardly implies that they did not regard them as being signs of their very nature. The fact that I am not always reading a book does not imply that I think it only has a significant content when, and because, I am reading it.

people regard as having some significant value, just because it has been agreed among them that they should have such a value, are human institutions; and some of them have been instituted as superfluous and extravagant luxuries, others as convenient and necessary adjuncts of life.

Thus if the signs which ballet dancers make in their dancing had their value from nature and not from human convention and agreement, there would have been no need in earlier times, when the ballet first came to Carthage, for an announcer to inform the people of the city what the dancer wished them to understand by his performance. Many senior citizens still remember this, as we have often heard them tell. And it is all the easier to believe, because even now when somebody unfamiliar with such trifles enters a theater, his attention to the performance will all be wasted unless someone else tells him what those movements mean. It is true, of course, that when people wish to signify something, they look for some kind of likeness, as far as possible, between the signs themselves and the things being signified. But because a thing can resemble something else in many ways, such signs will not mean anything to people, unless there is prior agreement about them.

39. With pictures, however, and statues, and other representative works of this sort,[88] especially those by skilled artists, nobody can go wrong, when he sees various representations, in recognizing what things they represent. And this whole category of signs is to be counted among the superfluous institutions of mankind, except when a difference is made by what is done, for what reason and where and when it is done, and by whose authority it is done. Finally there are thousands of fictions and fables and falsehoods, lies in which people take pleasure, which are all human institutions.[89] And nothing that human beings derive from themselves is to be reckoned as more proper to them than any kind of falsehood and lie.

But convenient and necessary signs that have been instituted by human beings among themselves are such things as they have agreed upon in dress and bodily adornment to distinguish the sexes or differences in rank, and countless other kinds of signification, without which human society either cannot carry on at all, or at least not so conveniently. And there are things that are peculiar to each city and nation, like weights and measures and distinct coinage, and other things of that sort, which would not vary between different peoples, nor be liable to be changed in each nation at the whim of their rulers, if they were not simply human institutions.

---

88. The only other sort that occurs to me is mosaics; but perhaps he may have been including straightforward stage plays, acting out a story.
89. Clearly Augustine would have had no more time for novels and for "light reading" than he had for theatrical performances. In modern times it looks as if he would have found himself at home in the strictest, one may say narrowest, Puritanical tradition. And yet he was not in fact a narrow-minded bigot; the bark of his bigotry, a characteristic rhetorical Ciceronian bark, was much more severe than its bite.

40.[90] But all such human institutions which contribute to the necessary ordering of life are certainly not to be shunned by Christians; on the contrary indeed, as far as is required they are to be studied and committed to memory.

26, For humanly instituted signs bear some sort of sketchy resemblance to natural ones. Those, as we have said, which refer to any association with demons are to be utterly abhorred and repudiated, while those which human beings share with one another are to be made use of, when they are not means of superfluous and self-indulgent extravagance. Chief among these are the shapes of letters, without which we cannot read, and a variety languages, as far as is required, which we have already discussed.[91] To the same class belongs shorthand, learned by those who are called shorthand-writers.[92] All these are useful arts, and it is not unlawful to learn them, nor do they involve you in superstition or dehumanize you with self-indulgence, provided they only take up as much of your time as does not distract you from more important matters, which they ought to be helping you to learn about.[93]

The value of history, and all other human sciences,
for the understanding of the scriptures

27, 41. But now we come to those arts and sciences which human beings have developed, not by inventing them but by investigating either what has happened in the past or what has been instituted by God; these cannot be regarded as human inventions. Of these some pertain to the bodily senses, while others are the province of the mind and its powers of reason. As for the ones which are attained by the senses of the body, we either believe them when told about them, or perceive them when they are shown to us, or assess them when we experience them.[94]

28, 42. Everything therefore that we are told about the past by what is called history is of the greatest help to us in understanding the holy books, even that kind that is learned apart from the Church at school, because we

---

90. In the text, both of CCL and the Maurists, section 40 begins with this sentence.
91. See sections 15—25 above.
92. Literally, "... notes, learned by those who are called notaries."
93. That is to say, the holy scriptures and how to expound them. Augustine does not want the clergy so to specialize in some secular branch of learning that they neglect their proper theological studies, and the application of them to their pastoral duties.
94. There he leaves these arts and sciences—his Latin just says "these things/matters"—which pertain to the senses. We have to remind ourselves that all the time he is talking about *signs*; and the only reason I do not translate here as "those signs," but as "those arts and sciences," is that we do not naturally talk about history, natural science, logic, etc., which he goes on to discuss at length, as signs.

So, coming to those which pertain to the senses, it will transpire that he includes history among them—I presume because it deals with external, physical events and realities; also astronomy and all practical arts and crafts.

often want to work out many dates by means of olympiads and the names of consuls,[95] and ignorance of the consulate in which the Lord was born and of the one in which he suffered has led not a few people astray, so that they have supposed that the Lord suffered when he was forty-six years old, because that was the number of years the Jews said it took to build the temple, which symbolically represented the Lord's body.[96]

Now we have it on the authority of the gospel that he was about thirty when he was baptized;[97] but how many years he then spent in this life, while it can be worked out from the account of his activities,[98] can still be ascertained with greater certainty and precision by collating Gentile history with the gospel, to avoid any cloud of doubt arising from any other source to obscure the truth. For then it will be seen that it was not for nothing that the temple was said to have taken forty-six years to build, because it will be impossible to refer this number to the Lord's age, and so it will then be referred to the more mysterious construction of the human body which the only Son of God, *through whom all things were made* (Jn 1:3), did not disdain to put on for our sake.

43. But as regards the value of history, if I may leave aside the Greek writers, there can be no denying what a big problem was solved by our Ambrose, against the false insinuations of the readers and lovers of Plato. They had the hardihood to say that all the sayings and maxims of our Lord Jesus Christ, which they cannot but admire and praise, were learned by him from Plato's books, since Plato lived long before the Lord's coming as a man. Did not this bishop I have named study the history of the nations, and discover that Plato traveled to Egypt in the time of Jeremiah, when

---

95. Respectively the official Greek and Roman methods of dating events. An olympiad was a period of four years between Olympic games, the first games having been traditionally celebrated in what we now call 776 B.C. As Roman consuls held office just for a year, dating events by who were the consuls that year was about the clumsiest method imaginable, requiring huge lists of consuls dating back to the expulsion of the kings from Rome. So a rather better way of dating was *ab urbe condita*, from the founding of the city, traditionally put in 753 B.C. Our AD/BC chronology was only introduced some 100 years after Augustine's death; and as is well known, the ingenious monk who invented it, Dionysius Exiguus, or Denis the Short, got it wrong by about 6 years, Jesus in fact being born about 6 B.C, seeing that Herod the Great, in whose reign he was born, died in 4 B.C. But we should not be too hard on Denis the Short; collating all those different calendar systems—there was also the Seleucid one of the Hellenistic kingdoms, dating events from "the year of the Greeks," from 312 B.C., to be found in the books of the Maccabees—must have been mind-boggling.
96. See Jn 2:20–21.
97. See Lk 3:23.
98. The accepted period of three years for Christ's ministry derives entirely from John's gospel. From the synoptic account it could have lasted as little as one year or as long as four or five. Presumably Augustine thought it lasted three years—but he is not really interested; his only concern here is to save the number 46 from being taken literally as applying to Christ's age, and so to preserve its mystical sense. See note 66 above.

that prophet was there; and then show that it was more likely that Plato was initiated into our literature by Jeremiah, thus being enabled to teach or write all those things that are so highly, and justly, commended?[99] For not even Pythagoras, from whose followers these people assert that Plato learned his theology, lived before the composition of the literature of the Hebrew people, among whom the worship of the one God was so prominent, and from whom our Lord came *according to the flesh* (Rom 9:5). Thus from a consideration and comparison of times and dates, it becomes much more credible that these men derived from our literature whatever good and true things they had to say, than that our Lord derived his teaching from the writings of Plato, which it is indeed the sheerest lunacy to believe.

44. But while it is in historical narratives that we are told about human institutions of the past, history itself must not be counted among human inventions, because what has been done in the past cannot now become undone; it has to be held in the succession of times, which have been established and are being controlled by God. It is one thing, after all, to tell the story of what has been done, another to teach what has to be done. History faithfully and usefully narrates what has been done, while the books of the soothsayers and similar literature have the intention of teaching what is to be done and what observances are to be kept, and this in the hectoring tones of a warning, not in the calm voice of reliable evidence.

29, 45. Narrative also resembles description, by which it is not past but present realities that are brought to the attention of those who are unaware of them. To this category belongs all that has been written about geography, and the nature of animals, trees, herbs, stones and other material bodies. We dealt with this category earlier on,[100] and taught that such knowledge is of value for solving the riddles of scripture, not suggesting, of course, that these should be treated as signs of a sort, to be used as remedial spells or tricks of the superstition trade,[101] since we have already set that kind of thing distinctly apart from this lawful and liberal realm of knowledge. It is one thing, after all, to say, "If you crush this herb and drink an infusion of it, your stomach pains will cease," and another to say, "If you hang this herb round your neck, your stomach pains will cease." In the first case one can approve of a wholesome infusion, in the other one must condemn a superstitious use of signs.

Though where no use is made of spells and invocations and "characters,"[102] it is often doubtful whether the thing that is tied, or otherwise attached to the body, as a cure, works by force of nature, in which case it

---

99. See the passage from *Revisions* given above, before Book I.
100. In section 24 above.
101. He is alluding, I presume, to the practice of using certain scriptural texts as protective charms, or in the concoction of love philtres and other suchlike superstitious tomfooleries.
102. See section 30 above. It is these "characters" that would often be little scriptural texts, frequently the divine name.

may be freely employed; or whether its effect comes from the significant symbolism of tying it on, in which case Christians should be all the more prudently on their guard against it, the more effectively it seems to work.[103] But when it is impossible to tell by what cause any such thing works effectively, what makes the difference is the spirit in which people make use of it, at least in the curing of bodies or mixing of ingredients, whether for medicinal or agricultural purposes.

46. Coming now to knowledge of the stars, this is not a matter for narrative but for description, and scripture has very little to say about it. But while most people know about the phases of the moon, which even govern the solemn annual celebration of the Lord's passion, very few indeed know anything with any certainty about the rising or the setting or the other movements of the rest of the firmament. Such knowledge of itself, while not involving people in superstition, is nevertheless of little, indeed practically no help at all in expounding the divine scriptures; in fact, unprofitable absorption in it is more of a hindrance than a help, and because it is so closely related to that most baleful error of those who chant the fatuous follies of Fates,[104] the most appropriate and correct thing to do is to ignore it. But besides its description of present realities, it also has this in common with the narrative of past events, that from the present positions and movements of the stars it is able according to its proper rules to trace their courses in the past.

According to the same rules it can also make predictions about their future courses, which are neither mere guesswork nor a taking of omens, but rationally calculated and certain; not that we should attempt to draw any conclusions from them about our own fates[105] and future experiences, like the ravings of the genethliacs,[106] but only about the stars themselves. Thus in the same way as the observer of the moon can tell us, from his observation of what phase it is in today, both what phase it was in however many years you like previously, and what phase it will be in in however many years you like in the future, so too about any one of the stars, those who are learned in observing them and making the necessary calculations have habitually been able to give correct answers. About this whole branch of knowledge I have candidly said what I think, as far as the use made of it is concerned.

---

103. That such a superstitious signification could be effective Augustine did not doubt; it would be so thanks to demonic collaboration.
104. *Fatua fata* in the Latin—or, as I am interpreting Augustine's mind, *fatua Fata*, the Fates as goddesses. So astronomy is cavalierly dismissed because of its close relationship with astrology; and to be fair to Augustine, the two arts/sciences were almost indistinguishable in the minds of nearly all his contemporaries, including almost all astronomers.
105. Reading *fata* with six manuscripts mentioned by the Maurists, instead of the *facta* "our deeds," of both the Maurists' and CCL's text. CCL does not even mention this alternative reading.
106. See section 32 above, note 74.

30, 47. Other arts and crafts too use their experience of the past to make conjectures about the future, such as those by which things are made that remain after the craftsman has done his work, like houses and benches and pots and other things like that; or those which cooperate with God as he works in the world, such as medicine and agriculture and seamanship, or those whose whole effect consists in the action, such as dancing and racing and wrestling. Clearly, none of the practitioners of any of these arts and crafts moves hand or foot in practicing them without combining memory of the past with what is expected in the future.

However, only a slight and cursory knowledge of these matters needs to be acquired in the course of this life—not of course for the practice of them, unless some duty should oblige us to it, which is not what we are dealing with at the moment, but for making an intelligent judgment, in case we should altogether fail to see what scripture is intending to suggest, when it brings in some figurative expressions from these arts and crafts.

31, 48. There remain those matters that belong not to the senses of the body but to the rational mind, where the disciplines of rational discourse and of mathematics hold sway. The discipline of rational discourse, indeed, is of the greatest value in penetrating and solving all kinds of problems which crop up in the holy literature. All that one has to be on guard against here is a passion for wrangling and a kind of childish parade of getting the better of one's opponents. There are, after all, many forms of argument called sophisms, false conclusions from reason which frequently look so like true ones that they can deceive not only the slow-witted but even sharp minds, when they are not paying careful attention. Thus someone put this proposition to the person he was talking to: "You are not what I am." And the other agreed; it was true after all, at least to this extent that one of them was crafty, the other simple. Then the first one added, "But I am human." When the other allowed this too, he concluded, "Therefore you are not human."

Scripture, in my opinion, expresses its detestation of such trickery in argument where it says, *Whoever speaks sophistically is hateful* (Sir 37:20), though even ways of speaking that do not involve such tricks, but strive for effect by using more flowery and inflated language than befits a serious speaker, are called sophistical.[107]

49. True logical inferences can also lead to false conclusions, which follow from the error of the person one is arguing with; but still these inferences can be drawn by a good and learned person, to shame the one whose error they follow from, and induce him to give up his error, because if he insists on sticking to it, he will necessarily be obliged also to hold the conclusions which he rejects. The apostle, after all, was not drawing true

---

107. Since public speaking and argument were, in civil life, almost exclusively confined to the law courts, it is lawyers and their tricks and their rhetorical *tours de force* that he primarily has in mind in this section.

conclusions when he said, *Neither has Christ risen again,* and that other thing, *Our preaching is vain; vain too is your faith* (1 Cor 15:13.14), and the rest that followed. These are all absolutely false conclusions, because Christ has risen again, and the preaching of those who proclaimed this was not vain, nor was the faith of those who believed it. But these conclusions validly and truly followed from the premise of those who were saying that there is no resurrection of the dead. But once you repudiate these false conclusions, which would be true if the dead do not rise again, it follows that there will be a resurrection of the dead.

So since there can be true and valid logical inferences from false as well as from true statements, it is easy to learn the rules of true and valid inference in those schools that have nothing to do with the Church. But the truth of the statements themselves has to be established by studying the holy books.[108]

32, 50. These valid rules of logic, however, have not been instituted by human beings, but observed and noted down by them, so that they can either learn or teach them, because they are inscribed in the permanent and divinely instituted rationality of the universe. Just as those, after all, who tell the story of successive ages do not themselves put those ages together, and those who point out the facts of geography, or the natures of animals or plants or stones, are not pointing out things instituted by human beings, and those who show us the stars and their motions are not showing us something instituted by themselves or anybody else; so too the one who says, "When the consequent is false, the antecedent must be false too," is saying something very true, and does not make it to be so himself, but is only pointing out that that is how it is.

This is the rule governing what we have just quoted from the apostle. The antecedent was that there is no resurrection of the dead, which is what those people were saying whose error the apostle wished to demolish. But the necessary consequent upon that antecedent statement, that there is no resurrection of the dead, is, *Neither has Christ risen again;* but this consequent is false, because Christ has risen again. Therefore the antecedent is also false, that there is no resurrection of the dead; accordingly there is a resurrection of the dead. This can all be put very briefly as follows: If there is no resurrection of the dead, then neither has Christ risen again; but Christ has risen again; therefore there is a resurrection of the dead.

So this rule, that if you deny the consequent you must necessarily deny the antecedent, was not instituted by human beings, but demonstrated. And it belongs to the truth or validity of logical inferences, not to the truth of propositions.

---

108. This, of course, is not itself a universal statement about the truth of all statements. We must again not forget that Augustine's work is concerned with teaching Christianity, and so the only statements or opinions he is interested in are religious and theological ones.

33, 51. But when we are dealing with this case of the resurrection, we find that both the rule about logical inference and the final conclusion are true. But with false propositions,[109] the truth of this rule of logic works like this. Let us suppose someone has conceded: "If a snail is an animal, it has a voice." Once this is conceded, and it is then proved that a snail does not have a voice, the conclusion follows that a snail is not an animal, because when you deny the consequent, you must necessarily deny the antecedent. This conclusion is a false statement, but it follows by a true logical inference from a falsehood that has been conceded. And so the truth of a statement or proposition stands on its own merits; but the truth of the logical inference[110] stands or falls with the opinion of the person one is dealing with, or of the point he has conceded.

The reason, though, why an inference is truly drawn that is in itself false is, as we said above, to make the person whose error we wish to correct be sorry for having maintained the antecedent, when he sees that its consequent has to be rejected. From all this it will now be easy to understand how, just as you can have true conclusions in false propositions, so too it is possible to have false conclusions in true propositions. Thus suppose someone has made the proposition, "If this man is just, he is good," and it has been conceded; and then that he has added the minor premise, "but he is not just"; and that when this has been granted too, he has drawn the conclusion, "therefore he is not good." Here, even though all the statements may be true, it is for all that not a truly or validly drawn conclusion. It is not, you see, the case that in the same way as when you deny the consequent you have to deny the antecedent, so when you deny the antecedent you have to deny the consequent. Because it is true when we say, "If he is an orator, he is a human being"; but if we then deny the first part of this proposition and say, "But he is not an orator," it will not be a true consequent, when you infer, "Therefore he is not a human being."

34, 52. That is why it is one thing to know the rules of logical relationships, another to know the truth of statements and propositions. The first involves learning what the meaning is of "consequent," "non-consequent," "repugnant." "If he is an orator, he is a human being" is a consequent propo-

---

109. The Latin word is *sententia*, which I have also been translating as "statement." Augustine is surely equivocating somewhat in his use of it. In the case of the resurrection we begin with a false *statement* that there is no resurrection of the dead; and we then in effect, to set our logical argument in motion, put it in the form of a true *proposition*: "If there is no resurrection of the dead, then neither has Christ risen from the dead"—a true proposition containing two false statements.

But now we are beginning with a false *proposition* (still a *sententia* in Augustine's Latin), "If a snail is an animal, then it has a voice," which starts from the true *statement*, "A snail is an animal."

110. Here, by the word *conexio*, which I have been translating "logical inference," he must mean the conclusion inferred, not the valid rule by which it is inferred.

sition; "If he is a human being, he is an orator" is an inconsequent one, a *non sequitur*; "If he is a human being, he is a quadruped" is a repugnant one. So here a judgment is being made about the logical inference or relationship. As regards the truth of statements or propositions, on the other hand, it is the statements in themselves, not their logical relationships that have to be considered. But when uncertain statements are joined to true and certain ones in valid logical relationships, they themselves are bound also to become certain.

But some people are so proud of themselves when they have grasped the truth of logical relationships that they think it is the truth of the statements themselves. And again there are some who hold onto the truth of a statement, but belittle themselves because they are ignorant of the laws of inference, though surely the person who knows that there is a resurrection of the dead is superior to the one who knows that it is a consequent proposition, that if there is no resurrection of the dead, then neither has Christ risen again.

35, 53. Again, although knowledge of how to define terms, to distinguish and distribute them, is often applied to false matters, it is not for all that false in itself, nor was it instituted by human beings, but discovered in the very nature and intelligibility of things. Yes, of course, the poets have been in the habit of applying it in telling their fanciful tales and voicing their erroneous opinions, and so have false philosophers and even heretics, that is to say false Christians; but this does not mean that it is false that the art of defining, distinguishing and distributing enables one to exclude irrelevant material, and also not to overlook matters that are relevant to the subject. This is true, even if the points that are defined and distributed are not true.

After all, we even define falsehood itself, when we say that falsehood means the signification of something that is not in fact as it is signified, or give some similar definition; and the definition is true, though falsehood cannot possibly be true. We can also distinguish it and say there are two kinds of falsehood, one asserting things that could not possibly be true, the other asserting things that are not true, though they could be. Thus if you say that seven and three make eleven, you are saying what cannot possibly be true, while if you say, for example, that it rained on January 1, although in fact it did not, you are still saying something that could have happened. So the definition and distinction of falsehoods can be very true, although the falsehoods themselves, of course, cannot be true.

36, 54. There are also rules governing a more copious, elegant style of discourse, which is called eloquence, and these rules are true, even though falsehoods can be persuasively put across by means of them;[111] but because the truth also can be, it is not this capacity that is blameworthy, but the crookedness of those who make bad use of it. Because here too it was no human institution that decided that the expression of esteem would win over an audience, or that a short, clear description would put across what the speaker intends, and that variety of expression would hold the attention of his hearers without boring them. And there are all the other little rules which are still true, whether applied in the cause of falsehood or of truth, insofar as they ensure something is known or believed, or as they move people's hearts to seek or to shun things; and they have been found to be effective like this, rather than instituted in order to be effective like this.

37, 55. But when this subject is learned, it is meant to be applied not so much to understanding things, as to putting across what we have understood, while that other one about conclusions and definitions and distinctions is of the greatest help to us in understanding things, provided only the error is avoided, which leads people to think that when they have learned these things, they have learned the truth about the happy life.[112] It freqently happens, however, that people find it easier to attain those objects for the attainment of which these things are learned, than to master the knotty and thorny discipline of such rules.[113]

It's rather as if someone wishing to give you rules about how to walk were to warn you not to lift the back foot until you have put down the front one, and then were to describe in detail the right way of moving the joints of your limbs and knees. Well, what he is saying is true, and there is no other way to walk. But people find it much easier to walk by doing these things than to notice them when they do them, and to understand when they are told about them. Those, however, who cannot walk are much less interested in such prescriptions, which they are quite unable to test by experience. In the same way a bright person will often see that a conclusion is invalid much sooner than he will grasp the rules that make it so, while someone who is slow on the uptake will not see this, but still will be much less able to grasp those rules.

---

111. The essential aim of eloquence in classical antiquity was to persuade, above all to persuade judges and juries, since it was before all else a forensic art.
112. The error of treating education as an end in itself, or of imagining that it is the infallible key to success and happiness in life. Nowadays it is more likely to be a scientific rather than a liberal education that is the subject of such mistaken ideas. For Augustine, of course, the happy life is not obtainable in this world; it is identical with the eternal life of the next.
113. This statement could be thought to call in question Augustine's whole enterprise in writing this work! Remember how it begins: "There are some rules for dealing with the scriptures, which I consider can be not inappropriately passed on to students."

And often from these rules of logic and discourse we get more pleasure at the spectacle of truth at work than help from them in conducting arguments and making judgments, though there is the point that they serve to sharpen our wits, provided they do not also make them more spiteful or more conceited, so that we either enjoy, that is to say, taking people in with specious arguments and questions, or else think that by having learned such things we have acquired something tremendous, which allows us to consider ourselves a cut above good and inoffensive people.

38, 56. Coming now, though, to the discipline of arithmetic, it must be clear to the dullest of wits that it has not been instituted by human beings, but rather discovered and explored. Yes, though the ancients pronounced the first syllable of *Italia* short, Vergil wanted it long, and long it became; but it is hardly possible in the same way for you to decide that three threes do not make nine, or that they cannot make a square figure, or that they are not three times three, and one and a half times six, and two times no number, because odd numbers[114] do not have halves. So whether numbers are considered in themselves, or are applied to the laws of shapes or of sounds and other motions,[115] they have their immutable rules which have in no way been instituted by human beings, but have been worked out by shrewd and sagacious minds.

57. However, take someone who loves knowing all these things just so that he can give himself airs among the uneducated, and does not rather go on to inquire why those things are true that he has simply perceived to be true,[116] and why some things are not only true but also immutable, which he has realized are immutable, and who then comes from the observation of material bodies to the human mind, which he finds also to be mutable, because it is now learned, now unlearned, but is all the same set between immutable truth above itself and other mutable things beneath itself, and who does not turn all this to the praise and love of the one God from whom he knows it all proceeds; such a person can seem to be very learned, but in no way at all can he be wise.

The proper frame of mind in which all such secular studies should be undertaken

39, 58. On all these counts it seems to me that the most salutary advice I can give to eager and bright young people who fear God and are seeking the blessed life[117] is that they should not impetuously and unconcernedly

---

114. The Latin calls them "intelligible numbers," *intellegibiles numeri,* which I find quite inexplicable and unintelligible, getting no help at all from dictionaries and encyclopedias.
115. To geometry, music, and astronomy.
116. The truth of which, that is, does not derive from human invention or institution.
117. These, in my view, are the young men we would now call seminarians or ordinands. There were no seminaries in those days, but there were boys and young

pursue any teachings that can be had outside the Church of Christ, as though these could ensure them a happy life; rather they should seriously and carefully distinguish between them, and if they find those of human institution to vary because of the different intentions of those who instituted them, and to be not highly thought of because suspected of error,[118] above all if they have any association with demons, entered into by anything like pacts or agreements about special signs, they should utterly repudiate and forswear them; they should also distance themselves from the study of the superfluous and dissolute arts which are of human institution.

But for the needs of this life, they should not neglect those humanly instituted arts and sciences which are of value for a proper social life. As for the other teachings, though, that are to be found among the heathen, apart from the history of past events, or the natural history of things present to the bodily senses, among which may also be counted the experience and the theories of the useful arts and crafts, and apart from logic, rhetoric and mathematics,[119] I reckon there is nothing among them of any use. In all these matters one should keep to the maxim, *Nothing too much*,[120] and above all in those that pertain to the senses, and are involved in space and time.

59. Now just as some people have taken all the Hebrew and Syrian[121] and Egyptian words and names, and those of any other language that can be found in the holy scriptures, which figure in them without a translation, and given translations of them in separate lists or booklets, and what Eusebius[122] has done for the history of the ages because of problems raised in the divine books which call for a reference to it, so what these scholars have done in these fields in order to save Christians a great deal of work in their research into just a few points, I see as something that could be done, if any of those who are capable of it would like out of the kindness of their hearts to undertake a work that would certainly be of the greatest use to the brethren, and to compile and commit to writing an explanatory encyclopedia of all the places, and all the animals, herbs and trees, stones and unknown

---

men who had received the minor orders of reader and acolyte, and who usually lived with the clergy of their town or village, to receive some kind of education from them; and perhaps they were sometimes sent by them to the equivalent of the local grammar school.

118. The text reads *et ignotas propter suspiciones errantium*, literally, "and unknown because of the suspicions of those who err"—a text with which I consider a translator is entitled to take as much liberty as is needed to make sense of it.

119. In the Latin, *praeter rationem disputationis et numeri*.

120. Terence, *Andria*, 61.

121. That is, Aramaic; its later form is known as Syriac, the language of several Christian liturgies.

122. The Church historian, a contemporary and sycophantic biographer of the Emperor Constantine I. Augustine is here probably referring, not to Eusebius' *Ecclesiastical History*, but to his *Chronicon*, a summary of world history. Eusebius did write a book on biblical topography, Bible place names, called the *Onomasticon*, which Augustine was presumably unaware of.

metals and any other species at all that are mentioned in scripture.[123] The same thing could also be done with numbers, and an explanation of the significance of only those numbers be written which scripture records.

Some or all of these things have perhaps been done already, just as I have found many works, which I had never realized existed, elaborated and written by good and learned Christians; but they have escaped general notice, whether as a result of simple neglect by the many, or of deliberate concealment by the envious. Whether the same sort of thing could be done for dialectic and the rules of discourse I do not know, and in fact I rather think not, because these are tied into the whole text of scripture as its very sinews. And thus they are of more help to readers in solving and explaining ambiguities, of which we shall speak later on, than in getting to know the meaning of unknown signs, which we are dealing with now.

40, 60. If those, however, who are called philosophers happen to have said anything that is true, and agreeable to our faith, the Platonists above all, not only should we not be afraid of them, but we should even claim back for our own use what they have said, as from its unjust possessors. It is like the Egyptians, who not only had idols and heavy burdens, which the people of Israel abominated and fled from, but also vessels and ornaments of gold and silver, and fine raiment, which the people secretly appropriated for their own, and indeed better, use as they went forth from Egypt; and this not on their own initiative, but on God's instructions, with the Egyptians unwittingly lending them things they were not themselves making good use of.[124]

In the same way, while the heathen certainly have counterfeit and superstitious fictions in all their teachings, and the heavy burdens of entirely unnecessary labor,[125] which everyone of us must abominate and shun as we go forth from the company of the heathen under the leadership of Christ, their teachings also contain liberal disciplines which are more suited to the service of the truth, as well as a number of most useful ethical principles, and some true things are to be found among them about worshiping only the one God. All this is like their gold and silver, and not something they instituted themselves, but something which they mined, so to say, from the ore of divine providence, veins of which are everywhere to be found. As they for their part make perverse and unjust misuse of it in the service of demons, so Christians for theirs ought, when they separate themselves in spirit from their hapless company, to take these things away from them for

---

123. An imperfect, as well as an excessively long sentence. I take it as indicating that while Augustine completed this work when he came to his *Revisions*, he did not in fact revise what he had already written.
124. See Ex 3:22; 11:2–3; 12:35–36. It is not quite clear why Augustine says they secretly (*clanculo*) despoiled the Egyptians. Perhaps it is because they asked their Egyptian neighbors to lend them these things, while having no intention of giving them back. How often most of us have been secretly plundered in this way, or secretly plundered others!
125. These, I imagine, would be superstitious practices and pagan rites.

the proper use of preaching the gospel. Their fine raiment too, meaning, that is, what are indeed their human institutions, but still ones that are suitable for human society, which we cannot do without in this life, are things that it will be lawful to take over and convert to Christian use.

61. For what else, after all, have so many of our good believers done? Can we not see how much gold and silver and fine raiment Cyprian was crammed with as he came out of Egypt, that loveliest of teachers and most blessed of martyrs? Or Lactantius, or Victorinus, Optatus, Hilary,[126] not to mention the living? Or countless Greek writers? This is what God's most faithful servant Moses had done before, of whom it is written that *he was educated in all the wisdom of the Egyptians* (Acts 7:22).

To none of these men would the superstitious culture of the heathen have lent the disciplines which they found useful, and especially not in those times when it was shaking off the yoke of Christ and persecuting Christians, if it had suspected that they were going to turn them into aids to the worship of the one God, by which the futile worship of idols would be extirpated. But they gave gold and silver and fine raiment to the people of God as they went forth from Egypt, quite unaware how the things they were giving would be restored to *the allegiance of Christ* (2 Cor 10:5). All that happened in the Exodus, after all, was a kind of acted parable, pointing in advance to all this.[127] Let me say that I have given my interpretation without prejudice to any other way of understanding the story that may be as good or better.

41, 62. But when students of the divine scriptures, instructed in this manner, begin to approach the task of searching them,[128] they should never stop reflecting on that maxim of the apostle's, *Knowledge puffs up, love builds up* (1 Cor 8:1). He is convinced, you see, that even if he comes forth from Egypt a rich man, still he cannot be saved unless he celebrates the passover. But *our passover, which is Christ, has been sacrificed* (1 Cor 5:7), and there is nothing that Christ's sacrifice teaches us more certainly than this, which he cried out himself, as though he could see them toiling away in Egypt under Pharaoh: *Come to me, all you who are toiling away and overburdened, and I will refresh you. Take my yoke upon you and*

---

126. Lactantius, an apologist, an older contemporary of Eusebius', who died about 320 as a very old man, and tutor to Constantine's eldest son Crispus, who was murdered by his imperial father a year or two later; Victorinus, an older contemporary of Augustine's, also an African, something of a philosopher, whose conversion in Rome fairly late in his life made a great impression on Augustine (*Confessions* VIII, 2); Optatus, also an older contemporary, and bishop of Milevis in Numidia, an anti-Donatist writer who died about 400; Hilary, bishop of Poitiers from about 353 till his death in 367, a staunch ally of Athanasius in the fight against Arianism. As Augustine does not mention Ambrose, for whom he had the greatest admiration, one may infer that he wrote this work, or at any rate reached this part of it, before Ambrose's death in 397.

127. See, for example, 1 Cor 10:1–11.

128. See Jn 5:39.

learn from me, since I am gentle and humble of heart, and you shall find rest for your souls. For my yoke is easy and my load is light (Mt 11:28–30). For whom is this so, if not for the gentle and humble of heart, who are not being puffed up by knowledge, but built up by love?

So they should remember how those who celebrated the passover at that time as a shadow and image of things to come,[129] after they had been told to mark or sign the door posts with the blood of the lamb, were themselves signed or marked *with hyssop* (Ex 12:22)—this is a humble and gentle herb, and there is nothing stronger or more penetrating than its roots—*so that rooted and founded in love, we may be able to comprehend with all the saints what is the breadth and length and height and depth*, that is to say, the Lord's cross. Its breadth refers to the cross-beam, where his hands are stretched out; its length to the part from the ground as far as this breadth, where his whole body from the arms down is fixed; its height to the part from the breadth upward to the top, where his head is; while the depth is what is hidden by being fixed in the ground. This sign of the cross encompasses the whole of Christian activity: doing good works in Christ and persevering in adhering to him; hoping for heavenly things, not profaning the sacraments.[130] Purified by this kind of activity, we shall have the capacity *to know also the love of Christ which surpasses all knowledge*, in which he through whom all things were made is equal to the Father, *so that we may be filled with all the fullness of God* (Eph 3:17–19).

Hyssop also has a purgative or purifying virtue, to prevent the lungs from swelling proudly as a result of anything they inhale, from being puffed up with knowledge about the riches taken away from Egypt: *You will sprinkle me with hyssop*, it says, *and I shall be cleansed; you will wash me and I shall be made whiter than snow. To my hearing you will give exultation and joy.* Then it goes on to add, in order to show that it is a purging of pride that is signified by hyssop, *and the bones that have been humbled shall exult* (Ps 51:7–8).

42, 63. But the supply of gold, silver and fine raiment which that people took with them from Egypt was much less, in comparison with the riches which they acquired later on in Jerusalem, which was most evident in the reign of King Solomon;[131] to the same extent all the knowledge derived from the books of the heathen, which is indeed useful, becomes little enough if it is compared with the knowledge of the divine scriptures. For whatever you learn outside them is there condemned if it is harmful, while if it is useful,

---

129. See Heb 10:1.
130. Doing good works in Christ is signified by the breadth of the cross on which his hands were stretched, hands standing for works; persevering in adhering to him is signified by its length, where his whole body was fixed; hoping for heavenly things is represented by its upper part where his head was, he the head of the body being now in heaven; not profaning the sacraments is represented by its depth hidden in the ground, because it meant observing the discipline of the secret.
131. See 1 Kgs 3:13.

it is also to be found there. And when you have found there everything of use that you can learn elsewhere, you will also find there in much greater abundance things that you cannot find anywhere else at all, things that can only be learned in the marvelous heights and equally marvelous lowliness and humility of those scriptures.[132]

So, dear reader, as soon as, furnished with this advice, you are no longer hindered by not knowing what signs mean—being gentle and humble of heart, submitting to Christ's easy yoke, and burdened with his light load, being founded and rooted and built up in love, and so not liable to be puffed up by knowledge—you must now approach the consideration and discussion of ambiguous signs in the scriptures. About these I will now attempt in the third volume to say what the Lord is good enough to grant me.

---

132. What Augustine probably meant by the lowliness or humility of scripture was its lack of the polished style of the classical Latin authors. It was this that had put him off Christianity and its scriptures as a very young, and very conceited, student and teacher of rhetoric.

Book III

Introduction

1, 1. Those who fear God are conscientious about seeking his will in the scriptures. And so, being gentle with the spirit of piety, to preserve them from a love of rivalry; well equipped too with a knowledge of languages, to save them from getting stuck over unknown words and expressions; well equipped also with a knowledge of a number of things that are necessary, lest they should be ignorant of the force and nature of things that are mentioned by way of comparison; assisted as well by the accuracy of their copies of the text, which a conscientious and expert work of correction has procured them—they must come now, thus well furnished, to the discussion and solution of the ambiguities of the scriptures.

But in order not to be led astray by ambiguous signs, as far as it is possible for them to be instructed by me—it could happen, though, that with the brilliance of their intellect or their more thorough enlightenment they scorn these ways I wish to show them as just childish—but still, as I had started to say, insofar as they are capable of being instructed by me, those who are in the right frame of mind to be instructed by me should know that the ambiguities of scripture are to be found in words used either in their proper or in their metaphorical senses, two ways of using words which we pointed out in the second book.

Ambiguities over phrasing

2, 2. But when ambiguities arise in scripture about the meaning of words used in their proper sense, the first thing we must do is see whether we have phrased or pronounced them wrongly. So when, on paying closer attention, you still see that it is uncertain how something is to be phrased, or how to be pronounced, you should refer it to the rule of faith, which you have received from the plainer passages of scripture and from the authority of the Church, about which we dealt sufficiently when we were talking in the first book about *things*. But if both possibilities, or all of them, if it is a multiple ambiguity, are consonant with the faith, it remains to refer to the whole context, to the sections that precede and that follow the ambiguous passage, holding it in the middle between them, so that we may see which of the several meanings that present themselves the context will vote for and allow to fit in with itself.

3. Straightaway now, consider some examples.[1] There is that heretical phrasing: *In principio erat Verbum et Verbum erat apud Deum et Deus erat,* adopted in order to give another meaning to the next phrase: *Verbum hoc erat in principio apud Deum*; this is a refusal to confess that the Word is God. But this is to be refuted by the rule of faith, which prescribes for us the equality of the three divine persons, so that we have to say, *et Deus erat Verbum*; and then add, *Hoc erat in principio apud Deum*[2] (Jn 1:1–2).

4. But there is another ambiguity of phrasing in which neither possibility is against the faith, and therefore the matter has to be settled by the context, where the apostle says: *And I do not know which to choose; but I am being constrained from two sides having a desire to cast off and be with Christ; for it is much the best; to remain in the flesh is necessary on your account* (Phil 1:23–24). It is uncertain, you see, whether it should be read *from two sides having a desire* or *I am being constrained from two sides*, to which is then added, *having a desire to cast off and be with Christ.* But since it goes on like this: *for it is much the best*, it is apparent that he is saying he has a desire for what is best, so that while he is being constrained from two sides, still he has a desire for the one, is under necessity from the other; desire, namely, to be with Christ, necessity to remain in the flesh.

This ambiguity is settled by one word that follows, the word *for*; the translators who omitted this little word inclined rather to the opinion that he was not only constrained from two sides, but also had a desire for the two. This then is how it should be phrased: *And I do not know which to choose; but I am being constrained from two sides*; this phrase is then followed by, *having a desire to cast off and be with Christ.* And as though he were asked why he had a desire for this rather than for the other, he says, *for it is much the best.* So why is he being constrained from two sides? Because he is under the necessity to remain, about which he adds, *to remain in the flesh is necessary on your account.*

5. Where, however, an ambiguity can be resolved neither by the standard of faith nor by the actual context of the passage, there is no objection to your phrasing it in any of the ways that are open to you. Like this to the Corinthians: *Has ergo promissiones habentes, carissimi, mundemus nos ab omni inquinatione carnis et spiritus perficientes sanctificationem*

---

1.   The examples that follow are, of course, all in Augustine's Latin text of scripture, and do not usually occur in an English translation, which may well have its own. So I regret that the rest of this section will be full of Latin texts, phrases and words, which will be translated and explained as necessary in the notes.
2.   "In the beginning was the Word, and the Word was with God, and God was"; so the next phrase reads, "This Word was in the beginning with God." The orthodox phrasing is, "… the Word was with God, and the Word was God; this was in the beginning with God."

in timore Dei capite nos; neminem nocuimus[3] (2 Cor 7:1–2). It is in doubt whether it should be read, *mundemus nos ab omni inquinatione carnis et spiritus,* according to that other text, *so that she may be holy both in body and in spirit* (1 Cor 7:34); or, *mundemus nos ab omni inquinatione carnis,* so that the next phrase would be, *et spiritus perficientes sanctificationem in timore Dei capite nos.* The phrasing, therefore, of such ambiguities is left to the discretion of the reader.

Ambiguities over pronunciation

3, 6. Now everything we have said about ambiguous phrasing is to be observed with ambiguities over pronunciation. These too, except where they arise from the carelessness of the reader, are to be settled either by the standard of faith, or by the context of what precedes and what follows; or if neither serves to resolve the doubt, then whichever way the reader pronounces the word, he will not be at fault.

For example, unless we were held back by the faith by which we believe that God is not going to accuse his chosen ones, and Christ is not going to condemn his chosen ones, we could pronounce the passage, *Who will bring an accusation against God's chosen ones?* as though the reply to this question followed immediately, *God, who justifies them*; and then again when the question is asked, *Who is it that will condemn them?* as though the answer came, *Christ Jesus who died* (Rom 8:33–34). But because it would be the last word in lunacy to believe that, it will be pronounced in such a way that first we have a challenging inquiry, and then this is followed by an interrogatory question. The difference between an inquiry and an interrogatory question,[4] according to the ancient authors, is that to an inquiry many answers can be given, while to an interrogatory question only a "no" or a "yes." So then it will be pronounced in such a way that after our inquiry, saying *Who will bring an accusation against God's chosen ones?* what follows is spoken in an interrogatory tone, *God, who justifies them?* so that the tacit reply to this is, "No." And again we inquire, *Who is it that will condemn them?* and once more ask the interrogatory question, *Christ*

---

3.   "Having therefore these promises, dearly beloved, let us purify ourselves from every defilement of the flesh and of the spirit perfecting sanctification in the fear of God receive us; we have done nobody wrong." The first alternative offered—the universally accepted one—is to phrase the sentence, "let us purify ourselves from every defilement of the flesh and of the spirit," so that it would continue, though he neglects to say this, "perfecting our sanctification in the fear of God. Receive us." The other is to phrase, "let us purify ourselves from every defilement of the flesh," so that the next part of the sentence would be, "and perfecting the sanctification of the spirit in the fear of God receive us"—that is, in more tolerable English, "And receive us as we perfect the sanctification of the spirit in the fear of God."

4.   In the Latin, between a *percontatio* and an *interrogatio.*

Jesus who died, or rather who rose again, who is at God's right hand, who is also interceding for us? so that all the time the tacit answer is "No."

On the other hand, in the passage where it says, *So then, what are we to say? That the nations who were not in pursuit of justice laid hold of justice* (Rom 9:30), unless to the inquiry, *So then, what are we to say?* the affirmative reply comes, *That the nations who were not in pursuit of justice laid hold of justice*, it would not be coherent with the following context. But in whatever tone you pronounce what Nathanael said, *A Nazareth potest aliquid boni esse*[5] (Jn 1:46); whether as though he were making an affirmation, so that the only interrogatory part would be *A Nazareth?* or as though the whole sentence expressed the questioner's doubt, I cannot see how it should be decided, the sense given in each case presenting no obstacle to faith.

7. Ambiguity can also arise over the sound and tone of syllables, and this of course is also a matter of pronunciation. Thus where it is written, *Non est absconditum a te os meum, quod fecisti in abscondito*[6] (Ps 139:15), it is not immediately clear to the reader whether he should pronounce "os" with a short or long vowel. If he makes it short, one understands the singular from which we get the plural "ossa," bones, while if he makes it long we understand the singular from which comes the plural "ora," mouths. But cases like this are settled by a look at the earlier language, because here in the Greek it has *ostoun*, not *stoma*,[7] which shows that very often the popular way of speaking is better for getting across the meaning of things than is literary correctness. I would rather it said, with a common barbarism, *Non est absconditum a te "ossum" meum*, than that a preference for good Latin should make its meaning less plain.

But sometimes a doubt about the right sound of a syllable can be settled from a word nearby in the same sentence, as in this from the apostle: *Quae pradico vobis, sicut praedixi, quoniam qui talia agunt, regnum Dei non possidebunt*[8] (Gal 5:21). If he had just said, *Quae praedico vobis*, and had not added, *sicut praedixi*, the only thing to do would have been to have recourse to a copy of the earlier language, to find out whether *praedico* should be pronounced with a short or long second syllable; but now it is plain that the syllable should be lengthened, since he does not say, "sicut praedicavi," but *sicut praedixi*.

---

5.   "Can anything good come from Nazareth?" The alternative in the Latin to this universally accepted way of reading the sentence is; "From Nazareth? Something good can come"—very far-fetched, even in the Latin.
6.   "My bone/mouth is not hidden from you, which you have made in secret."
7.   The Greek for "bone" and "mouth" respectively.
8.   "About which I am warning you, as I have warned you before, that those who do such things will not gain possession of the kingdom of God"; *praedico* with a long i, perfect *praedixi*, meaning literally "say beforehand." The alternative, *praedico* with a short i, perfect *praedicavi*, means to preach or proclaim.

Ambiguities over grammatical construction

4, 8. But besides these instances, similar considerations also apply to ambiguities which are not concerned with phrasing or pronunciation, like this to the Thessalonians: *Propterea consolati sumus fratres in vobis*[9] (1 Thes 3:7). The doubt is whether it should be "O fratres" or "hos fratres." Neither reading, indeed, is against the faith; but the Greek language does not have the same form for these two cases, and thus a glance at the Greek reveals that it is the vocative, that is, "O fratres." But if the translator had been prepared to say, "propterea consolationem habuimus, fratres, in vobis," he would have been keeping less closely to the words of the original, but there would have been less doubt about the meaning—or at least if he had added "nostri"; practically nobody, after all, could doubt that it was the vocative case, on hearing, *Propterea consolati sumus, fratres nostri, in vobis.*[10]

But now adding a word like this is rather risky, and only rarely to be permitted.[11] The same sort of thing was done in the passage to the Corinthians, where the apostle says, *I die every day by your glory, brothers, which I have in Christ Jesus* (1 Cor 15:31). One translator, you see, says, *I die every day, "I swear" by your glory*, because in the Greek it is clearly an oath without any ambiguity.[12] It is extremely rare, then, and indeed very hard, to find any ambiguity in the literal meaning of words, as far as the books of the divine scriptures are concerned, which cannot be settled either from the context of the word, which indicates the intention of the writers, or from a comparison of different versions, or from an examination of the original language.

Ambiguities in metaphorical language; enslavement to the letter

5, 9. But ambiguities arising from metaphorical language, about which we have to talk from now on, call for no ordinary care and attention. For in the first place, you have to beware of taking a figurative expression literally. And this is where the apostle's words are relevant, *The letter kills, but the spirit gives life* (2 Cor 3:6). When something that is said figuratively, you see, is taken as though it were meant in its proper literal sense, we are

9. "That is why we have taken comfort, brothers, among you." But the alternative, he says, could be to read "brothers" as accusative, not vocative—and also incidentally, though he does not mention this, to read *consolati sumus* as a deponent active verb, rather than as passive reflexive—which would give the sense, "For this reason we have comforted the brothers among you."
10. "That is why we have taken comfort, our brothers, among you."
11. Literally he says, "But now this"—that is, adding a word—"is permitted rather riskily." But the instance he goes on to give does not illustrate how risky this procedure can be, but how it is occasionally permissible.
12. In the Latin, and literal English, "I die every day by your glory" could be taken to mean "Your glory is making me die every day." M adds the Greek word *ne*, which indicates the swearing of an oath, the text running, literally, "because in the Greek the voice of one swearing (*ne*) is clear..."

being carnal in our way of thinking. Nor can anything more suitably be called the death of the soul than when that in it too, which surpasses the brute beasts, that is to say its intelligence, subjects itself to the flesh by following the letter.[13]

When you follow the letter, you see, you take in their proper literal sense words that are being used metaphorically, and fail to refer what is signified in this proper sense to the signification of something else; but if, for example, you hear the word "sabbath," and all you understand by it is this one of the seven days which recurs week by week; and when you hear the word "sacrifice," your thoughts do not go beyond what is usually done with victims from the flock and the fruits of the earth. This, precisely, is the wretched slavery of the spirit, treating signs as things, and thus being unable to lift up the eyes of the mind above bodily creatures, to drink in the eternal light.

6, 10. Such slavery, however, in the Jewish people was something different by far from the deadness[14] of the other nations, seeing that the Jews were subjected to temporal things in such a way that in all of them the one God was being brought to their attention. And although they observed the signs of spiritual things[15] as things in their own right, quite unaware of what they should be referred to, it was still second nature to them to suppose that by such a slavery they were pleasing the one God of the universe, whom they could not see. This, the apostle writes, was like being in the custody of a minder of children.[16] And that is why those who clung so stubbornly to such signs could not tolerate the Lord, who made light of them when the time had already come for unveiling their real meaning, and why their leaders piled up charges against him that he cured people on the sabbath, and why the people, in bondage to those signs as though they were the ultimate realities, could not believe that one who refused to take any notice of them, in the way they were observed by the Jews, could be God or could have come from God.

But those of them who came to believe, who formed the first Church in Jerusalem, showed well enough how very useful it had been for them to be kept under that child-minder; it meant that the signs which had been imposed on them as slaves for a time had tied the ideas of those who observed them to the worship of the one God *who made heaven and earth* (Ps 121:2).

---

13. A grossly exaggerated statement which I am sure he would have modified, had he really revised this work, as well as completing it.
14. Reading *a ceterarum gentium morte* with one venerable manuscript mentioned by the Maurists, but not by the CCL editor, instead of *a ceterarum gentium more*, "from the custom of other nations," of the CCL and M text. Can one manuscript so outweigh all the rest? Yes, if it has the right feel to it, and if it is less likely to represent a copyist's or stenographer's correction than the alternative.
15. As, for example, the laws about the sabbath and about sacrifices.
16. A pedagogue; see Gal 3:24.

Thus because they had been close to spiritual things already (for in those actual temporal and carnal signs and votive offerings, although they were unaware of how they were meant to be understood spiritually, they had at least learned that only the one eternal God was to be honored), they turned out to be so ready for the Holy Spirit that they sold all their possessions, and *laid the price at the feet of the apostles* (Acts 4:35), to be distributed to the poor; and in this way they dedicated themselves totally to God as a new temple, the earthly image of which, that is the old temple, they used to be enslaved to.

11.[17] It is not written anywhere, after all, that any other Churches did this, and that is because they had not been found to be so near,[18] since they had held images made with hands to be gods.

7, And if ever any of them, as pagans, tried to explain those images as signs, they related them to some creature to be worshiped and honored. But what good does it do me, after all, to be told that some idol of, let us say, Neptune is not to be regarded as a god, but that it represents the whole sea, or even all the other waters that gush forth from springs? As he is described by one of their poets, if I remember rightly, speaking as follows:

Thy brow, O father Neptune, is hoary white
With thundering surf, and ever from thy beard
Great Ocean flows, and rivers from thy locks
Do curl their winding ways.[19]

This little shell, this pod is shaking and rattling its little stones in a sweet-tasting husk; but it is the food of pigs, not of men. Those who know the gospel will know what I am saying.[20]

So what use is it to me that the idol of Neptune is given that symbolic meaning, except perhaps to warn me off worshiping either of them? For me, after all, neither any statue at all, nor the entire sea, is God. Still, I must admit that those who regard the works of men as gods are more deeply sunk in falsehood than those who so regard the works of God. We, though, are commanded to love and worship the one God who made all these things, the idols of which the pagans venerate either as gods or as the signs and images of gods. So if taking a sign, which was instituted for a useful purpose, as

---

17. In the text, both of the Maurists and of CCL, section 11 begins with this.
18. See Eph 2:17.
19. Author unknown. The Latin text runs:
    Tu, Neptune pater, cui tempora cana crepanti
    Cuncta salo resonant, magnus cui perpete mento
    Profluit oceanus, et flumina crinibus errant.
20. That he is alluding to Lk 15:16, in the parable of the prodigal son. The general reference of Augustine's simile is to the gourd used as a rattle in the percussion department of a band—certainly of an African band. But that one could have used the pods of the carob tree—which is what the prodigal son would have liked to eat, according to my Greek-English Lexicon of the New Testament—as a musical rattle seems to me improbable.

being the very thing it was established to signify is a form of enslavement to the flesh, how much more so must it be to take the signs of useless things for the things themselves? If you refer them to the things they signify, and oblige your spirit to worship these, you are still nonetheless not ridding yourself of a servile, carnal burden and veil.[21]

Liberation from enslavement to the letter

8, 12. That is why those who were found by Christian liberty to be serving under useful signs were found to be near;[22] and by explaining the signs to which they were subjected, this liberty raised them up to the substantive realities, the things they were signs of, and so set them free. It was from these people that the Churches of the holy Israelites were formed. As for those whom it found serving under useless signs, it cut out not only their slave labor under such signs, but also the signs themselves and got rid of them all, so that the nations might be converted from the corruption of a multitude of fake gods, which scripture often and rightly calls fornication, to the worship of the one God, and this, not by enslaving themselves now to those useful signs, but rather by exercising their minds in the spiritual understanding of them.

9, 13. Those, you see, who practice or venerate some kind of thing which is a significant sign, unaware of what it signifies, are enslaved under signs, while those who either carry out or venerate useful signs established by God, fully understanding their force and significance, are not in fact venerating what can be seen and passes away, but rather that reality to which all such things are to be referred. Such people are spiritual and free even during the time of slavery, in which it is not yet opportune for carnal spirits to have those signs openly explained to them, because they still need to be broken in under their yoke. Such spiritual people, however, were the patriarchs and prophets, and all those in the people of Israel through whose ministry the Holy Spirit has provided us with the help and the consolation of the scriptures themselves.

In this time, though, after the clearest indication of our freedom has shone upon us in the resurrection of our Lord, we are no longer burdened with the heavy duty of carrying out even those signs whose meaning we now understand. But the Lord himself and the discipline of the apostles has handed down to us just a few signs instead of many, and these so easy to perform, and so awesome to understand, and so pure and chaste to celebrate, such as the sacrament of baptism, and the celebration of the Lord's body and blood. When people receive these, they have been so instructed that they can recognize to what sublime realities they are to be referred,

---

21. For the veil, in this grossly overloaded use of figurative language, see 2 Cor 3:12—4:4.
22. See Eph 2:17.

and so they venerate them in a spirit not of carnal slavery, but rather of spiritual freedom.

But just as following the letter and taking signs for the things signified by them is a matter of slavish weakness, so too interpreting signs in a useless way is a matter of error going badly astray.[23] Those, however, who do not understand what a sign signifies, and still understand that it is a sign, are also not being oppressed by the yoke of slavery. But it is better even to be oppressed by signs that are useful though not understood than by interpreting them in a useless manner to withdraw one's neck from the yoke of slavery, only to insert it in the noose of error.

Rules for telling what are figurative expressions and what are not

10, 14. To this warning against treating figurative expressions, that is metaphorical ones, as though they were meant in the literal, proper sense, we also have to add this one, to beware of wanting to treat literal, proper statements as though they were figurative. So first of all we must point out the method for discovering if an expression is proper or figurative. And here, quite simply, is the one and only method: anything in the divine writings that cannot be referred either to good, honest morals or to the truth of the faith, you must know is said figuratively. Good honest morals belong to loving God and one's neighbor, the truth of the faith to knowing God and one's neighbor. As for hope, that lies in everybody's own conscience,[24] to the extent that you perceive yourself to be making progress in the love of God and neighbor, and in the knowledge of them. All this formed the subject of the first book.

15. The human race, however, is inclined to judge sins, not according to the gravity of the evil desire involved, but rather with reference to the importance attached to their own customs. So people frequently reckon that only those acts are to be blamed which in their own part of the world and their own time have been customarily treated as vicious and condemned, and only those acts to be approved of and praised which are acceptable to those among whom they live. Thus it can happen that if scripture either commands something which does not accord with the customs of the hearers, or censures something which does fit in with them, they assume they are dealing with a figurative mode of speech—if, that is, their minds are bound by the authority of God's word.[25] Scripture, though, commands

---

23. A reference to heretical sects, primarily to the Donatists, who did not appreciate that the ultimate thing, or *res*, signified by the sacraments is the grace of unity, the Catholic unity of the Church, the body of Christ. The persons referred to in the next sentence are presumably the ignorant Catholic faithful who have not been well instructed and who still bring an Old Testament mentality to the practice of their religion.
24. He has in mind 1 Tm 1:5, where love and faith are mentioned, while hope only figures in the guise of a good conscience.
25. If they are not, they will simply treat such precepts as false and invalid.

nothing but charity, or love, and censures nothing but cupidity, or greed, and that is the way it gives shape and form to human morals.

Again, if people's minds are already in thrall to some erroneous opinion, whatever scripture may assert that differs from it will be reckoned by them to be said in a figurative way. The only thing, though, it ever asserts is Catholic faith, with reference to things in the past and in the future and in the present. It tells the story of things past, foretells things future, points out things present; but all these things are of value for nourishing and fortifying charity or love, and overcoming and extinguishing cupidity or greed.

16. What I mean by charity or love is any urge of the spirit to find joy in God for his own sake, and in oneself and one's neighbor for God's sake; by cupidity or greed any impulse of the spirit to find joy in oneself and one's neighbor, and in any kind of bodily thing at all, not for God's sake. Now what unrestrained greed does by way of corrupting the human spirit and its body can be called infamous, while whatever it does to harm someone else can be called criminal.[26] And all sins fall into these two categories, but infamous deeds come first. When these have drained the spirit dry and reduced it to a kind of want, it bursts out into criminal acts in order to eliminate obstacles to its infamous behavior, or to secure assistance in it.

Again, what charity does, or love, to profit self is usefulness, while whatever it does to profit the neighbor is called kindness. And here usefulness comes first, because one cannot profit one's neighbor with what one does not have oneself. For the more the kingdom of greed is whittled away, so much the more is that of love increased.

11, 17. So then anything we read of in the scriptures as coming from the person of God or his saints that sounds harsh and almost savage in deed and word is of value for whittling away the kingdom of greed. And if its meaning is crystal-clear, it is not to be referred to something else, as though it were said figuratively, like this from the apostle: *He is storing up for himself wrath on the day of wrath and of the revelation of the just judgment of God, who will pay back each and all according to their works; to those indeed who by patient endurance in doing good are seeking glory and honor and imperishability, eternal life; to those however who are given to quarrels and who distrust the truth while they trust iniquity, wrath and indignation. Tribulation and distress upon every human soul that works evil, Jew first and also Greek* (Rom 2:5–9). But this is being addressed to those who are being overthrown together with their greed,[27] because they have been unwilling to overcome it.

---

26. The two Latin words to which he thus gives his own very strict definition are *flagitium* and *facinus*. Their opposites in the next paragraph are *utilitas* and *beneficentia*.

27. He actually says, "those with whom greed itself is being overthrown," *evertitus*, a very curious way of putting it. So one sympathizes with the copyist of one manuscript who substitutes *versatur* for that word, giving the sense, "those with whom greed itself is dwelling."

But when the kingdom of greed is being undermined in those people it used to dominate, we have this plain statement: *But those who are Jesus Christ's have crucified their flesh, with its passions and lusts* (Gal 5:24), except that in these instances too some words are to be treated as metaphorical, such as "the wrath of God" and "have crucified"; but they are not so many, or so placed, as to obscure the plain sense and make it all into an allegory or a riddle, which is what I properly call a figurative expression. But coming to what Jeremiah was told, *Behold, I have set you today over nations and kingdoms, to pull down and to destroy, and to scatter and to rout* (Jer 1:10), it is undoubtedly all a figurative utterance, to be referred to that end which we have mentioned.

12, 18. Those things, however, that strike the ignorant as infamous, whether they are only said, or also done, whether attributed to God or to men whose holiness is being commended to us, they are all to be taken as figurative, and their secret meanings have to be winkled out for the nourishment of charity. Anyone,[28] though, who makes use of passing things more sparingly than is customary with those among whom he lives, is either temperate or superstitious, while anyone who makes use of them in a way that exceeds the bounds that are acceptable to the good people among whom he spends his time is either signifying something, or is behaving infamously. In all such cases it is not the use of things, but the caprice of the user that is at fault.

Nor will any in their right mind even begin to believe that the Lord's feet were anointed by the woman with precious ointment[29] in the same sort of way as wantonly extravagant and worthless people are familiar with, in those orgies of theirs which we abominate. The good odor, after all, stands for the good reputation which those of good life will have from their works, while they follow in Christ's footsteps, and as it were shed over his feet the most precious fragrance. Thus what is generally infamous in other persons is, in the person of God or a prophet, the sign of some important reality. Certainly, association with a harlot is one thing in men of abandoned morals, another in the prophetic activity of Hosea; nor, if it is infamous conduct to strip off your clothes in drunken and licentious parties, does that mean that it is equally infamous to be naked in the baths.[30]

19. So we have to pay careful attention to what befits places and times and persons, in order not to judge behavior rashly as infamous. It can happen, after all, that a wise person will make use of the most expensive food without a hint of the vice of self-indulgence or greediness, while a fool will be disgustingly on fire with gluttony for the cheapest stuff imaginable. And sane people would much rather eat fish as the Lord did than lentils in

---

28. He means, almost certainly, anyone in the pages of scripture.
29. See Jn 12:3.
30. He means the public baths.

the way Esau, Abraham's grandson, did,[31] or oats the way horses do. Just because most wild animals, after all, live on less refined kinds of food than we do, this does not mean that they are more self-restrained than we are. For in all matters of this kind it is not the nature of the things we make use of, but our reason for making use of them and the manner in which we set about getting them, that decides whether what we do deserves approval or disapproval.

20. The just men of old in the earthly kingdom pictured the heavenly kingdom to themselves, and foretold it.[32] Provision of offspring was the reason for the blameless custom of one man having several wives at once; and that is why it was not also decent for one woman to have many husbands, because that does not make her any the more fruitful. To seek either gain or children by sleeping around is simply the disgraceful style of the prostitute. In this sphere of morals scripture does not find fault with whatever the holy men of those times did without lustfulness, although they did what today can only be done out of lust or lechery. And all such stories as are told there are not only to be interpreted literally as historical accounts, but also to be taken figuratively as prophetic in some way, pointing to that end of the love of God or of neighbor, or of both.

Thus it was a matter of infamy among the ancient Romans to wear ankle-long, long-sleeved tunics, whereas now it is infamous for those born to high station not to wear them,[33] even when they are informally dressed. In the same sort of way we have to observe that such lustful inclinations should be banished from every other kind of use we make of things; for not only do they vilely abuse the very customs of the people among whom one is living, but they will even exceed all bounds and erupt, very often, in the most infamous display of their ugliness, which was previously lurking concealed behind the enclosure walls of conventional morals.[34]

13, 21. But anything that fits in with the customs of those among whom this life has to be spent, and is either imposed on one by necessity or undertaken out of duty, is to be seen as directed by good and important people to the end of usefulness and of kindness,[35] either literally, which is how we too should do it, or even figuratively, as befits the prophets.

14, 22. When unlearned people who have other customs come across such deeds in their reading, they think, unless checked by authority, that

---

31. See Lk 24:42–43; Gn 25:29–34.
32. See Heb 11.
33. *Non eas habere flagitium est.* This could, I suppose, be translated, "it is not an infamy to wear them"; so the BAC Spanish translation, Madrid, 1957. But if Augustine had really meant that, I am sure he would have dictated, *eas habere flagitium non est.*
34. I have to confess that I really have no idea what he is talking about in this sentence, except to say that *libido* can rear its ugly head in all sorts of ways; nor can I see how this is illustrated by the changes in what fashion decreed that Roman gentlemen should wear.
35. See section 16 above.

they are acts of infamy, and they are quite unable to appreciate that the whole of their own way of life, in their marriages, or their parties, or their clothing, and in all other aspects of human life and culture, would seem infamous to other nations and other times. Some people, moved by the variety of innumerable customs, and half asleep, if I may so put it, being neither sunk in the deep slumber of folly, nor able to wake up fully to the light of wisdom, have supposed that there is no such thing as justice in itself, but that each nation takes it for granted that its own customs are just; as these differ from nation to nation, while justice ought to remain immutable, it becomes obvious, they conclude, that there is no justice anywhere.

They have not understood, to mention just one point, that *What you do not wish done to you, do not do to another* (Tb 4:15)[36] can suffer no variation through any diversity of national customs. When this maxim is referred to love of God, all infamous conduct dies; when to love of neighbor, all crimes. We none of us, after all, like our dwellings ruined; so we ought not to ruin God's dwelling, namely ourselves. And we none of us wish to be harmed by anyone else; therefore let us not harm anyone else ourselves.

15, 23. The tyranny of cupidity or greed being thus overthrown, charity or love reigns supreme with its just laws of loving God for God's sake, and oneself and one's neighbor for God's sake. So this rule will be observed in dealing with figurative expressions, that you should take pains to turn over and over in your mind what you read, until your interpretation of it is led right through to the kingdom of charity. But if this is already happening with the literal meaning, do not suppose the expression is in any way a figurative one.

16, 24. If it is an expression of command, either forbidding infamy or crime, or ordering usefulness or kindness, it is not figurative. But if it seems to command infamy or crime, or to forbid usefulness or kindness, then it is figurative. *Unless you eat,* he says, *the flesh of the Son of man and drink his blood, you shall not have life in you* (Jn 6:53). He seems to be commanding a crime or an act of infamy; so it is said figuratively, instructing us that we must share in the Lord's passion, and store away in our minds the sweet and useful memory that his flesh was crucified and wounded for our sakes.

Scripture says, *If your enemy is hungry, feed him; if he is thirsty, give him a drink.* Here there can be no doubt that it is enjoining a kindness upon us. But with what follows: *For in doing this you will be heaping coals of fire upon his head* (Rom 12:20; Prv 25:21–22), you might suppose a spiteful crime is being commanded. So you must have no doubt that it is said figuratively; and while it can be interpreted in two ways, in one for doing harm, in the other for giving support, let charity rather call you back to kindness, and to understanding by coals of fire the red hot pangs of repentance, which heal the pride of the man, who is grieved at having been the enemy of the person he is being helped by in his plight.

---

36. See also Mt 7:12.

Again, when the Lord says, *Whoever loves his life, let him throw it away*[37] (Jn 12:25), he must not be supposed to be forbidding those useful acts by which we all ought to preserve our lives. But "let him throw away his life" is said figuratively; that is, let him do away with and lose that use he now makes of it, namely a perverse and topsy-turvy use, so taken up with temporal things that he gives no thought to eternity.

It is written, *Give to the kindhearted person, and do not support the sinner* (Sir 12:4). The second part of this maxim seems to be forbidding a kindness, in saying *do not support the sinner*. So you should understand that "sinner" is put figuratively for sin, and thus it means you must not support him in his sin.

Various other rules and considerations

17, 25. But it often happens that those who have reached a higher stage of the spiritual life, or think they have, consider that instructions meant for the lower stages are said figuratively; for example, those who have embraced the celibate life, and *have castrated themselves for the sake of the kingdom of heaven* (Mt 19:12), will argue that whatever the holy books enjoin about loving and ruling wives[38] must be taken metaphorically and not properly; and anyone who has decided to keep his virgin unmarried[39] will attempt to give a figurative interpretation of the text, *Give your daughter in marriage, and you have accomplished a great work* (Sir 7:25).

Among points, therefore, to be observed in trying to understand the scriptures there will also be this one, that we should realize that some things are enjoined universally upon everybody, others upon this or that particular class of person; thus medicine is provided not only to ensure a general state of good health, but also to cope with each member's own peculiar weakness. What cannot be raised up to a higher class is of course to be cured in its own lower one.

18, 26. Again one has to be on one's guard against supposing that whatever in the Old Testament, with respect to the condition of those times, is not an infamy nor a crime either, even when understood literally and not figuratively, can be transferred also to these times and put into practice in life today. Not unless cupidity or greed is lording it over you, and seeking the support of the very scriptures which are meant to udermine it, will you do such a thing. If you do, you are miserably failing to understand the value of such things being set down there; it is to help persons of good hope to come to the salutary realization both that a custom which they abhor can have

---

37. Reading *perdat* with four manuscripts instead of *perdet*, "will throw it away" with M and CCL. These four are surely correct, in view of what he goes on to say. *Perdet* is the Vulgate reading, to which copyists were inclined to correct their author.
38. For example, Eph 5:25.
39. See 1 Cor 7:37.

a good use, and that one they favor can be condemned, if they look in the first case to the love and in the second to the greed of those who observe it.

27. The fact is, if one person, given the time he lived in, could be chaste in his association with many wives, another can be lustful in his association with one. I have more respect, you see, for the man who makes use of the fertility of many wives for the sake of something else than for the one who finds enjoyment in the flesh of one for its own sake. In the first instance an advantage is being sought suitable to the needs of the times, in the second an appetite wrapped up in passing pleasures is being satisfied. And those men to whom the apostle allows carnal congress, each with his own one wife, by way of concession on account of their lack of self-restraint,[40] were at a lower stage in their progress toward God than those who, though they each had several wives, were only looking in their sexual relations with them to the procreation of children, like the wise man whose only consideration in food and drink is bodily health. And so if they had still been found alive when the Lord came, when it was no longer *a time to throw away stones, but a time to gather stones together* (Eccl 3:5), they would straightaway have castrated themselves for the sake of the kingdom of heaven;[41] you only find it difficult, after all, to go without something, when you are greedy to possess it.

Those men of old did indeed know that even within marriage one could be guilty of wanton self-indulgence, as the prayer of Tobias shows, which he prayed when he was bedded with his wife. Thus he said, *Blessed are you, Lord God of our fathers, and blessed is your holy name for ever and ever. May the heavens and all creation bless you. You it was who made Adam, and gave him Eve as a helper. And now, Lord, you know that it is not out of self-indulgent lust that I am taking this sister of mine, but in all sincerity, so that you may have mercy on us, Lord* (Tb 8:5-7).

19, 28. But men who let themselves go to seed in their unbridled lust, and roam around from debauch to debauch, or even those who with their own wives not only exceed the limit allowed for the procreation of children, but even with a quite shameless licentiousness make use of a kind of slavish freedom to pile up the filth of a scarcely human self-indulgence;[42] such people do not believe it was possible for the men of old to make temperate use of many women, doing nothing in such use but performing the duty of begetting offspring as required in those times. And they assume that what they themselves, tangled in the snares of lust, cannot practice even with only one wife could not possibly be done with many.

29. But these people can also say that good and holy men should not even be honored and praised, since they themselves, when they are hon-

---

40. See 1 Cor 7:2.7.
41. See Mt 19:12.
42. This is the recent professional rhetorician piling up the useless rhetoric of vituperation.

ored and praised, swell up with pride like turkey cocks, being all the more avidly eager for the vanity of empty fame, the more frequently and widely they are fanned with the breeze from flattering tongues. This makes them so light-headed that the slightest breath of a rumor, whether it is considered favorable or adverse, can carry them into the whirlpools of any kind of infamy, or dash them on the rocks of any sort of crime.[43] So let them reflect how hard and difficult it is neither to be lured by the bait of praise nor pierced by the darts of abuse, and refrain from measuring others by the standard of themselves.

20. They should rather believe that our apostles were neither puffed up when they were looked up to by people, nor cast down when they were looked down upon. Those men were indeed spared neither test, because on the one hand their praises were sung far and wide by believers, and on the other they were defamed by the curses of their persecutors. So just as these men made use of all this as the times and occasions demanded, and were not corrupted, in the same way those men of old used the custom of polygamy in a way suitable to their times, and did not endure the domination of that lust of which these people, who do not believe such things, are the slaves.

30. And that is why these people would in no way restrain themselves from giving way to an unforgivable hatred for their own sons, on learning that they had violated or seduced their fathers' wives or concubines, should such a thing ever happen to them.

21, But when King David suffered such an injury from his impious and monstrous son, he not only tolerated him in his ferocious hostility, but even bewailed him on hearing of his untimely death.[44] He was not caught fast, you see, in the nets of carnal jealousy, and so it was not at all the wrong done to himself, but the sins of his son that troubled him. That is why he gave orders forbidding him to be killed if he was defeated, so that duly chastened he might have the chance to repent; and because this turned out to be impossible, it was not his own bereavement that he grieved over in the young man's death, but he knew what pains awaited such an impiously adulterous and parricidal soul.[45] Because previously for another son, who was innocent, he had afflicted himself while the child was sick, but rejoiced when he died.[46]

31. And this following instance shows better than anything else with what moderation and self-restraint those men made use of the custom of polygamy. This same king, carried away by a kind of turmoil of feelings

---

43. The Scylla and Charybdis theme; sailors were lured to their destruction in the whirlpools or on the rocks by sweet Siren voices.
44. See the story of David and Absalom, 2 Sm 15—18, especially 16:21–22 and 18:32–33.
45. Here Augustine is reading back Christian or late Jewish conceptions of heaven and hell to the time and consciousness of David, who in all probability had no such ideas.
46. See 2 Sm 12:15–23.

common at his age, and by the success of his temporal enterprises, had unlawfully taken one woman, and also given orders for her husband to be killed. He was taken to task by the prophet, who came to him to convict him of his sin; he did this by putting to him a parallel case of a poor man who had one ewe lamb, and whose neighbor, who had many sheep, took his poor neighbor's one and only ewe lamb to provide a meal for a guest of his who had just arrived. David was enraged at his conduct, and ordered him to be put to death,[47] and fourfold restitution of the sheep to be made to the poor man—thus condemning himself unawares, though he had sinned with full awareness. When this was made plain to him, and God's sentence upon him was pronounced, he washed away his sin by repentance.

But for all that, in this parallel case, it was only his sexual misconduct that was signified by what happened to the poor neighbor's ewe lamb; but with his elimination of the woman's husband, that is with the putting to death of the poor man himself who had just the one ewe lamb, David was not taxed in terms of this parallel case, so that he only condemned and passed sentence on himself for adultery. From which we should understand with what self-restraint he had many women, when he was obliged to punish himself over just one, with whom he overstepped the mark.[48] But in this man such ungoverned lust was not something habitual, but a passing instance; that is why even the prophet, in his veiled accusation, called this illicit desire a passing guest. He did not say, you see, that the man had presented his poor neighbor's ewe lamb as a feast for his king, but for his guest. But in David's son Solomon this kind of lust did not come and pass on like a guest, but established its permanent reign; and scripture did not keep quiet about this, but found fault with him for having been a lover of women. In his early days, though, he had had a burning desire for wisdom; and having won her by a spiritual kind of love, he lost her through carnal love.[49]

22, 32. So then, all the doings, or practically all of them, which are contained in the books of the Old Testament, are to be taken not only in their literal sense, but also as having a figurative sense. All the same, when the people in the narratives, which the reader takes in the proper literal sense,[50] were praised for doing things that are abhorrent to the manners of good men and women who keep God's commandments after the Lord's coming, the reader should not take the actual deeds as models for moral behavior, but should try to understand their figurative meaning. There are many things, after all, which at that time were done out of duty that now can only be done out of lust.

---

47. Not quite accurate; he said the man deserved to die. See 2 Sm 12:1–14.
48. What a quite extraordinary inference!
49. See 1 Kgs 3:3–14; 11:1–13. The parallel account in 2 Chr 1—9 precisely does keep quiet about Solomon's aberrations.
50. As Augustine certainly insisted all the historical narratives should be taken, among which he and his contemporaries, and their successors up to modern times, included narratives we now know to be mythical or fictional, like the stories of Job and Jonah, and most of Gn 1—11.

23, 33. If, however, you read about any sins of great men, and yet are able to notice and explore in them some figurative representations of future realities,[51] you should still turn the proper literal meaning of the thing done to this good use: that as a result of seeing the tempests such men were in danger from and the shipwrecks they had to bewail, you should never even think of congratulating yourself on what you have done rightly, or of looking down upon other people as sinners from the vantage point of your own justice. The recording even of these men's sins, you see, had this purpose, to make that judgment of the apostle's strike terror on all sides, *Therefore let anyone who seems to stand see to it that he does not fall* (1 Cor 10:12). There is, in fact, almost no page of the holy books in which the lesson is not echoed, that *God withstands the proud, but gives grace to the humble* (Prv 3:34; Jas 4:6; 1 Pt 5:5).[52]

Some further, more technical rules of interpretation

24, 34. And so the thing that has to be ascertained above all else is whether the passage we are trying to understand is intended to be taken literally or figuratively. For on being assured of its figurative nature, it is easy, by applying the rules we set out in the first book, to turn the passage over this way and that until we arrive at its true meaning, especially when our use of these rules is reinforced by being exercised devoutly and reverently. But we discover whether the passage is to be taken literally or figuratively by considering all that has been said above. 25, When this becomes clear,[53] the words employed in the expression will be found to be drawn from similar things or from things approximating more or less closely.

35. But because there are many ways in which things are seen to be like other things, we should not think it is *de rigueur* for us to assume that a thing always has to signify what it happens to signify in one passage by its resemblance to something else. Thus the Lord talked of yeast in a negative sense when he said, *Beware of the yeast of the Pharisees* (Mt 16:6), and in a positive sense when he said, *The kingdom of heaven is like*

---

51. Such as the famous one Augustine thought he could detect in the way Jacob cheated Esau out of his father's death-bed blessing, Gn 27:1–40; saying about Jacob's flagrant lie, verse 24, *Non est mendacium sed mysterium* (*Against Lying*, 10, 24), "It is not a lie but a mystery"—the mystery of Christ identifying himself with us sinners, and taking our sins upon himself, like the kid skins on Jacob's arms and neck. See Book I, note 45
52. See also Mt 23:12; Lk 14:11; 18:14.
53. In fact, that the passage or expression is to be taken as figurative. He assumes no further assistance is needed for understanding the literal meaning—it means what it says! But this whole section does rather strike one as being pure flannel—something he would surely have either cut out or given some substance to, had he really revised the work.

a woman who hid some yeast in three measures of flour, until it was all leavened (Lk 13:21).[54]

36. Observation, therefore, will show that this variety takes two forms: thus things can signify this as well as that in such a way that they signify either contraries or merely diverse realities. Contraries, that is to say, when the same thing is put as a simile for something good in one place, something bad in another, like what I have just said about yeast. Such too is the case with the lion, which signifies Christ where it says, *The lion from the tribe of Judah has conquered* (Rv 5:5); and also signifies the devil where it is written, *Your adversary the devil goes about roaring like a lion, seeking whom he may devour* (1 Pt 5:8). In the same way we have the serpent in a good sense: *As cunning as serpents* (Mt 10:16); while in a bad sense, *The serpent seduced Eve by his cunning* (2 Cor 11:3). Bread in a good sense: *I am the living bread, who have come down from heaven*; in a bad sense: *Eat hidden loaves of bread with pleasure* (Prv 9:17). And these instances I have mentioned, of course, leave no doubts about their meaning, because to illustrate the point it was necessary to mention only clear cases.

There are others, however, where it is uncertain in what sense, good or bad, they should be taken, like: *A goblet of pure wine in the hand of the Lord is full and mixed.* It is uncertain whether it signifies the wrath of God, but not down to the final punishments, that is down to the dregs, or whether it rather signifies the grace of the scriptures passing from the Jews to the nations, because *he turned it this way and that*, while there remained with the Jews the observances which they understand in a carnal, literal sense, because *its dregs have not been emptied out* (Ps 75:8). But as an example of a thing put to signify, not contraries, but simply diverse realities, we have water signifying the people, as we read in the Apocalypse,[55] and the Holy Spirit in the text, *Rivers of living water shall flow from his belly* (Jn 7:38), and anything else that water can be taken to signify in other places where it is mentioned.

37. In the same way there are other things which, considered not in their general use, but in any particular instance, signify not only two different things but sometimes even several, depending on the place the sentence occurs in.[56]

---

54. It is here that Augustine laid the work aside, some time in 396 or 397, and only completed it some 30 years later. See Translator's Note and the extract from the *Revisions* that follows it.
55. See Rv 17:15; 19:6.
56. In the Latin text this one sentence paragraph begins section 37. I am not at all certain what it means. It begins *Sic et aliae res non singulae, sed unaquaeque earum...*; and trying to distinguish between the meaning of *singulae* and *unaquaeque earum* makes my head spin. If he means what I say he means, an instance of one figurative thing meaning several things at once, a case in point would be the text he has just quoted from Ps 75.

26. But wherever their meaning is clear, there we must learn how they are to be understood in obscurer places. After all, there is no better way of understanding what was said to God in the verse, *Take up arms and shield, and arise to help me* (Ps 35:2), than from that other place where we read, *Lord, you have crowned us as with the shield of your good will* (Ps 5:12). This does not mean, however, that wherever we read of a shield as some kind of defense we should only take it to mean God's good will; it says elsewhere, after all, *And the shield of faith, with which you can quench all the fiery arrows of the wicked one* (Eph 6:16). Nor again, in spiritual equipment of this sort, should we confine faith only to the shield, since another place also talks of the breastplate of faith: *Putting on*, he says, *the breastplate of faith and love* (1 Thes 5:8).

27, 38. But when from the same words of scripture not just one, but two or more meanings may be extracted, even if you cannot tell which of them the writer intended, there is no risk if they can all be shown from other places of the holy scriptures to correspond with the truth. However, those who are engaged in searching the divine utterances must make every effort to arrive at the intention of the author through whom the Holy Spirit produced that portion of scripture. But as I say, there is nothing risky about it, whether they do get at this, or whether they carve out another meaning from those words which does not clash with right faith, and is supported by any other passage of the divine utterances. That author, in fact, possibly even saw this very meaning in the same words which we wish to understand; and certainly the Spirit of God who produced these texts through him foresaw without a shadow of doubt that it would occur to some reader or listener; or rather he actually provided that it should occur to them, because it is upheld by the truth.[57] How, after all, could the divine scriptures make more abundant and generous provision, than by ensuring that the same words could be understood in several ways, which are underwritten by other no less divine testimonies?

28, 39. But where a possible meaning emerges which cannot be made entirely clear by other certain testimonies of the holy scriptures, it remains to elucidate it with arguments from reason, even if the writer whose words we are trying to understand did not perhaps intend that meaning.[58] But this habit is risky; it is really much safer to walk along with the divine scriptures; when we wish to examine passages rendered obscure with words used metaphorically, either let something emerge from our scrutiny that is not controversial, or else if it is so, let the matter be settled from the same scripture by finding and applying testimonies from anywhere else in the sacred books.

---

57. Here he is making the very important point that the Holy Spirit, as well as being active in inspiring the authors of the scriptures, is also present to inspire the readers and hearers, if their minds are open to his suggestions and his illumination.
58. I really do not know what meaning emerges from this sentence! The meanings he is talking about, of course, are the figurative or secondary ones, what a later systematized theology of exegesis will call the spiritual senses.

29, 40. Educated readers, however, should know that our authors used all the figures of speech, to which grammarians give the Greek name of tropes, much more freely and abundantly than people who are unfamiliar with them, and who have learned about these things in other writings, could possibly guess or believe. Still, those who know these tropes will recognize them in the holy texts, and will to some extent be helped by this knowledge in understanding them. But this is not the right place for handing them on to those who are ignorant of them; else I might seem to be teaching the art of grammar. My advice certainly is that this should be learned elsewhere, though I have already given this advice above, that is in the second book, where I was discussing what knowledge of languages is necessary.[59] Letters, after all, from which grammar gets its name—the Greeks, you see, call letters *grammata*—are of course signs of the sounds making up the articulated words we talk with.

Not only, though, are there examples in the divine books of all these tropes, but even the names of some of them can be read there, like allegory, enigma,[60] parable. As a matter of fact, though, practically all these tropes, which are said to be learned in the liberal art of grammar, are also to be found in the speech of people who have never taken any courses in grammar, and are quite happy with the speech of common people. Is there anybody, after all, who never says, "May you blossom like that,"[61] which is the trope called metaphor? Or who does not call any pool a fish pond, even though it has no fish in it, and was not even made for fish? And yet it got its name from fish; this trope is called catachresis.

41. It would take too long to run through the rest of the tropes in this way; after all, common speech gets as far as using those which are all the more surprising, because they signify the opposite of what is said, such as the one called irony or antiphrasis. But irony indicates by the tone of voice what is intended to be understood, as when we say to a person behaving badly, "You *are* behaving well," whereas antiphrasis manages to signify the opposite of what it says, not by the tone of voice, but either by having its own words, which derive from the opposite meaning, like calling a grove a *lucus*, though it is almost devoid of *lucis*, light, or by saying something in that way, although it can also be said without meaning the opposite, as when we ask for something which is not there, and are told, "There's plenty," or when we show by the context of our other words that what we say is to be understood in the opposite sense, as if we were to say, "Beware of that fellow, because he's a good man."

---

59. See Book II, section 16 above.
60. This word will almost certainly not occur in any English translations; it occurs in the Greek and Latin versions in 1 Cor 13:12, and in Num 12:8. The best English equivalent, to my mind, is "riddle."
61. Is there anybody who ever does say this in English? But evidently the Latin, *Sic floreas,* was a common expression of good wishes; an English translation that we hardly think of now as metaphorical would be "May you flourish like that." The same consideration applies to fish pond, *piscina,* in the next sentence.

And are there any uneducated people who do not use such expressions, though they do not have the slightest idea of what tropes are, or what they are called? The reason knowledge of them is necessary for unraveling the ambiguities of the scriptures is that when the sense of the words, if they are taken literally, is absurd, we have of course to inquire whether the passage we do not understand was said according to this or that trope; and in this way, often enough, the meaning of what was obscure is laid bare.[62]

The seven rules of Tychonius

30, 42. There was a man called Tychonius, who wrote against the Donatists in a manner that it is quite impossible to refute, and whose unwillingness to part company with them completely reveals the utter absurdity of his attachments. He composed what he called a book of *Rules*, because in it he worked out seven rules by which the hidden meanings of the divine scriptures might be unlocked, as with keys. The first of them he states as being "about the Lord and his body"; the second, "about the twofold body of the Lord"; the third, "about the promises and the law"; the fourth, "about species and genus"; the fifth, "about times"; the sixth, "about recapitulation"; the seventh, "about the devil and his body."

When looked at indeed as employed by him, they are of no small assistance in penetrating the hidden meanings of the divine utterances. All the same, not everything that is so written as not to be easily understood can be deciphered by these rules; but a number of other ways are required which this man did not include in his list of seven, to the extent, indeed, that he himself explains many obscurities without applying any of these rules, since in fact they are not needed there. Nothing like them, in fact, is employed or looked for, where he is inquiring in John's Apocalypse how the angels of the seven Churches are to be understood, to whom he is commanded to write;[63] and he produces many arguments to conclude that we should understand the Churches themselves as being the angels. In this wide-ranging discussion there is no mention of these rules, and it is a very obscure point that is being examined there. That must be sufficient by way of an example, because it would take far too long and be much too

---

62. The most important, and neglected, trope in this respect is in my opinion irony— especially perhaps in the gospels where our Lord's words are being reported. We can no longer hear his tone of voice, and irony is the last thing most readers will suspect Jesus of indulging in; I, though, suspect quite the contrary, that it was a way of speaking he made frequent use of—for example in Lk 7:43, in his answer to his host, the Pharisee Simon. If you take his words, "You have judged rightly" as ironic—because surely Jesus would not agree that love could be bought—the whole episode springs to life. On tropes, and in particular on enigma, see *the Trinity*, XV,15.

63. See Rv 1:11.20. Tychonius' *Book of Rules* was edited and published by Burkitt (Cambridge, 1894). See that edition, pages 1–9. The text may also be found in PL 18, 15.

much trouble to list all the places in the canonical scriptures which are so obscure that none of these seven keys may be expected to unlock them.[64]

43. When this man, though, was putting these forward as rules, he attributed such effective force to them, that if only we knew and applied them well, we would be enabled to understand everything that we find stated obscurely in the law, that is in the divine books. At least, he opened this very book with these words: "I considered it necessary, before all the other ideas I have, to write a little book of rules, and to forge as it were keys and lamps for the hidden secrets of the law. For there are certain mystical rules which can gain admittance to the inner chambers of the whole law, and render visible the treasures of truth that are invisible to some people. If my account of these rules is accepted ungrudgingly, in the spirit in which I offer it, all closed doors will be opened and dark places lit up, so that anyone strolling through the vast forest of prophecy will be protected by these rules from error, being guided by them, so to say, along paths of light."

Here, if he had said, "for there are certain mystical rules which can gain admittance to not a few of the inner chambers of the law," or even, "which can gain admittance to the important inner chambers of the law," and not what he actually did say, "the inner chambers of the whole law," and if he had not said, "all closed doors will be opened," but "many closed doors will be opened," what he said would have been true, and he would not have raised false hopes in those who wish to read and know his extremely painstaking and useful work, by giving it a bigger boost than the actual matter calls for. The reason I thought this had to be said is that on the one hand this book ought to be read by serious students, because it is of the greatest help in understanding the scriptures, and on the other one should not hope to get from it what it cannot provide. It certainly needs to be read with caution, not only because of some points on which he erred just by being human, but supremely because of the things he says precisely as a Donatist heretic. But let me now briefly indicate what these seven rules teach or advise us.

31, 44. The first one is "about the Lord and his body." We know that we are sometimes being given hints that head and body, that is Christ and Church, constitute one person—after all, it was not without reason that the faithful were told *Then you are the seed of Abraham* (Gal 3:29), although there is only one seed of Abraham, which is Christ. So according to this first rule we should not let it baffle us when a text passes from head to body and from body to head, and yet still refers to one and the same person. It is one person speaking, you see, where it says, *He placed a turban on my head as on a bridegroom, and adorned me with ornaments as a bride* (Is 61:10); and yet of course we have to understand which of these two fits the head, which the body; which fits Christ, that is, and which the Church.

---

64. What he says literally is "... that none of these seven is to be looked for in them"—a rather careless form of expression.

32, 45. The second one is "about the twofold body of the Lord." It should not in fact have been called that, because that which will not remain with him for ever in eternity is not really the body of the Lord; but it should have been called "about the true and the mixed body of the Lord," or "the true and pretended body," or something else like that; because it is not only in eternity but even now that hypocrites should not be said to be with him, even though they appear to be in his Church. Hence this rule could also have been given a name and title such as "about the Church as a mixture."

This rule calls for wide-awake understanding, when a text, which is in fact already addressed to others, seems to be addressed to the very people whom it was addressing[65]—as though both sorts belonged to one body, because they are temporarily mixed up together, and share the same sacraments. This from the Song of Songs, for example: *I am swarthy and beautiful as the camps of Kedar, as the tents of Solomon* (Sg 1:5). She did not say, you see, "I was dusky as the camps of Kedar, and I am beautiful as the tents of Solomon," but she said she was each of them at the same time because of the temporary unity within a single net of both good and bad fish together. The camps of Kedar, after all, belong to Ishmael, who will not be an heir with the son of the free woman.[66]

So too, while God says about the good sort, *I will lead the blind along a road which they have not known, and they shall tread paths which they have not known, and I will turn darkness into light for them, and make what is crooked straight; these are the words I will perform, and I will not abandon them*, he goes on immediately to say, *They however turned backward* (Is 42:16–17), although others are now being meant by these words, namely the other bad sort that are mixed in together with the good.[67] But since they are now all in one body together, he appears to be speaking about the same ones as he was speaking about first; they will not, however, always be in one and the same body. This in fact is that servant mentioned in the gospel, whose master, when he comes, *will divide him and put part of him with the hypocrites* (Mt 24:51).[68]

33, 46. The third rule is "about the promises and the law," which could otherwise be called "about the spirit and the letter," which is what I myself called it when I wrote a book on this topic. It could also be called "about grace and commandments." It strikes me, though, as being more a very

---

65. A most peculiar sentence.

66. See Gn 25:13; 21:10; Gal 4:30.

67. I have rephrased what he says to make it clearer, because he does in fact phrase it very badly! What he says literally is: "He immediately says about the other sort, which has been mixed in badly, *They however turned backward*, although others are now being meant by these words."

68. An ingenious, but clearly inadmissible, way of interpreting a difficult text—the servant represents the whole Church, which is divided at the last judgment, in the next chapter of Matthew, into the wise and foolish virgins, the good and faithful servants as against the wicked and idle servant, and lastly into the sheep and the goats.

large question, than a rule to be applied to the settling of questions. This is the thing the Pelagians failed to understand, and so either laid the foundations of their heresy or built more on them. Tychonius did some good work in his treatment of it, but still left something to be desired. While discussing faith and works, he said that our works are given to us by God on the strength of our faith, but that faith itself comes from us in such a way that we do not have it from God.[69] He failed to notice what the apostle says, *Peace to the brethren, and charity with faith from God the Father and the Lord Jesus Christ* (Eph 6:23).

But then he had had no experience of this heresy, which has arisen in our time, and has engaged us so much in defending against it the grace of God that comes to us through our Lord Jesus Christ; and according to the apostle's words, *There must be heresies, so that those who are tried and tested may be shown up* (1 Cor 11:19), it has made us much more vigilant and alert, so that we notice in the holy scriptures what escaped the attention of Tychonius, lacking as he did an enemy to make him wary, namely that faith too is a gift of the one who *assigns the measure of it to each one* (Rom 12:3). By the same token others were told, *To you it has been granted for Christ's sake, not only that you should believe in him, but also that you should suffer for him* (Phil 1:29). Who then, on hearing with faithful intelligence that each thing has been granted, could doubt that each is a gift of God? There are also many other passages that could be quoted to support the point, but this is not what we are dealing with at the present moment; we have, though, dealt with it often enough in all sorts of other places.[70]

34, 47. Tychonius' fourth rule is "about species and genus." That, you see, is what he calls it, wishing "species" to be understood as the part, "genus" as the whole, of which that is a part which he calls species. Thus any city[71] is of course a part of the totality of nations; so he calls it a species, while he calls all the nations the genus. Nor do we have in this case to make the subtle distinction which is taught by the logicians, who go in

---

69. The original Pelagian statement, as criticized by Augustine, was that our good works proceed entirely from our own free will and not from God's grace. Later, under presssure from his arguments, they conceded that, in Paul's language, we are justified by faith and not by works, that good works without faith in Christ are valueless; but then they maintained that this faith is entirely our own act.

70. In addition to some fifteen anti-Pelagian treatises listed as such among Augustine's writings, there are innumerable references to this heresy in his later letters. It was the great pre-occupation, not to say obsession, of the last fifteen to twenty years of his life.

71. Though no city states survived in Augustine's time, he still inhabited a culture inherited from Greece and ancient Rome, in which "city" could as often as not mean "state." Indeed, at first I thought of so translating it, but what he goes on to say rather ruled that out.

Augustine does not spell out how this rule actually works; but one gathers that it is simply a matter of sometimes applying what is said about the part, or species, to the whole, or genus.

for very keen arguments about the difference between "part" and "species." The same rule applies if anything of the sort is found in the divine literature, not about some city, but about some province or single nation or kingdom. It is not only, for example, a matter of something being said about Jerusalem or some other city of the nations, whether Tyre or Babylon or any other you like, that exceeds its limitations and is suited rather to all the nations, but also of what is said about Judea, about Egypt, about Assyria and any other nation in which there is any number of cities. Such countries, all the same, are not the whole world but parts of it, and things are sometimes said about them that exceed their limits and are applicable rather to the whole of which they are parts—or in this man's terms to the genus of which they are the species.

It is from this usage, in fact, that these words have entered the common language, so that even the uneducated understand what is of special and what is of general application in any imperial decree. The same rule also applies to people, as when things said about Solomon exceed his limitations, and become luminously clear when referred to Christ or the Church, of which Solomon is a part.

48. Nor is the species always exceeded or surpassed. Things are often said, after all, which obviously apply to it, or even perhaps apply to it alone. But it is when the transition is made from species to genus, while scripture still seems to be speaking about the species, that readers should be most wide awake and attentive, in order not to seek in the species what can be better and more certainly found in the genus. Clearly, it is easy to see that what the prophet Ezekiel says: *The house of Israel has dwelt in the land, and they have defiled it with their ways and with their idols and their sins; their ways have become like the uncleanness of a menstruating woman before my face. And I have poured out my wrath upon them, and have scattered them among the nations and winnowed them into distant regions; according to their ways and according to their sins have I judged them* (Ez 36:17–19)—it is easy, I say, to understand this about that house of Israel of which the apostle says, *Observe Israel according to the flesh* (1 Cor 10:18), because these are all things that the fleshly people of Israel both did and suffered.

What follows can also be understood as fitting the same people. But when he starts saying, *And I will sanctify my holy name, that great name, which has been defiled among the nations, which you have defiled in the midst of them, and the nations shall know that I am the Lord*, the reader should now be alert to notice how it is going beyond species and touching on genus. He goes on to say, you see, *when I sanctify myself among you before their eyes. And I will take you back from the nations and gather you together from all lands, and I will bring you back to your own land. And I will sprinkle you with clean water, and you shall be cleansed of all your images; and I will cleanse you and give you a new heart and put a new spirit in you, and I will take away the stony heart from your flesh and give you a heart of flesh. And I will put my spirit in you, and make you walk in my justices and keep and carry out my judgments. And you shall dwell in the land which I gave to your fathers, and you shall be my people, and I will be your God, and I will cleanse you from all your uncleannesses* (Ez 36:23–29).

You only have to notice that *the bath of rebirth* (Ti 3:5) is also promised here, something we now see bestowed on all nations, and you will be in no doubt that this whole passage is a prophecy of the new covenant, which embraces not only that one nation in its remnant, about which it is written elsewhere, *Even if the number of the children of Israel is like the sands of the sea, only a remnant will be saved* (Is 10:22; Rom 9:27), but also the other nations which were promised to their fathers, who are also ours.[72] And there is also what the apostle said, when he was putting forward the grace of the new covenant as surpassing that of the old: *You yourselves are our letter, not written in ink but in the Spirit of the living God, not on tablets of stone, but on the fleshly tablets of the heart* (2 Cor 3:2–30); he is here looking back and observing that this comes from the very place where our prophet says *And I will give you a new heart and put a new spirit in you, and I will take away the stony heart from your flesh and give you a heart of flesh.* A heart of flesh, of course—from which the apostle gets his phrase *the fleshly tablets of the heart*—he wished to be distinguished from a stony heart by its having life and feeling, and by feeling he meant intelligence. In this way the spiritual Israel consists not of one nation but of all, which were promised to the fathers in their seed, *which is Christ* (Gal 3:16).

49. So this spiritual Israel is distinguished from that Israel of the flesh, which is one nation, by newness of grace, not by privilege of race, and by attitude of mind rather than by nationality of any kind.[73] But the profundity of prophecy, while speaking about, or addressing itself to the former, will pass unperceived to the latter, and while it is still speaking about or addressing itself to this latter will still seem to be referring to the former. It does this, not because it is unfriendly and grudges us our understanding of the scriptures, but because it is giving our understanding some very salutary therapeutic exercise. Thus the text, *And I will bring you back into your own land,* and its repetition a little later, *And you will dwell,* he says, *in the land which I gave to your fathers* (Ez 36:24.28), should be taken by us as referring, not in a fleshly manner to the Israel of the flesh, but in a spiritual manner to the Israel of the spirit.

The Church that is to say, *without spot or wrinkle* (Eph 5:27), gathered together out of all the nations and destined to reign for ever with Christ, is itself the land of the blessed, *the land of the living* (Ps 27:13), and is to be understood as what was given to the fathers, when it was promised them by the sure and immutable will of God. This land which the fathers believed

---

72. See Gn 17:15; Rom 4:16–17.
73. *Novitate gratiae, non nobilitate patriae, et mente, non gente, distinguitur.*

was to be given in its own time was already given them, as a matter of fact, in the very firmness of the promise or of God's predestining decision, as the apostle also says about the grace which is given to the saints, in his letter to Timothy: *Not according to our works, but according to his own purpose and grace, which was given to us in Christ Jesus before the eternal ages, but has been manifested now through the coming of our Savior* (2 Tm 1:9–10). He says that grace was given, when there was not even anyone yet for it to be given to, because in the plan and predestining decision of God, what was going to happen in its own time, which he calls being "manifested," had already happened.

These texts, though, could also be understood of the land of the age to come, when there will be *a new heaven and a new earth*, in which the unjust will not be able to live (2 Pt 3:13; Rv 21:1). And that is why it was quite right for the godly to be told that theirs is the land, of which not a single particle will belong to the ungodly, because it too was likewise given, when it was definitively confirmed that it was to be given.[74]

35, 50. Tychonius lays down a fifth rule, which he calls "about times." By it much can be discovered or inferred that is hidden in the holy scriptures about the length of times. Now he says that this rule works in two ways, either by the figure of speech called "synecdoche," or by proper numbers.[75] The figure of synecdoche leads one to understand either the whole from the part or the part from the whole; thus one evangelist says something happened after eight days, which another says happened after six, when in the presence of only three disciples on the mountain, *the Lord's face shone like the sun and his clothes like snow* (Mk 9:1–3; Lk 9:28–29). Each of the things said about the number of days, after all, could not be true, unless the one who said *after eight days* is understood to have included the last part of the day on which Christ foretold it would happen, and the first part of the day on which he shows it was fulfilled, as two whole and complete days, while the one who said *after six days* is taken to have counted only the whole and complete days in between.

It is by this manner of speech, in which the whole is signified by the part, that that problem about the resurrection of Christ is solved. After all, unless the last part of the day on which he suffered is taken for a whole day, that is to say with the previous night joined to it, and unless the night in the last part of which he rose again is taken as a whole day, namely with

---

74. The CCL edition here suggests that he may be alluding to Mt 5:5, *Blessed are the meek, for they shall inherit the earth*—"earth" and "land" being of course both *terra* in Latin. But in his frequent quotations of the beatitudes, he never refers to the recipients of this blessing as the *pii*, which is the word he uses here, but always as either the *mites* or the *mansueti*. I think he is in fact referring in a more general way back to Ez 36, which he has been continually quoting.
75. *Legitimis numeris* in the Latin. Perhaps it was a recognized technical term in ancient arithmetic. See Book II, 56, and note 14. There he talks about *intelligibiles numeri*, which the context requires me to translate "odd numbers."

the Lord's day that was dawning joined onto it, you cannot get the *three days and three nights* during which he foretold he would be *in the heart of the earth* (Mt 12:40).

51. By proper numbers, though, he means those which divine scripture gives pride of place to, like seven or ten or twelve and any others there may be, which careful readers will be happy to recognize. Often enough, you see, such numbers stand for the whole time; thus *Seven times a day will I praise you* (Ps 119:164) means exactly the same as *His praise is always in my mouth* (Ps 34:1). They have the same value too when they are multiplied, either by ten like seventy and seven hundred—thus Jeremiah's *seventy years* (Jer 25:11) can also be taken spiritually for the whole time in which the Church finds itself among foreign nations; or by themselves, like ten times ten making a hundred, and twelve times twelve a hundred and forty-four, the number that signifies the total company of the saints in the Apocalypse.[76] Thus it is clear that it is not only problems about times that are soluble by these numbers, but that their meanings spread much more widely, and worm their way into many places. This number in the Apocalypse, after all, does not refer to times but to people.

36, 52. Tychonius calls the sixth rule "about recapitulation," which he discovered by being particularly wide awake in his attention to the obscurities of scripture. There are some things, you see, that are said in such a way that they seem to follow in the order of time, or to be told in continuation of some narrative, while in fact the narrative is being imperceptibly turned back to earlier events that had been left out; and unless they are understood by this rule, mistakes can be made. Thus in Genesis, *The Lord God*, it says, *planted a paradise in Eden to the east, and placed there the man whom he had fashioned; and God further produced from the earth every tree that was beautiful and good for food* (Gn 2:8–9). This seems to be saying that this was done after he had placed the man he had made in paradise, though in fact after briefly mentioning each thing, that is that *God planted paradise, and placed there the man whom he had fashioned*, the writer goes back by way of recapitulation, and adds what he had left out—how, that is to say, paradise had been planted: that *God further produced from the earth every tree that was beautiful and good for food*.

Next he went on to add, *And the tree of life in mid-paradise and the tree of knowing good and evil*. Finally the river by which paradise was to be watered is spread out by *being divided into four heads* (Gn 2:9–10) of four streams; and all this belongs to the setting up of paradise. When he had come to an end of all this, he repeated what he had already said, and indeed what he now said really did follow: *And the Lord God took the man whom he had molded, and placed him in paradise*, and so on (Gn 2:15). The man was placed there after all this was done, as the order of the narrative now shows; it is not that all this was done after the man was placed there,

76. See Rv 7:4; 14:3.

as he might at first have been thought to have said, unless the recapitulation is intelligently observed, by which he went back to matters that had been left out earlier.

53. Again, it said in the same book, when the generations of the sons of Noah were being listed, *These are the sons of Ham in their tribes, according to their languages, in their regions and in their nations* (Gn 10:20). Then after also listing the sons of Shem, it says, *These are the sons of Shem in their tribes, according to their languages in their regions and in their nations.* And it adds about them all, *These are the tribes of the sons of Noah according to their generations, according to their nations. And from these the islands*[77] *of the nations were scattered over the earth after the flood. And the whole earth was one lip and one voice for all* (Gn 10:32—11:1). And so this bit added at the end, *And the whole earth was one lip and one voice for all,* that is, they all had one language, seems to be said as though still at the time in which they were scattered over the earth according to the islands of the nations they all had one common language, which undoubtedly conflicts with what was said a few words earlier on, *in their tribes, according to their languages.* After all, the various tribes would not have been said to have had each their own language, which made them into each their own nation, when they all had one common language.

And thus we see that it was by way of recapitulation that he added, *And the whole earth was one lip and one voice for all,* with the narrative going back imperceptibly to tell us how it came about that from having one language, they were divided by many.[78] And straightaway the story is told of the building of that tower, where this punishment for pride was meted out to them by God's judgment, after which they were scattered through the earth according to their languages.

54. There can be even more obscure cases of this recapitulation, as where in the gospel the Lord says, *On the day that Lot came out of Sodom, he rained down fire from heaven and destroyed them all; that is how the day of the Son of Man will be, on which he is revealed. In that hour, whoever is on the roof, and his tools in the house, let him not come down to fetch them; and whoever is in the field, let him likewise not come back. Let him remember Lot's wife* (Lk 17:29–32). Is it really only when the Lord is revealed that these things have to be observed, that one should not look back, should not hanker, that is, for the past mode of life one has renounced, and not rather during this present time, so that when the Lord is revealed

---

77. Faithfully translating the Greek Septuagint, which mysteriously inserts these islands here. I have kept the whole translation of the biblical text here absolutely literal. But it must have sounded as peculiar in the Latin as it does in the English.

78. Augustine was unable to explain this incoherence, and others like it, in the way modern commentators will, by observing that Gn 10 and 11 each comes from a different original source or narrative, which a final editor stitched together without worrying about such little inconsistencies: in this case, Gn 10 from the priestly narrative, P; Gn 11 from the earlier Yahwist narrative, J.

due retribution may be awarded according to what each one has observed or ignored? And yet because it says, *In that hour,* one would naturally think that these things are to be observed at the moment when the Lord is revealed, unless one's senses were alert while reading to understand a case of recapitulation.

We are helped to do this by another text which cried out, still in the time of the apostles, *Children, it is the last hour* (1 Jn 2:18). So the very time during which the gospel is being preached, up until the Lord is revealed, is the hour in which these things have to be observed, because that revelation of the Lord belongs itself to the same hour, which will come to its end on the day of judgment.[79]

37, 55. Tychonius' seventh and last rule is "about the devil and his body." He too, after all, is a head, but of the ungodly, who are after a fashion his body, and going to go with him into the torment of eternal fire, just as Christ is *the head of the Church, which is his body* (Eph 1:22), that will be with him in the kingdom and everlasting glory. So just as with the first rule, which he calls *about the Lord and his body,* one has to be on the alert to understand, when scripture is speaking about one and the same person, what fits the head and what the body; in the same way too with this last rule, something can sometimes be said against the devil which could more properly be acknowledged as not referring to him so much as to his body. He has this, not only in those who are manifestly *outsiders* (1 Cor 5:12), but also in those who, while belonging to him, are for a time mixed up in the Church, until each one departs this life, or the chaff is separated from the wheat at the final winnowing.

What is written in Isaiah, for example: *How he has fallen from heaven, Lucifer rising in the morning,* and the rest, which was all said under the figure of the king of Babylon about or against the same person, is in the actual context of the passage to be understood of course of the devil. And yet what it goes on to say there in the same place, *He has been crushed into the earth, the one who sends to all the nations* (Is 14:12), does not altogether fit the head himself. Because even if it is the devil who sends his angels to all the nations, still it is his body, not himself, that is crushed into the earth—except that he himself is in his body, which on being crushed becomes *dust which the wind chases away from the face of the earth* (Ps 1:4).

56. All these rules, however, except the one which is called "about the promises and the law," result in one thing being understood from another; and this is the peculiarity of figurative speech, which extends far wider than can be all grasped, as far as I can see, by any one person. Because wherever it appears that one thing is said for another to be understood, you have a case of figurative speech, even if the name of that figure is not found in the formal theory of rhetoric. When this occurs where it is usual for it to do so, the understanding can follow without any difficulty. But

79. See Rom 2:5; 13:11.

when it occurs where it is not usual, there is difficulty in understanding it, for some people more, for others less, according as different people have greater or lesser talents from God, or receive more or less help from him.

Accordingly we would remind students of this venerable literature of what we said above in discussing words used in their proper sense, where things are to be understood just as they are stated,[80] and warn them that in the same way in their metaphorical use, which introduces figurative expressions, in which one thing is to be understood from another, which we have now dealt with sufficiently up to this point, as I think, they should familiarize themselves with the kinds of expression employed in the holy scriptures and be on the alert to observe how things are commonly said in them, and to commit it to memory. But much more important than that, and supremely necessary, is that they should pray for understanding. After all, in this very literature which they are eager to study, they read that *the Lord gives wisdom, and from his face come knowledge and understanding* (Prv 2:6). From him indeed it is that they have received their interest and eagerness to study, if it is qualified by loving piety.

But that is enough said now about signs, so far as words are concerned. It remains for me to speak in the next volume what the Lord may grant me to say about communicating the things we come to understand.

---

80. See Book II, 10.

Book IV

*The value of rhetorical skills; but this will not be a textbook
of rhetoric*

1, 1. I originally divided this work of ours, which has the title *Teaching Christianity*, into two parts. After the prologue, in which I gave my answer to those who were going to find fault with it, I said, "There are two things which every treatment of the scriptures should strive for: a way of attaining to an understanding of their meaning, and a way of communicating what has been understood. We shall first discuss how to understand them, and next how to communicate their meaning" (Book I, 1). Because we have already said much about ways of understanding them, and have filled three volumes with this one part, we shall now with the Lord's help say a few things about communication, and so conclude it all, if possible, with one last book, and finish the whole work in four volumes.

2. And so first of all I must preface my remarks by dashing the expectations of any readers, who may think perhaps that I am going to give them the rules of rhetoric which I myself learned and taught in the secular schools. I hereby warn them not to expect such things from me, not because they are of no use at all, but because even if they are of some use, they are to be learned elsewhere, if any good man should chance to have the leisure to study this subject too. Only they should not be looked for from me, either in this work or in any other.

2, 3. Rhetoric, after all, being the art of persuading people to accept something, whether it is true or false, would anyone dare to maintain that truth should stand there without any weapons in the hands of its defenders against falsehood; that those speakers, that is to say, who are trying to convince their hearers of what is untrue, should know how to get them on their side, to gain their attention and have them eating out of their hands by their opening remarks,[1] while these who are defending the truth should not? That those should utter their lies briefly, clearly, plausibly, and these should state their truths in a manner too boring to listen to, too obscure to

---

1.   A rather free paraphrase, I have to admit. He is stating what any public speaker must set out to do from the moment he first opens his mouth; he must render his audience, literally, "benevolent, attentive, and docile."

understand, and finally too repellent to believe? That those should attack the truth with specious arguments, and assert falsehoods, while these should be incapable of either defending the truth or refuting falsehood? That those, to move and force the minds of their hearers into error, should be able by their style to terrify them, move them to tears, make them laugh, give them rousing encouragement, while these on behalf of truth stumble along slow, cold and half asleep?

Could anyone be so silly as to suppose such a thing?[2] So since facilities are available for learning to speak well, which is of the greatest value in leading people either along straight or along crooked ways, why should good men not study to acquire the art, so that it may fight for the truth, if bad men can prostitute it to the winning of their vain and misguided cases in the service of iniquity and error?

3, 4. But be that as it may, whatever the rules whose observance makes for what is called fluency and eloquence, when habitually applied by a skillful tongue in its choice of a wide and colorful vocabulary, they should be learned apart from what I am writing here, in the proper time and place set aside for such work, and at the most suitable age, by those who can learn them quickly. For even the leading lights of Roman eloquence did not hesitate to say that unless you can master this art quickly, you can never master it at all. Whether this is true or not, what need is there for us to decide? For even if they could eventually be mastered by the slower spirits, we do not consider them of such importance that we would wish to impose the learning of them upon men of mature or even venerable age. It is enough that this subject should be the concern of the young, and not even of all of those whom we desire to have educated for the service of the Church, but only of those who are not yet busy with more urgent requirements, which undoubtedly take precedence over this one.[3]

The fact is that, given a bright and eager disposition, eloquence will come more readily to those who read and listen to eloquent speakers than to those who pore over the rules of eloquence. Nor is there any lack of ecclesiastical writers, over and above the canon of scripture that has been

---

2.   A play on words in the Latin: *Quis ita desipiat, ut hoc sapiat?*
3.   This passage bears out my contention in the Translator's Note that the whole work had been undertaken as a kind of manual to help the clergy with their preaching. Augustine does not propose to send the priests and deacons, grown men, back to the schools of rhetoric—though he hopes they may be able to study the subject in their spare time. No, it is the *adolescentes* among the clergy, that is to say the lectors or readers, who were frequently boys in their teens, that could advantageously be sent along to the schools of rhetoric. We must remember that there were no seminaries in those days, and these young lectors would be receiving their "ecclesiastical" education, at least in a Church organized like Augustine's at Hippo Regius, and possibly Aurelius' at Carthage, in a house of clergy from senior priests. And some of them, the older ones, would already be involved in pastoral duties, from which they should not be taken in order to go and study rhetoric.

set for our salvation at the summit of authority, by whose style a capable man will be influenced when he reads them, even if that is not his concern, but he is only interested in what they have to say; and he will put this to good use when he has occasion to write, or dictate, or finally even to preach what he has in mind that accords with piety and the rule of faith.

But if such a disposition is lacking, then these rules of rhetoric cannot be grasped; or even if they can be to some extent and with great effort impressed on a person and understood, they will not be of any use, seeing that those who have learned them and are fluent and attractive speakers cannot all think about them, in order to speak in accordance with them, while they are speaking, unless they are actually discussing them. Indeed I imagine that there are scarcely any of them who can do both at the same time, that is speak well, and in order to do this think about those rules for public speaking while they are speaking. You would have to take care, after all, not to let what you had to say escape your mind, while you were giving all your attention to saying it artistically. And yet in the speeches and the style of eloquent speakers you will find that the rules of eloquence have been implemented, which they were not thinking about either in order to speak, or while they were speaking, and this whether they had learned them formally, or never even encountered them. They implement them because they are eloquent, they do not apply them in order to be eloquent.

5. So then, infants only become speakers by learning the speech and pronunciation of speakers; why cannot people become eloquent without any formal training in the art of public speaking, but simply by reading and hearing the speeches of the eloquent and, as far as they have the chance to follow this up, by imitating them? Why, we have surely all experienced examples of this, have we not? I mean, we know a great many people, quite innocent of the rules of rhetoric, who are much more eloquent than a great many people that have learned them; but we don't know anybody like this who has not read and heard the debates and the style of eloquent speakers.

Even the art of grammar, after all, in which we learn about correctness of speech, would not need to be taught to boys, if they had the good fortune to grow up and live among people who spoke correctly. That is to say, without knowing any of the names of grammatical faults, their own sound habits of speech would enable them to point out and avoid faulty grammar on the lips of any speaker, in the way townspeople, even though illiterate, will find fault with the speech of rustics.

4, 6. The interpreter and teacher of the divine scriptures, therefore, the defender of right faith and the hammer of error, has the duty of both teaching what is good and unteaching what is bad; and in this task of speaking it is his duty to win over the hostile, to stir up the slack, to point out to the ignorant what is at stake and what they ought to be looking for. When, though, he finds them friendly, attentive, willing to learn, or renders them so himself, further tactics have to be employed, as the case requires. If the listeners need to be instructed, this calls for the narrative style, provided, at least, that they need to be informed about the subject being dealt with, while for the clearing up of doubts and the establishment of certainty, reasoned arguments and documentary proofs are needed.[4]

But if the listeners are to be moved rather than instructed, so as not to become sluggish in acting upon what they know, and so as to give a real assent to things they admit are true, more forceful kinds of speaking are called for. Here what is necessary is words that implore, that rebuke, that stir, that check, and whatever other styles may avail to move the audience's minds and spirits. And in fact practically nobody, when it comes to public speaking, neglects doing the things I have said.

5, 7.[5] Some people, of course, do it all in a dull, unattractive and cold sort of way, while others do it with wit, elegance and feeling. In any case, those who can speak and discuss things wisely, even though they cannot do so eloquently, must now undertake the task we are concerned with[6] in such a way as to benefit their listeners, even though less than they would have benefited them if they could also speak eloquently. Beware, on the other hand, of those whose unwisdom has a flood of eloquence at its command, and all the more so, the more their audience takes pleasure in things it is profitless to hear, and assumes that because they hear them speaking fluently, they are are also speaking the truth. This consideration did not even escape those who thought the art of rhetoric was worth teaching; for they admitted that "wisdom without eloquence is of little use to society, while eloquence without wisdom is frequently extremely prejudicial to it, never of any use."[7] If those therefore who have propounded the rules of eloquence have been obliged, in the very books in which they have done this, to make such a confession at the instigation of truth, even though they were ignorant of the true, that is to say the heavenly, wisdom which *comes down from the Father of lights* (Jas 1:17); how much more ought we to have no other opinion, seeing that we are sons and ministers of this wisdom?

Now a person is all the more or the less able to speak wisely, the more or the less progress he has made in the holy scriptures. I don't mean just in reading them frequently and committing them to memory, but in understanding them well and diligently exploring their senses. There are people, after all, who read them and neglect them—read them in order to have them at their finger tips, neglect trying to understand them. Unquestionably far

---

4.   Here he may well have had debates with the Donatists in mind, or talks to Catholics about Donatism; the true story of the original schism had to be told again and again, and appeal to be made to the documents of the case, whether to the court records of the time of Constantine, or also, as the dispute widened to include theological disagreements, to the works of Cyprian.

5.   In the Latin text this section begins with the previous sentence; but the older editors before the Maurists put their chapter division here—I think with better judgment.

6.   That is, in a word, preaching. He is writing for the African clergy, in particular, perhaps, for their bishops.

7.   Cicero, *On Rhetoric* (*De Inventione Rhetorica*) 1, 1.

and away to be preferred to these are people who do not have their words at their finger tips, but can see into the heart of them with the eyes of their own hearts. But better than either is the man who can both quote them at will and understand them as they deserve.

8. For the man, therefore, who has the duty of saying wisely even what he cannot say eloquently, it is supremely necessary that he should have the words of the scriptures at his finger tips.[8] For the poorer he perceives himself to be in his own words, the richer it behooves him to be in those of scripture. In this way he can prove what he says in his own words from the words of scripture, and what carried less weight said in his own words[9] can somehow or other grow weightier with the support of that greater testimony. For though he may not be so good at pleasing his audience by the way he states his point, he will please them by proving it.

There is the man, on the other hand, who wishes to speak not only wisely but eloquently, since he will surely be of more use if he can do both. Him I much prefer to send off to read or listen to eloquent speakers and to practice imitating them, rather than instructing him to devote his time to teachers of the art of rhetoric, provided, that is, that those whom he reads or listens to are genuinely and reliably renowned for having spoken, or for speaking, wisely as well as eloquently. Those, you see, who speak eloquently are listened to with pleasure, those who speak wisely, with wholesome profit. That is why scripture does not say, "A multitude of eloquent men" but *A multitude of wise men is the health of the world* (Wis 6:24). Now just as bitter but wholesome things often have to be taken, so pernicious sweet things have to be shunned. But what could be better than the pleasantly wholesome, or the wholesomely pleasant? The more eagerly, after all, what pleases is sought here, the easier it is for what is wholesome to be imparted. There are, then, churchmen who have commented on the divine utterances not only wisely but also eloquently;[10] it is more a matter of there not being time enough to read them than of their not being available to those who have the will and the leisure to do so.

Examples of eloquent wisdom from biblical authors: Saint Paul

6, 9. Here, no doubt, someone may ask whether our authors, whose divinely inspired writings have provided us with a canon of the most salu-

8. Not entirely consistent with what he has just said in the previous paragraph—he uses the same expression in both places, *verba tenere*. But here he is urging clergymen of the second category of that paragraph, those who see into the heart of the scriptures, to rise to the category of those who can also quote them at will—particularly if they lack the skill of eloquence.
9. *Qui propriis verbis minor erat*, in the text—while he was less in his own words, he can also grow. I emend to *quod propriis verbis minus erat*.
10. Saints Cyprian of Carthage and Ambrose of Milan were his prime models of sound ecclesiastical eloquence; Saint Hilary of Poitiers very definitely in third place.

tary authority, are only to be called wise, or also eloquent. This is indeed a question that it is the easiest thing in the world for me to answer, and for those who agree with what I say in this matter. The fact is that where I understand these authors, it seems to me that not only could there be nothing wiser, but also nothing more eloquent. And I make bold to say that all who rightly understand what these authors are saying also thereby understand that they could not and should not have said it in the least differently. For just as one sort of eloquence goes with youth, while another suits riper years—and it should not in fact be called eloquence if it does not match the person of the speaker—so too there is a kind that becomes men thought worthy of the highest authority and in fact of being called divine. This is the style in which they spoke, and no other becomes them, nor does this one become any other persons. With them it accords perfectly, whereas the more lowly it appears, the higher does it soar above other writers, not by any kind of windiness, but by its very solidity.

Where, however, I do not understand them, their eloquence is indeed less apparent to me, but I do not doubt that it is of the same quality as where I do understand. It was also right for this obscurity of the divine and saving utterances to be mixed in with such clear eloquence, because in order for us to make progress in our understanding we need the mental exercise of wrestling with the text as well as the intellectual satisfaction of discovering what it means.[11]

10. Here are these people, rating their style above the style of our authors because it is more inflated, not because it is grander; well, I could show them all the strengths and graces of eloquence, on which they so preen themselves, in the sacred writings of those authors, whom divine providence has provided us with, to instruct us and transfer us from this crooked age into one of blessedness.[12] But it is not what these men have in common with the orators or poets of the Gentiles that delights me more than I can say in their style of eloquence. What really amazes and astonishes me is that through another kind of eloquence of their own they employed this eloquence of ours[13] in such a way that it was neither lacking nor obtrusive in their writings, because it was important that it should be neither rejected nor paraded by them. The first would be true if they avoided it altogether, the second could be thought to be the case, if it was too easily recognized in their writings. And in those passages where it can perhaps be detected by the learned, such things are being said that the words they are said with seem to spring spontaneously from the subject matter, rather than to be contributed by the writer, so that you could almost imagine wisdom stepping out from her own house, that is from the breast of the wise man, followed by eloquence as her inseparable, even if uninvited, lady in waiting.

---

11. A rather wordy paraphrase of an excessively succinct, and hence obscure, sentence. For the thought, see Book II, 7–8 above.
12. See Col 1:13.
13. Here "ours" means that of the Gentile—Latin—classics.

7, 11. Could anybody fail to see, for example, what the apostle was wishing to say here, and how wisely he said it: *We glory in tribulations, knowing that tribulation results in patience, patience in approbation, approbation in hope, while hope does not confound, because the love of God has been poured out in our hearts through the Holy Spirit which has been given to us* (Rom 5:3–5)? Were any inexpert expert, if I may so put it, to maintain that here the apostle was observing the rules of the art of rhetoric, would he not be laughed out of court by Christians both learned and unlearned? And yet one can here observe the figure of speech which in Greek is called *klimax*, while in Latin some people called it *gradatio*, because they were unwilling to say "ladder"; when words or meanings are linked together, one being spun from another, as here we can see patience spun from tribulation, approbation from patience, hope from approbation.

There is also another embellishment to be observed, that after some phrases, each terminated by a pause,[14] which our people call "clauses" or just "phrases," while the Greeks call them *kolons* and *kommas*, there follows a round or circuit, which they call a *periodos*, whose clauses are held in suspense by the voice of the speaker, until it ends with the last of them. Thus the first of the clauses that precede the period[15] is *that tribulation results in patience*, the second is *patience in approbation*, the third *approbation in hope*. Then the period is joined on, consisting of three clauses, of which the first is *while hope does not confound*, the second *because the love of God has been poured out in our hearts*, the third *through the Holy Spirit which has been given to us*. Now this is the sort of thing that is taught in courses on the art of eloquence. So while we are not saying that the apostle deliberately observed the rules of eloquence, we are still not denying that eloquence waited upon his wisdom.

12. Writing to the Corinthians in the second letter, he confuted certain people, who were pseudo-apostles from the Jews, and were slighting him; and because he is obliged to blow his own trumpet, he puts this down to himself as folly—and how wisely he says it, and how eloquently! But he does it as the companion of wisdom, the leader of eloquence, following the former, going ahead of the latter, and not spurning her as she follows: *Again I say it*, he declares, *let nobody take me for a fool; or else accept me as a fool, so that I too may do a little boasting. In what I have to say I am not speaking according to God, but as in a fit of folly, in this serious matter of boasting. Since many, indeed, are boasting according to the flesh, I too will boast. For you suffer fools gladly, being so wise yourselves. For you*

---

14. Literally, "by a voice of pronunciation," *pronuntiationis voce*; presumably a technical use of the word *pronuntiatio*. Here and in the rest of this section the allusions are mostly to Cicero and Quintilian, the arch-grammarian. Most English names for the figures of speech referred to derive from the Greek rather than the Latin, and have come to signify punctuation marks, which the ancients quite innocent of, rather than kinds of phrase.

15. The first of the *kolons* that precede the round, or period.

put up with it if anyone reduces you to slavery, if anyone swallows you up, if anyone takes you in, if anyone pushes himself forward, if anyone slaps you in the face. I am speaking in an ignoble way, as though we too have grown weak. But in whatever respect anyone puts on a bold face—I speak in folly—I do so too. Are they Hebrews? I am too. Are they Israelites? I am too. Are they the seed of Abraham? I am too. Are they ministers of Christ? I speak as a fool—I am more so. In labors endlessly, in prisons more frequently, in beatings beyond measure, at the point of death more often. From the Jews five times have I received forty strokes less one. Three times have I been beaten with rods, once I have been stoned, three times shipwrecked. I have been a night and a day in the depth of the sea. Often on journeys in danger of rivers, in danger of robbers, in danger from my kin, in danger from the nations, in danger in the city, in danger in the wild, in danger in the sea, in danger among false brethren; in toil and distress, too often going without sleep, in hunger and thirst, too often fasting, in cold and nakedness; apart from those outward matters, the daily assault on me, my anxiety for all the churches. Who is weakening, and I do not feel weak? Who is being scandalized, and I am not on fire? If boasting is required, I will boast about what concerns my weakness (2 Cor 11:16–30). Wide-awake readers can see with what wisdom all this is said; with what a flow of eloquence it all runs will be noticed even by someone who is snoring.

13. In fact, though, anyone who knows about it will acknowledge that these phrases which the Greeks call *kommas*, and the clauses and periods which I discussed a short while ago, being woven together with the most seemly variety, are what constitute the whole beauty of this passage, and its very countenance as it were, which moves and delights even the unlearned. Thus at the point where I began to insert this passage, there are some periods. The first is the smallest, consisting of two clauses; periods, you see, cannot have fewer than two clauses, though they can have more. So this was the first: *Again I say it, let nobody take me for a fool.* There follows another of three clauses: *Or else, accept me as a fool, so that I too may do a little boasting.*[16] The one that follows in the third place has four members: *In what I have to say, I am not speaking according to God, but as in a fit of folly, in this serious matter of boasting.* The fourth has two: *Since many indeed are boasting according to the flesh, I too will boast.* And the fifth has two: *For you suffer fools gladly, being so wise yourselves.* The sixth also is of two clauses: *For you put up with it, if anyone reduces you to slavery.*[17]

There follow three phrases: *If anyone swallows you up, if anyone takes you in, if anyone pushes himself forward.* Then three clauses: *If anyone slaps you in the face, I am speaking in an ignoble way, as though we too*

---

16. The first clause, or *membrum*, here is, I think, the single word *Alioquin*, Or else.
17. From here on his analysis at times seems very idiosyncratic. But he was, unlike his translator, a trained rhetorician! Also, however, again unlike his translator, he did not have the benefit of punctuation in his texts.

have grown weak. A three-clause period is added: *But in whatever respect aynyone puts on a bold face—I speak in folly—I do so too.* From this point he now puts three phrases as short questions, and again three phrases in answer: *Are they Hebrews? I am too. Are they Israelites? I am too. Are they the seed of Abraham? I am too.* To the fourth phrase put as a question he replies, not with a counter-phrase, but with a counter-clause: *Are they ministers of Christ? I speak as a fool—I am more so.* Now the four following phrases tumble out, the question and answer form being very suitably dropped: *In labors endlessly, in prisons more frequently, in beatings beyond measure, at the point of death more often.* Then a brief period is inserted, which has to be divided by a slight pause: *From the Jews five times,* so that that is one clause, to which the next is tied on: *have I received forty strokes less one.* Then there is a return to phrases, and three are put down: *Three times have I been beaten with rods, once I have been stoned, three times shipwrecked.* There follows a single clause: *I have been a night and a day in the depth of the sea.*

Next fourteen phrases come flowing out with a most becoming force: *Often on journeys, in danger of rivers, in danger of robbers, in danger from my kin, in danger from the nations, in danger in the city, in danger in the wild, in danger in the sea, in danger among false brethren; in toil and distress, too often going without sleep, in hunger and thirst, too often fasting, in cold and nakedness.* After that he inserts a three-clause period: *Apart from those outward matters, the daily assault on me, my anxiety for all the churches.* And to this he adds two clauses as rhetorical questions: *Who is weakening, and I do not feel weak? Who is being scandalized, and I am not on fire?* Finally, this whole breathless passage ends with a two-clause period: *If boasting is required, I will boast about what concerns my weakness.*

But it is quite impossible to find words to express how neat and pleasing it is, that after this energetic, forceful flood of words he should somehow come to rest, and bring his hearers to rest in a little narrative that he inserts. He goes on to say, you see, *The God and Father of our Lord Jesus Christ, who is blessed for ever, knows that I am not lying* (2 Cor 11:31). And then he tells very, very briefly how he had been in peril and how he had escaped.

14. It would take too long to go through the rest of the passage, or to demonstrate these things from other places in the holy scriptures. And what if I had also chosen to point out the figures of speech this art teaches, which are to be found at least in these texts I have quoted to illustrate the apostle's eloquence?[18] Would not serious people readily conclude[19] that I was going beyond what any student might think sufficient? All these

---

18. All he has done so far is analyze the eloquent structure of the passages quoted; he has not noted the apostle's use of such figures of speech as irony, metaphor, hyperbole—or, in English, underand over-statement, comparisons, and so forth.
19. I have supplied some such word as *existimarent*; the text does seem defective here.

things, when taught by professionals, are highly regarded, are bought at a high price, sold with high-flown self-advertisement. This is the kind of self-advertisement I too fear I may reek of, while I am holding forth like this. But I had to answer those less than learned people who think our authors are to be lightly dismissed, not because they lack, but because they do not parade, the eloquence of which these people are altogether too fond.

Examples from biblical authors: Amos

15. But perhaps you may think I have chosen the apostle Paul as being our only eloquent writer. Where he says, after all, *Even if unskilled in speaking, but not in knowledge* (2 Cor 11:6), he seems in speaking that way to have been granting his detractors something for the sake of argument, not to have been admitting it as if it were really true. If he had said, "Unskilled indeed in speaking, but not in knowledge," it could only have been understood as meaning what it said. He certainly did not hesitate to claim knowledge, without which he would never have qualified as *teacher of the nations* (1 Tm 2:7). Certainly, if we are offering anything of his as an example of eloquence, we do it, naturally, from those letters which were admitted even by his detractors, who wanted his speech when present in person to be considered beneath contempt, to be *weighty and forceful* (2 Cor 10:10).[20]

So I see that I must say something also about the eloquence of the prophets, where many things are veiled under a figurative manner of speech. The more thoroughly indeed they seem to be wrapped up under metaphorical expressions, the sweeter they taste when they are finally unpacked.[21] Here, however, where I quote such a passage, I am not to be required to expound what is said, but only to draw attention to the way it is said. And I will do this most effectively from the book of that prophet who said he was a shepherd or herdsman, and was taken away from that by God and sent to prophesy to God's people. I will not take it, however, from the version of the Seventy translators,[22] who were also divinely inspired in their translation, and for that reason appear to have said some things rather differently from the original, in order to encourage the reader to concentrate on searching out the spiritual sense, which is why much of their text is more obscure, because couched in more figurative language. Instead I will quote it as translated from Hebrew into Latin speech by the presbyter Jerome, who was well versed in both languages.

---

20. He forgets that one of his selected passages came from Romans.
21. See above, Book II, 7.
22. The Greek Septuagint, or LXX for short. I think this may be the only place in which he states a preference for Jerome's Vulgate over earlier versions based on the Septuagint—perhaps as a kind of posthumous olive-branch to that redoubtable man, who had died in 420.

16. So then, when this rustic prophet, or rustic turned prophet, was attacking the godless, the proud, the lovers of luxury, who were thereby utterly neglectful of the demands of brotherly love, he cried out with the words, *Woe to you who are opulent in Sion, and place your trust in the mountain of Samaria, aristocrats, heads of peoples, pompously pacing into the house of Israel! Pass over to Calneh and see, and go from there to Hamath the great; and go down to Gath of the Philistines, and to each of their best kingdoms, if their boundaries are wider than your boundaries. You that have been set apart for the evil day, and are drawing near to the throne of iniquity; who sleep on beds of ivory and sport wantonly on your quilts; who eat lamb from the flock and veal from the midst of the herd; who sing to the voice of the psaltery. They imagined they had instruments of song like David, drinking wine in goblets and smearing themselves with the finest ointments; and they felt nothing for the grinding down of Joseph* (Am 6:1–6).

Would these so-called learned and well-spoken people, who despise our prophets as unlettered men unfamiliar with eloquence, would they really have wished to say that differently, if they had to say anything of the sort to that sort of persons—those of them, that is, who would not have liked to be thought crazy?

17. What more, after all, could sober ears desire than this piece of eloquence? First of all, with what a roar is that invective hurled at, so to say, sleep-sodden senses to make them wake up! *Woe to you who are opulent in Sion, and place your trust in the mountain of Samaria, aristocrats, heads of peoples, pompously pacing into the house of Israel!* Next, to show how ungrateful they were for God's favors in giving them ample lands for their kingdom, since they were placing their trust in the mountain of Samaria, where of course they were worshiping idols, *Pass over*, he says, *to Calneh and see, and go from there to Hamath the great; and go down to Gath of the Philistines, and to each of their best kingdoms, if their boundaries are wider than your boundaries.* Simultaneously with this point being made, the utterance is decorated with place names as with lights: Sion, Samaria, Calneh, Hamath the great, and Gath of the Philistines. And then the words which are connected to these places have such a nice variety: "are opulent," "place your trust," "pass over," "go," "go down."

18. It goes on to announce that the captivity which is to be experienced under an iniquitous king is drawing near, when it adds, *You that have been set apart for the evil day, and are drawing near to the throne of iniquity.* Then it details the love of luxury that deserved this: *Who sleep on beds of ivory and sport wantonly on your quilts; who eat lamb from the flock and veal from the midst of the herd.* These six clauses have been set out in three two-clause periods. For he did not say, "You that have been set apart for the evil day, you that are drawing near to the throne of iniquity, you that sleep on beds of ivory, you that sport wantonly on your quilts, you that eat lamb from the flock, you that eat veal from the midst of the herd." If it were said

like that, it would indeed be very fine, with all six clauses flowing along from the one pronominal phrase repeated each time, and each indicated by the reciter's inflection. But it has turned out much finer, with their being connected to the same pronoun in pairs, and so unfolding themselves in three sentences; one concerned with foretelling the captivity: *You that have been set apart for the evil day, and are drawing near to the throne of iniquity*; the next with lechery: *Who sleep on beds of ivory, and sport wantonly on your quilts*; while the third is concerned with gluttony: *Who eat*, he says, *lamb from the flock, and veal from the midst of the herd*. Thus it remains the reciter's choice whether to make six clauses by closing each one, or whether to raise his voice slightly at the first and third and fifth, and by threading the second onto the first, the fourth onto the third and the sixth onto the fifth, to make three of the neatest two-clause periods—one pointing to the imminent catastrophe, the next to the unchaste bed, the third to the wastefully lavish table.

19. Next he savages the self-indulgent pleasure of the ears.[23] Now music can be wisely engaged in by the wise; so after saying, *Who sing to the voice of the psaltery*, with a marvelous, beautiful finesse he eased off the violence of his invective, and went on now to speak not to them but about them, as a reminder to us to distinguish between a wise man's music and that of a self-indulgent man. So he did not say, "who sing to the voice of the psaltery, and imagine you have instruments of song like David"; but first he told them what the self-indulgent needed to hear: *Who sing to the voice of the psaltery*; and then, to point out somehow to others their ignorant vulgarity, he added, *They imagined they had instruments of song like David, drinking wine in goblets, and smearing themselves with the finest ointments*. These three clauses are best recited if the voice is slightly raised after the first two, and the period is brought to an end by dropping the voice at the third.

20. We come finally to what concludes all this: *And they felt nothing for the grinding down of Joseph*; it can be said in a continuous breath, as one clause, or more elegantly divided by a pause after *and they felt nothing*, and then with this distinction made, rounded off by *for the grinding down of Joseph* as a two-clause period. But in either case, it was an admirably charming touch that he did not say, "And they felt nothing for the grinding down of their brother," but instead of "their brother" put *Joseph*. In this way you could take any brother at all as being signified by the proper name of that one whose fame stood out among his brethren, whether in the evils he suffered at their hands or in the good he repaid them with.[24] Whether

---

23. Which Augustine himself, so he tells us, was all too prone to indulge. See *Confessions* X, 33.

24. He is alluding to the story of Joseph and his brothers here, Gn 37, 39—45. But Amos in all probability simply meant the northern kingdom of Israel by the name "Joseph," its two principal tribes being those descended from Joseph's sons, Ephraim and Manasseh; see Gn 48. Augustine alludes to him with a play on words which I cannot reproduce in English: *vel in malis quae pendit, vel in*

indeed this trope, by which we are led to understand any brother you like in Joseph, is propounded in that art of rhetoric which I both learned and taught, I do not know.[25] What a beautiful touch it is, though, and how it moves those who read and appreciate it, there is no point in anybody being told, if he cannot perceive it for himself.

21. And there are yet more things indeed, relating to the rules of eloquence, which can be discovered in this very same passage that we have presented as an example. But the good listener will not so much be instructed by its being diligently analyzed as fired by its being passionately recited. It was not, after all, composed by mere human industry, but it poured out as a divine message both wisely and eloquently from the prophet's mind, its wisdom not being preoccupied with eloquence, but its eloquence not withdrawing from wisdom. For if, as some of the most eloquent and percipient of men have been able to see and have said, things that appear to be learned in the art of oratory would never have been observed and noted down and put into form as this systematic doctrine, unless they had first been there in the minds and natural capacities of the orators,[26] small wonder, surely, if they are there to be found in these men, who were sent by the maker of minds and natural capacities. Accordingly, let us acknowledge that our canonical authors and teachers were indeed eloquent as well as being wise, with the kind of eloquence that befitted persons of that category.

Further suggestions and advice for preachers

8, 22. But while we have taken some examples of eloquence from their writings which can be understood without difficulty, we certainly must not think that they are to be imitated by us in those things which they said with a useful and salutary obscurity, to exercise and after a fashion to hone the minds of readers, and to break the fastidious habits[27] and whet the appetite of those who are eager to learn, while also casting a veil over[28] the minds of the ungodly, whether to prompt their conversion to a more God-fearing frame of mind, or to ensure their exclusion from sacred mysteries. Those prophets did in fact speak in such a way that later generations, who would

---

bonis quae rependit. You can pay penalties in English, in the sense he uses *pendit* here, but not evils.

25. Why doesn't he know? Perhaps because it was so long since he had taught rhetoric. But this profession of ignorance is really just another device for insinuating that it is not really necessary formally to study the art of rhetoric in a school of rhetoric.

26. In their *ingenia*, a word for which there seems to be no good English equivalent. These eloquent and percipient men could doubtless be reduced to Cicero and Quintilian.

27. *Ad rumpenda fastidia.* I take it he is remembering his own fastidiousness as a conceited young rhetorician, which had blocked his appreciation of the scriptures, owing to the "rusticity" of their Latin.

28. Reading *velandos* for the *celandos*, covering, of the text, there being, I take it, an allusion to 2 Cor 3:15.

understand them rightly and expound them, would be able to uncover the other kind of grace, different indeed, but following upon the first kind[29] in the Church of God.

Their expositors, therefore, should not speak in the same sort of way, as though putting themselves forward with a similar authority to be expounded; but in all their commentaries and sermons they should first and foremost and supremely work away at being intelligible with what[30] lucidity of diction they can muster. It is important that the cause of what we say being less readily or easily understood should not lie in our manner of speaking, but that it should be attributable either to the person who does not understand being very slow-witted, or to the things we are wishing to explain and point out being so difficult and subtle.

9, 23. For there are some things, in fact, which of their very nature are hard or impossible to understand, however much and in whatever way, as plainly as you like, they are gone over and analyzed by the speaker; and such things are only rarely, if there is some urgent need, or absolutely never to be presented in the hearing of the people. It is another matter though with books, which are so written that they hold the reader's attention when they are understood, and when they are not understood need not vex those who decline to read them. In conversations, too, with some people we should not shirk the duty of helping them to understand truths which we ourselves have already grasped, however hard they are to understand, and however laborious the effort of discussing them may be. That is, of course, if our listeners, or those we are having a conversation with, evince an eager desire to learn and do not lack the mental capacity in some way or other to grasp what is being suggested. In this case the teacher has to worry, not about how eloquently he is teaching, but how convincing his evidence is.

10, 24. A diligent quest for such evidence is sometimes neglectful of the more polished words, and is interested, not in those that sound well, but in those that indicate and suggest what the speaker wishes to prove. So a certain authority, when dealing with this kind of speech, says that there is to be found in it a certain "diligent negligence."[31] This, however, while cutting out embellishments, does not go so far as to cultivate the uncouth. Good teachers, though, will or should be so concerned with teaching, that if a word can only be correct Latin if it is obscure or ambiguous, while in common speech it has an incorrect form that avoids ambiguity or obscurity, they will speak it in the way the uneducated, not the way educated people are used to. For if our translators did not shrink from saying, *I will not assemble their conventicles from bloods* (Ps 16:4), since they felt it was

---

29. Following upon the law, which the prophets were sent to remind Israel of.
30. Reading with M, *ea quantum possunt perspicuitate dicendi*, instead of CCL's *et quantum possunt*. This would attach the phrase to the next clause/sentence, in which the main verb has been changed rather carelessly from the third to the first person plural.
31. Cicero, *The Orator* 23, 75.

pertinent to the context to put this noun in the plural, though in the Latin language it is only used in the singular,[32] why should the dedicated teacher, speaking to the unlearned, shrink from saying *ossum* rather than *os*,[33] to avoid the single syllable being thought to belong to the plural *ora* rather than to the plural *ossa*, when African ears cannot distinguish between short and long vowels?

What is the point, after all, of correctness of speech which the hearers are unable to follow and understand, seeing that there is absolutely no point in speaking at all, if the people do not understand, whom we are speaking to precisely in order that they may understand? So the person who is teaching will avoid all words that do not in fact teach; and if instead of them he can correctly use others that are understood, he will prefer to choose them. But if he cannot, either because there are none such, or because they do not occur to him at that moment, he will also use words that are not so correct, provided the matter itself is being taught and learned correctly.

25. And it is not indeed only in conversation, whether with one or several persons, but also and above all in preaching to the people, that we should make every effort to be understood. In conversations, after all, everyone has the chance to ask questions. But where all are silent so that one may be heard, and all faces are turned expectantly toward him, neither custom nor good manners allow anyone to ask about what they have not understood; and for that reason the speaker should take every care to help the silent listener.

For the multitude greedy for knowledge usually indicates by its movements whether it has understood; and until it does so, the matter in hand should be gone over with every possible variety of approach and utterance. Now this is something that is simply not in the power of those who recite sermons they have prepared and learned by heart, word for word. As soon, though, as it is evident that the point has been understood, the preacher should either stop, or pass on to another point. For just as a speaker who clears up things people want to know is welcome, so too one who drums in things they already know is burdensome—to those listeners, at least, whose whole expectation was hanging on the solution of the difficulties in the matters being set before them. Because if you also aim at giving the

---

32. The word "bloods," *sanguinibus* in the Latin. In fact the translators both of the Latin from the Greek and of the Greek from the Hebrew were simply being excessively literal, and not worried very much about the result being somewhat meaningless. No doubt they assumed, as Augustine did, that this indicated the divine mysteriousness of the text, and was grist to the mill of those seeking spiritual meanings.

33. A bone. As a matter of fact, Lewis & Short, under *os*, does give *ossum* as a "collateral form," on the authority of Varro; but perhaps Varro quoted it as a vulgar solecism. Since African ears did not, as Augustine goes on to say, distinguish short from long syllables, they might understand *os* to mean a mouth (plural *ora*) rather than a bone (plural *ossa*). See Book III, note 5, 6, and 7.

audience pleasure, you can also say things they already know very well; but here it is not what is said, but the way it is said that holds their attention.

But if the hearers are already familiar with this too, and enjoy it, then it makes almost no difference whether the speaker is reading it aloud, or saying it of his own. It is the common experience, after all, that things that are well written are not only read with enjoyment by those who come to them for the first time, but also do not fail to be enjoyed when read again by those who know them and whose memory of them has not faded away. Such writings, of course, are also listened to with pleasure by both kinds of person. But when people are reminded of what they have already forgotten, they are being taught.

However, I am not now discussing ways of pleasing an audience; I am talking about how those who wish to learn are to be taught. This is done in the best way when listeners both hear something true and understand what they hear. When this end is attained, the point should not be labored any further as though it had to go on and on being taught; perhaps, though, they need to be urged to take it to heart and remember it. If that seems to be the case, it must be done discreetly, to avoid irritating and boring them.

11, 26. Precisely this is eloquence, then, in the matter of teaching: to ensure, not that what was thought repellent should be found to be pleasing, or that something disliked should still be done, but that a point that was obscure or simply missed should be indicated and cleared up. If this is done, however, in a disagreeable way, only a few listeners will get any profit from it, and those the most serious, who are eager to know what there is to be learned, however dismally and crudely it is expressed. When they have attained this object, they feed enjoyably on truth itself; it is indeed the characteristic trait of good minds and dispositions to love in words what is true, not the words themselves.

What, after all, is the use of a golden key if it cannot open what we want, or what is wrong with a wooden key if it can, since all we are looking for is that closed doors should be opened to us? But yes, there is a certain similarity between feeding and learning; so because so many people are fussy and fastidious, even those foodstuffs without which life cannot be supported need their pickles and spices.

Three functions of eloquence: to teach, to delight, to sway

12, 27. An eloquent man once said, you see, and what he said was true, that to be eloquent you should speak "so as to teach, to delight, to sway." Then he added, "Teaching your audience is a matter of necessity, delighting them a matter of being agreeable, swaying them a matter of victory."[34] Of these three, the one put first, that is the necessity of teaching, is to be

---

34. Cicero, *The Orator* 21, 69: *ut doceat, ut delectet, ut flectat; docere necessitatis est, delectare suavitatis, flectere victoriae.* In fact Cicero wrote *ut probet* etc…; *probare necessitatis est*…—a slightly more stringent requirement than *docere*.

found in the things we are saying, the remaining two in the way we say it. Therefore the person who is saying something with the intention of teaching should not consider he has yet said anything of what he wants to the person he wishes to teach, so long as he is not understood. Because even if he has said something he understands himself, he is not to be regarded as having said it to the person he is not understood by, while if he has been understood, he has said it, whatever his way of saying it may have been.

If on the other hand he also wishes to delight the person he is saying it to, or to sway him, he will not succeed in doing so whatever his way of saying it may have been; but in order to do so, it makes all the difference how he says it. Now just as the listener needs to be delighted if you are to hold his attention and keep him listening, so he needs to be swayed, if you are to move him to act. And just as he is delighted if you speak agreeably, so in the same way he is swayed if he loves what you promise him, fears what you threaten him with, hates what you find fault with, embraces what you commend to him, deplores what you strongly insist is deplorable; if he rejoices over what you declare to be a matter for gladness, feels intense pity for those whom your words present to his very eyes as objects of pity, shuns those whom in terrifying tones you proclaim are to be avoided; and anything else that can be done by eloquence in the grand manner to move the spirits of the listeners, not to know what is to be done, but to do what they already know is to be done.

28. But if they still do not know, they must, of course, be taught before being moved. And perhaps when they are simply informed of the matters in hand, they will be moved in such a way that there is no need for them to be moved any more by greater eloquence of a more forceful kind. When there is a need of this, however, it must be done; and the need arises precisely then, when they know what should be done, and do not do it. And thus teaching is a matter of necessity. People, after all, are able both to act and not to act upon what they know; who though would ever say that they should act upon what they do not know? And that is why swaying an audience is not a matter of necessity, because it is not always needed, if the listener gives his full assent to the person who is teaching, or also delighting him. The reason, though, why it is a matter of victory is that an audience can be taught and delighted, and still not give their full assent to the speaker. And what use will those two be if this third thing is lacking?

But neither is delighting an audience a matter of necessity, seeing that when things that are true are being pointed out in a speech, which is what the function of teaching is about, it is not the concern of the speaker, nor is it expected of him, that either his matter or his speech should give delight; but his matter by itself, being true, delights simply by being shown to be so. Which is why it frequently happens that even falsehoods give delight when they are convincingly laid bare and revealed to an audience. It is not because they are false, you see, that they delight, but because it is true that they are false, the speech by which this is shown to be true also gives delight.

13, 29. There are, however, fastidious people who do not take pleasure in the truth if it is presented in any old fashion, but only if it is presented in such a way that the speaker's style too is pleasing; and that is why no slight place in the art of eloquence is also allotted to the function of giving delight. Adding it, all the same, is not enough for the hardened cases who do not profit either from having understood or from having been delighted by the style of the person teaching them. What good, after all, do these two things do the man, who both admits that what has been said is true, and has high praise for the speech it has been said in, and still does not yield that full assent, which is the only thing the speaker is concentrating his attention on, when he is trying by what he says to persuade to a particular course of action?

For if the things that are being taught are of the kind which it is sufficent to believe or know, consenting to them simply means admitting that they are true. When, however, something is being taught that has to be done, and is precisely being taught so that it may be done, in vain does the way and style in which it is said give pleasure, if it is not put across in such a way that action follows. It is the duty, therefore, of the eloquent church-man, when he is trying to persuade the people about something that has to be done, not only to teach, in order to instruct them; not only to delight, in order to hold them; but also to sway, in order to conquer and win them. There still remains, in fact, that type to be swayed by eloquence in the grand manner to give his full assent, in whom that result has not been produced by his admitting the truth of what has been demonstrated, even when this has been done in the most agreeable style.

14, 30. There are so many base and evil things that, so far from being practiced, should on the contrary be shunned and detested; and yet there are people who have spent so much effort upon this matter of an agreeable style that they have presented such things with the most persuasive elo-quence to base and evil men, not for them to give them their consent, but simply and solely for the delectable pleasure of reading about them over and over again.[35] But may God spare his Church from experiencing what the prophet Jeremiah states about the synagogue of the Jews, when he says, *Amazement and horrid things have come upon the land; prophets were prophesying iniquity, and priests clapped their hands in applause, and my people loved it thus. And what will you do in the future?* (Jer 5:30–31). Oh what eloquence, all the more terrifying for being so simple, and all the more forcefully effective for being so down to earth! Oh indeed *an axe splitting the rocks* (Jer 23:29)! For that is what God himself, through this very prophet, said that his word is like, which he has pronounced through his holy prophets.

---

35. He presumably has in mind the stylish and elegant pornography which is what much of Latin literature was, or would certainly have seemed to be in his eyes—all those passages in the Loeb editions which the translators have left untranslated.

And so, far be it, far be it from us that priests should applaud those who utter iniquity, and that the people of God should love it thus. Far from us, I repeat, be such madness; for what shall we do in the future? And certainly, let the things that are said among us be less understood, less pleasing, less moving; but at least let things that are true and just be said, not iniquity be listened to gladly—which assuredly would not happen, if it were not put forward agreeably.

31. But a grave and serious-minded people, of whom it is said to the Lord, *In a grave people I will praise you* (Ps 35:18), will not even find delight in that kind of agreeable style, which is not indeed uttering iniquity, but is decking out slight and fragile goods with a frothy crest of words, of a kind that not even great and enduring matters should be decently and seriously embellished with. There is something of this sort in a letter of the most blessed Cyprian; and the reason I think it occurred, or was deliberately produced, was so that posterity might know precisely what great tongue had been recalled from this superfluous excess by the soundness of Christian teaching, and confined to a graver and more moderate eloquence, such as can be safely admired in his later letters, and religiously emulated, though achieved only with the greatest difficulty. So he says in one passage:

> Let us occupy this seat; the neighboring arbors provide us with privacy; here, while the wandering loops of tendrils wind their way in drooping twists and knots round the canes that carry them, the leafy roof has made a porch of the vine.[36]

This is all said, to be sure, with a marvelously copious and fertile fluency, but it offends against proper gravity with its over-lavish profusion. Those who like this sort of thing, though, will automatically assume that authors who do not say things in this way, but speak in a more restrained manner, are unable to speak in this way, not that they show good judgment by avoiding the style. That is why this holy man both showed that he could speak like this, because he did so on one occasion, and also that he did not choose to, because he never did so again on any other.

Pray before preaching

15, 32. And so this eloquent speaker of ours is at pains, when he has just and good and holy things to say—he ought not, after all, to be saying anything else; so he is at pains to ensure as far as he can, when he says these things, that his listeners understand them, enjoy them, obey them. And he should not be in the slightest doubt that if he can ensure this, and to the extent that he can, it is more the piety of prayer than the ready facility of orators that enables him to do so; by praying then both for himself and for

---

36. Cyprian, *To Donatus* 1 (3, 12–14 H)

those he is about to address, let him be a pray-er before being a speaker.[37] At the very moment he steps up to speak, before he even opens his mouth and says a word, let him lift up his thirsty soul to God, begging that it may belch forth what it has quaffed, or pour out what it he has filled it with.

About any of the matters, after all, that have to be dealt with in terms of faith and love, there are many things that can be said, and many ways they can be said in by those who are well versed in such work; but who knows what is the right thing for us to say, or for someone to hear from us, at precisely this time, but the one who can see into the hearts of us all? And who can ensure that we say what is needed and in the way it is needed, but the one *in whose hands are both we and our words* (Wis 7:16)? This being so, by all means let the man, who wishes both to know and to teach, learn all the things that are to be taught, and acquire proficiency in speaking, as befits a man of the Church. But at the actual moment he is due to speak, let him reflect that what really suits the good mind much better is what the Lord said: *Do not give thought to how or to what you are to speak; for it will be given to you in that hour what you are to speak; for it is not you who are speaking, but the Spirit of your Father who is speaking in you* (Mt 10:19–20). So if the Holy Spirit is speaking in those who are handed over to the persecutors on Christ's account, why not also in those who are handing Christ over to the learners?

16, 33. But anyone who says that people do not need to be given rules about what or how they should teach, if the Holy Spirit is making them teachers, can also say that we do not need to pray either, because the Lord said, *Your Father knows what you need before you ask it of him* (Mt 6:8); or that the apostle Paul should not have instructed Timothy and Titus on how they were to instruct others—three letters of the apostle, by the way, which anyone charged with the role of teacher in the Church ought always to have before his eyes.

Do we not read in the First Letter to Timothy. *Proclaim these things and teach them* (1 Tm 4:11)? What they are, he had just said earlier on. Does this not occur there: *Do not rebuke an elder, but entreat him like a father* (1 Tm 5:1)? Is he not told in the second letter, *Hold on to the form of sound words which you have heard from me* (2 Tm 1:13)? Is he not also told there, *Keep busy, presenting yourself to God as a reliable worker, with nothing to be ashamed of, handling the word of truth straightforwardly* (2 Tm 2:15)? There too is this to be found: *Preach the word, keep at it, in season, out of season; reprove, exhort, rebuke, with all long-suffering and teaching* (2 Tm 4:2). And again, does he not say to Titus that a bishop ought to be *persevering in teaching the faithful word, so that he may be well able in sound teaching also to confute those who gainsay it* (Ti 1:9)? He also says there, *You, though, speak as befits sound doctrine; that the old men are to*

---

37. He is punning on the two meanings of the word *orator*; an orator and a pray-er, and its close connection with *oratio*, prayer (without the hyphen).

be sober, and what follows (Ti 2:1–2). And again in that letter: *Speak out about these things, and exhort and rebuke with all command. Let no one ignore you. Admonish them to be subject to rulers and authorities*, etc. (Ti 2:15—3:1).

So what are we to think? Not, surely, that the apostle is taking up a position against himself, when after saying that teachers are made by the working of the Holy Spirit, he goes on himself to instruct them about what and how to teach? Or is it to be understood that even with the Holy Spirit giving bountifully to teachers in the things they have to teach, their functions as men are not canceled out; and yet all the same, *neither the one who plants is anything, nor the one who waters, but the one who gives growth, which is God* (1 Cor 3:7)? So it is, too, that from the ministrations of holy men, or even of holy angels, nobody can correctly learn what is involved in living with God, unless he has been made docile to God by God, who is asked in the psalm, *Teach me to do your will, since you are my God* (Ps 143:10). So it is, too, that the same apostle says to Timothy himself, teacher speaking of course to disciple, *You, though, persevere in the things which you have learned and which have been handed over to you, knowing from whom you learned them* (2 Tm 3:14). Medicines for the body, after all, which are provided for people by human beings, only do good to those whose health is restored by God; and he can cure without them, while they cannot do so without him, and yet they are still provided and applied—and if this is done out of kindness it is counted among the works of mercy, or as a good deed. So in the same way the assistance of sound doctrine provided by a human teacher is only then any good to the soul when God is at work to make it any good, seeing that he was able to give the gospel to man, even without its coming from men or through man.[38]

More advice from Cicero

17, 34. The man, therefore, who is striving by speaking to persuade people to do what is good, bearing in mind each of those three things, namely that he is meant to be teaching, delighting and swaying them, should pray, and take pains to ensure, as we said above,[39] that he is listened to with understanding, with enjoyment, and with obedience. When he does this in a fitting and suitable manner, he can be not undeservedly called eloquent, even if he does not win the assent of his audience. For to these three things, that is teaching, delighting and swaying, that other trio seems to have been attached, according to the mind of the great founder of Roman eloquence himself, when he said in similar vein, "That man therefore will be eloquent, who can talk about minor matters calmly, about middling ones moderately,

---

38. A rather baffling concluding sentence, seeing that it is presumably the gospel of Jesus Christ that he has in mind. But as usual with Augustine, Christ's divinity tends to overshadow his humanity; he was not "a mere man."

39. At the beginning of section 32.

about great matters grandly."[40] It's as if, were he to add those other three as well, he could set it all out in one and the same judgment by saying, "That man therefore will be eloquent who, in order to teach, can talk about minor matters calmly; in order to delight, about middling matters moderately; in order to sway, about great matters grandly."

18, 35. Now he could have illustrated these three modes, as stated by him, with instances taken from the law courts, but not from ecclesiastical occasions, which this man whom we wish to instruct will be concerned with in his public speaking. There, you see, those are minor matters in which a judgment is being sought in questions about money; great matters are those in which the welfare, even the life of persons is at stake, while occasions on which no such judgment has to be given, and nothing is done to get the listener to act or to make a decision, but only to delight him, they put in between the two, so to say, and thus called them middling.[41]

But in our sphere we have to refer everything we say, above all what we say from our higher position[42] to our congregations, to the welfare of persons, to their eternal, not merely temporal, welfare what's more, which also means warning them to beware of eternal perdition. So here everything we say is a great matter, to the extent that not even what the ecclesiastical teacher has to say about money and acquiring or losing it should be regarded as a minor matter, whether it's a minor or major sum of money involved. Justice, after all, is not a minor matter, and this of course we must maintain even where trifling sums are at stake, seeing that the Lord says, *Anyone who is faithful in a minimal amount is also faithful in a great amount* (Lk 16:10). So a minimal amount is certainly minimal, but being faithful in a minimal amount is a great thing. The essence of roundness, that is where the lines from the center to the edge are all equal, is the same in a large dish as in a tiny coin; in the same way, where minor matters are dealt with justly, this does not diminish the greatness of justice.

36. In any case, when the apostle was talking about secular judgments and lawsuits (what kind, to be sure, if not ones to do with money?), he said, *Does any of you dare, when he has a case against another, to seek a judgment from the wicked, and not have recourse to the saints? Or do you not know that the saints will judge the world? And if the world is being judged by you, are you unfit to pass judgment on trifling matters? Do you not know that we shall judge angels, let alone secular matters? If therefore you have secular lawsuits, set those who are contemptible in the Church, yes set them to judge them. I say it to your shame. So, is there really nobody*

---

40. Cicero, *The Orator* 29, 101.
41. *Modica.* He adds,...*hoc est, moderata. Modicis enim "modus" nomen imposuit; nam modica pro parvis abusive, non proprie dicimus.* For it is "mode" that has given its name to modest things, because we use "modest" for minor things by an abuse of language, not properly. None of this applies in English.
42. Meaning both from the pulpit and from our higher official position as bishops and priests.

*among you wise enough to be able to judge between his brothers? But
brother goes for judgment against brother, and this before unbelievers. It
is already indeed a serious fault that you have lawsuits among yourselves
at all. Why not rather put up with injustice? Why not rather let yourselves
be cheated? You, though, act unjustly and cheat, and your own brothers
at that. Or do you not know that the unjust will not inherit the kingdom of
God?* (1 Cor 6:1–9).

Why is it that the apostle is waxing so indignant, so censorious, so
vehemently reproachful, so threatening? Why is it that he shows the intensity of his feelings by such frequent and such harsh changes of tone? Why
is it, finally, that he speaks so grandly about minimal matters? Did secular
lawsuits merit such treatment from him? Surely not. But he is taking this
line on account of justice, of charity, of mutual respect, which nobody of
sound and sober mind will doubt are great things, however trifling and
minimal the matters they are concerned with.

37. Certainly, if we were advising people how they should conduct
their secular business, whether on their own account or that of their clients,
before ecclesiastical judges, we would rightly advise them to present it
calmly, as a minor matter.[43] But when we are discussing the proper style of
speaking for the man whom we wish to be a teacher of the truths by which
we are delivered from eternal evils and conducted to eternal good things,
wherever these are being presented, whether to the people, or privately to
one person or several, whether to friends or enemies, whether in unbroken
discourse or in conversation, whether in treatises or in books, whether in
letters either lengthy or brief—they are great matters.

Unless, of course, because a cup of cold water is a trifling thing, and
worth practically nothing, this means that the Lord was saying something
trifling and and worthless, when he said that whoever gives one to a disciple
of his *shall not lose his reward* (Mt 10:42); or that when this teacher gives
a sermon on this point in church, he should reckon he is talking about a
minor matter, and therefore should not speak either in the grand manner
or even moderately, but only calmly. Is it not the case that when we have
happened to speak to the people on this point, and God has helped us to
say something suitable, it's as though a flame has leapt up out of that cold
water, and fired even people with the coldest of hearts to perform works
of mercy out of hope of a heavenly reward?

19, 38. And yet, while this teacher ought always to be setting forth
great matters, he does not always have to say them in the grand manner.
But he should do it calmly when he is teaching, moderately when he has
something to blame or praise. But when it is something to be done, and we

---

43. Ecclesiastical judges—that is, bishops—had to hear a great deal of secular liti-
    gation, disputes about inheritances and so forth brought to them for arbitration.
    This was an imposition which Augustine resented deeply, but could not get out
    of.

are addressing people who ought to do it, and yet are not willing to, that is when great matters are to be uttered in the grand manner, and in a way suited to swaying minds and hearts. And sometimes one and the same great matter is spoken of calmly if it is being taught, moderately if it is being proclaimed and preached,[44] and grandly if spirits that have turned away from it are being urged to turn back and be converted.

What, after all, could be greater than God himself? Does that mean that we cannot learn about him? Or that someone who is teaching the unity of the Trinity ought to discuss the matter other than calmly, so that a subject involving such difficult distinctions may as far as God may grant be understood? Is it rhetorical flourishes that are required here, and not rather instructive models? Does the hearer have to be persuaded and swayed to do something, and not rather assisted to learn something? But when God is being praised, either in himself or in his works, what a vast prospect of beautiful and glowing language will occur to the speaker, in order to praise as best he can the one whom nobody can praise as befits him, nobody can fail to praise somehow or other! But if he is not being worshiped, or if idols or demons, or any creatures are being worshiped together with him or instead of him, then of course the grand manner is called for, to declare how wrong and wicked this is, and to turn people back from this wickedness.

Further examples of different styles

20, 39. There is an example of the calm manner in the apostle Paul, to illustrate the point more clearly, where he says: *Tell me, you that wish to be under the law, have you not heard the law? For it is written that Abraham had two sons, one by a maidservant, one by a free woman; but the one by the maidservant was born according to the flesh, while the one by the free woman through a promise; which is all an allegory. For these are the two testaments, one indeed bringing forth from Mount Sinai into slavery, and that is Hagar. For Sinai is a mountain in Arabia, which is linked to this Jerusalem that now is, and is in slavery with her children. But the Jerusalem which is above is free, which is our mother*, etc. (Gal 4:21–26).

And again, where he is presenting an argument and says, *Brethren, I speak in merely human terms; still, nobody can invalidate or supersede a man's will and testament, once it has been probated. The promises were made to Abraham and his seed. It does not say "and seeds," as in the plural, but as in the singular, "and to your seed," which is Christ. But what I say is this: a law made four hundred and thirty years later cannot annul a testament probated by God, and make the promises void. For if the inheritance is by law, it is no longer by promise. But God granted it to Abraham by a promise* (Gal 3:15–18). And because the thought could occur to someone

---

44. The difference between *catechesis*, or instruction, and *kerygma*, or the proclamation of the word.

hearing this, "So why was the law given, if the inheritance is not settled by it?" he put this objection to himself, and as if questioning himself said, *Why then the law?* Then he answered, *It was laid down because of trans-gression, until the seed should come, arranged by angels in the hand of a mediator, to which the promise had been made. But a mediator is not of one, while God is one.* And here the objection occurred to him, which he stated himself: *Is the law therefore against the promises of God?* And he answered, *Surely not,* and gave his reason, saying, *For if a law had been given which could bring to life, then justice would certainly have come from the law. But scripture locked all things up under sin, so that the promise from faith in Jesus Christ might be given to those who believe* (Gal 3:19–22), and the rest, or if there is anything in the same vein.

So it is part of the teacher's responsibility, not only to open closed doors and to unravel knotty problems, but also while this is being done to meet other problems that may perhaps arise, in case what we say should be called in question or refuted by them, provided, that is, that the solution of these problems occurs to us at the same time, or we may start something we can-not dispose of. It does happen, though, that when other problems intruding upon a problem, and then further problems intruding upon these intrusive ones, are dealt with and solved, the argument stretches on and on to such lengths, that unless the disputant has an extremely good and disciplined memory, he is unable to get back to the original point he started from. It is, however, a very good thing if anything that can be gainsaid should be refuted as soon as it crops up, in case it should also crop up on an occasion when there is nobody who can answer it, or where such a person is indeed present but keeps quiet, and the person who raised it should go away, his mind not put at rest.

40. The apostle adopts a moderate style in these words: *Do not rebuke an older man, but entreat him as a father, younger men as brothers, old women as mothers, young women as sisters* (1 Tm 5:1-2). And again in these: *But I implore you, brothers, by the compassion of God, to present your bodies as a living sacrificial victim, holy, pleasing to God* (Rom 12:1). And almost the whole of that passage of exhortation displays a moderate kind of oratory—particularly fine, where things that are appropriately due in appropriate circumstances follow one another handsomely like debts being paid, in this way: *Having gifts that vary according to the grace that has been given to us, whether prophecy according to the rule of faith, or service in serving, or the one who teaches in teaching, or the one who encourages in encouragement, or the one who is bountiful in simplicity, or the one who is in charge in solicitude, or the one who takes pity in cheerfulness. Love without pretense, hating what is evil, cleaving to the good, loving one another with fraternal charity, vying with one another in mutual respect, not sluggish in zeal, fervent in spirit, serving the Lord, rejoicing in hope, patient in trouble, punctilious in prayer, sharing with the saints in their needs, pursuing hospitality. Bless those who persecute you, bless and do*

not curse. Rejoicing with those who rejoice, weeping with those who weep, sharing each other's thoughts (Rom 12:6–15).

And how beautifully all this, after pouring out like that, is rounded off with a two-clause period: *Not thinking highly of yourselves, but going along with the lowly* (Rom 12:16). And a little later: *Persevering*, he says, *in this very thing, pay to all their due, taxes to whom taxes, tolls to whom tolls, fear to whom fear, honor to whom honor.* This flow of clauses, one after the other, is also rounded off with a period, stitched together from two clauses: *Owe nobody anything, except to love one another* (Rom 13:6–8). And a little later on: *Night is far advanced*, he says, *while day has drawn near. And so let us cast aside the works of darkness, and clothe ourselves with the armor of light; let us walk decently as in the day. not in revels and drunkenness, not in sleeping around and shamelessness, not in wrangling and jealousy; but clothe yourselves with the Lord Jesus Christ, and do not make provision for the flesh in its lusts* (Rom 13:12–14). If someone were to phrase this "and for the flesh in its lusts make no provision," he would undoubtedly be wooing the ears with a more rhythmical conclusion;[45] but the more sober translator preferred also to keep the order of words of the original. How it sounds in the Greek language which the apostle spoke, those who are more learned in that language even as regards these points of style can tell; still, it doesn't seem to me that what has been translated for us, keeping the same order of words, runs with a very smooth rhythm.

41. It must be admitted, certainly, that this embellishment of a speech, which consists of rhythmic concluding phrases, is wanting in our authors. Whether this is the fault of the translators, or whether (as I am inclined to think) the authors deliberately avoided these agreeable niceties, I dare not judge, since I confess I do not know. What I do know, for all that, is that if anybody skilled in this matter of rhythm were to rewrite the translators' concluding phrases according to the rules of such rhythms, which can be done very easily by substituting some words with the same meaning, or by changing the order of the words found there; he will acknowledge that nothing he learned in the schools of grammar or rhetoric that is considered important was wanting in the writings of those God-sent men; and he will find many turns of phrase of real elegance, which are indeed elegant in our language, but above all in theirs, and none of which are to be found in the literature which these people are so proud of.

But one must beware of detracting from the weight of grave divine statements, while adding to their rhythm.[46] For the subject of music, in which

---

45. What he is saying here really only applies in the Latin. The text runs, *et carnis providentiam ne feceritis in concupiscentiis*, translating the Greek word for word in the same order. Augustine is saying that to have written *et carnis providentiam in concupiscentiis ne feceritis* would have made a more rhythmic conclusion, *clausula numerosior*.

46. The word I am translating "rhythm" is *numerus*, literally number; and he is here alluding to the text of Wis 11:20.

this matter of number or rhythm is most fully studied, was to be found so prominently in our prophets that Jerome, the most learned of men, even recorded the meters of some of them, at least in the Hebrew language; but in order to keep the true meaning of the words, he did not transfer these meters into Latin.[47] For my part, though, to express my own sentiments, which are of course better known to me than to other people and than other people's sentiments, while I do not neglect these concluding rhythms in my own speaking, as far as I consider can decently be done, still what gives me more pleasure in our authors is that I find them there so very infrequently.

42. As for the grand manner of speaking, it is as far removed as can be from this moderate kind, being not so much a matter of elegantly stylish language as of the impetuous expression of very deep feelings. For it seizes on almost all those elegant embellishments, but if it doesn't have them to hand it doesn't look for them. It is in fact carried along by its own vehemence, and if it stumbles on some beauty of expression, it carries it along in virtue of its subject, rather than choosing it with a careful eye on appearances. It is sufficient, you see, for the subject which engages it that suitable words, rather than being picked by the deliberation of the tongue, should follow upon the ardor of the breast. After all, if a mighty man of valor should be armed with steel that has been gilded and set with gems, intent upon the battle he does indeed do what he does with those arms, not because they are valuable, but because they are arms. He is still himself, and

> supremely valiant, even when
> anger makes a weapon of whatever he breaks off.
>
> (Vergil, *Aeneid* VII, 508)

The apostle is in full swing, concerned that for the sake of the ministry of the gospel the evils of this time should all be patiently borne, with the consolation of God's gifts. It is a great matter, and it is handled in the grand manner, while the embellishments of speech are not wanting either: *Behold, he says, now is the acceptable time, now is the day of salvation. Giving no offense in any matter, that the ministry may not be objected to, but commending ourselves in all things as ministers of God in much patience, in tribulations, in necessities, in tight straits, in blows, in prisons, in riots, in labors, in vigils, in fasting, in chastity, in knowledge, in long-suffering, in kindness, in the Holy Spirit, in charity unfeigned, in the word of truth, in the power of God, with the weapons of justice in the right hand and in the left, through glory and dishonor, through ill repute and good repute, as seducers and yet truthful, as ones unknown and we are known, as though dying and behold we are alive, as fenced in and not done to death, as sad but always rejoicing, as in want but enriching many, as having nothing and possessing all things.* See him still on fire: *Our mouth is open to you,*

---

47. See the prologue to Jerome's commentary on Job.

O Corinthians, our heart is enlarged (2 Cor 6:2–11), and the rest, which it would take too long to continue with.

43. Here he is again in full swing to the Romans, concerned that the persecutions of this world should be overcome with charity, in the certain hope of God's help. He handles it, though, both in the grand and the decorative manner. *We know*, he says, *that for those who love God all things work together for good, for those who have been called according to plan. For those whom he foreknew beforehand, he also predestined to be replicas of the image of his Son, so that he might be the firstborn among many brethren. And those whom he predestined he also called, and whom he called, them he also justified, and whom he justified, them he also glorified. What therefore shall we say to this? If God is for us, who can be against us? The one who did not spare his own Son, but handed him over for us all, how has he not also with him granted us all things? Who will bring charges against the chosen ones of God? God who justifies them? Who is it that may condemn them? Christ Jesus who died, or rather who rose again, who is at the right hand of God, who is also interceding for us? Who will separate us from the love of Christ? Tribulation, or distress, or persecution, or hunger, or nakedness, or danger, or the sword? As it is written, "For your sake we are being done to death all day long, we are counted as sheep for the slaughter." But in all these things we do more than conquer through him who loved us. For I am certain that neither death nor life, neither angel nor princedom, neither things present nor things to come, neither might nor height nor depth, nor any other creature will be able to separate us from the love of God, which is in Christ Jesus our Lord* (Rom 6:28–39).

44. As for the Letter to the Galatians, although the whole of it is written in the calm style of speaking, except for its first and last parts,[48] where you have the moderate style, still he does insert one place of such heartfelt emotion, that without any embellishments indeed of the sort to be found in the passages we have quoted just now, it could still only be spoken in the grand manner. *You observe days*, he says, *and months and years and seasons. I am afraid about you, lest perchance I have labored over you for nothing. Be as I am, since I too am as you are, brothers, I beg you. You have done me no harm. You know that it was through a weakness of the flesh that some time ago I preached the gospel to you, and you did not spurn the trial you underwent in my flesh, nor reject me, but you took me to your heart like an angel of God, like Christ Jesus. So what was your blessedness? I bear you witness that if it had been possible, you would have plucked out your eyes and given them to me. So have I become an enemy to you by preaching the truth? They are zealous for you in a way that is not good, but they wish to exclude you, so that you may be zealous for them. But it is good to*

---

48. *Nisi extremis partibus.* I think *extremis* must refer, so to say, to both sides of the middle, not just to the end—to the letter's two extremes. But it is an odd expression of an extremely odd judgment.

*be zealous in the good at all times, and not only when I am present among
you, my little children, with whom I am again in labor, until Christ takes
shape in you. But I wish I were now present among you and could change
my tone, because I do not know what to make of you* (Gal 4:10–20).

Do we have here any words balanced against each other in contrast,
or linked to each other in any kind of progression, or has there been any
music of phrases and clauses and periods? And yet that did not result in
any tepidity in the grandeur of the emotion, with which we sense the whole
passage to be so highly charged.

Examples from ecclesiastical writers: Cyprian and Ambrose

21, 45. But these passages from the apostle are clear in such a way that
they are also profound, and so written and committed to memory that they
call not only for a reader or a hearer, but also for an expositor, for anyone
who is not content with their surface meaning, but wishes to plumb their
depths. For that reason, let us take a look at these different kinds of speaking
in those authors who by reading these have made advances in the knowledge
of matters pertaining to divinity and salvation, and have ministered that
knowledge to the Church.

The blessed Cyprian employs the plain, calm manner of speaking in
the book where he discusses the sacrament of the cup.[49] In it, that is to say,
the question has been raised and is settled whether the Lord's cup should
have only water in it, or water mixed with wine. But we must give an extract
from it by way of example. So after the letter's opening salutation he is now
getting down to settling the question that has been raised:

> But you must know, he says, that we have been admonished, in of-
> fering the cup, to keep to what has been handed down to us from
> the Lord, and that nothing different should be done by us from what
> the Lord did for us first; so that the cup which is offered in com-
> memoration of him should be offered with wine mixed in it. For
> since Christ says, *I am the true vine* (Jn 15:8), the blood of Christ is
> assuredly not water, but wine; nor can his blood, by which we have
> been redeemed and given life, be seen to be in the cup when wine
> is lacking in the cup. For it is by wine that Christ's blood is shown
> forth, and by which it is proclaimed by the sacramental symbolism
> and testimony of all the scriptures.

> For we find in Genesis, as regards the sacramental symbolism,
> that Noah was a forerunner in this very case, and presented a rep-
> resentation of the Lord's passion there, in that he drank wine, got
> drunk, stripped himself naked in his own home, and was lying on
> his back with his thighs naked and spread out; in that his nakedness
> was pointed out by his middle son, but covered by the eldest and

---

49. Letter 63 to Caecilius, 2–4: CSEL 3,702, 7–703, 8.

youngest;[50] and the rest which there is no need to run through, as this is enough on its own to show Noah as a type of the true reality to come, since he drank wine, not water, and thus presented an image of the Lord's passion.

Again, we can see in the priest Melchizedek a sacramental prefiguration of the Lord's sacrifice, according to the testimony of the divine scripture, where it says, *And Melchizedek king of Salem brought out bread and wine. Now he was priest of God Most High, and he blessed Abraham* (Gn 14:18–19). Now that Melchizedek represented Christ is declared by the Holy Spirit in the psalms, saying to the Son in the person of the Father, *Before the daystar I begot you; you are a priest for ever according to the order of Melchizedek* (Ps 110:4).

This, and the rest of the letter that follows, keeps to the style of calm diction, which readers can easily discover for themselves.

46. Saint Ambrose too, when dealing with the great matter of the Holy Spirit, to demonstrate his equality with the Father and the Son, employs a plain, calm style of speaking, since the subject he has undertaken does not call for flowery language, or for emotional fireworks to sway people's spirits, but requires instructive examples and illustrations of the matters proposed. So among other things, he says at the beginning of this work:[51]

Gideon was moved by this oracle, and on hearing that the Lord would deliver his people from their enemies through one man, even in the absence of thousands of the people, he offered a kid of the goats, and following the angel's instructions placed its flesh and unleavened bread on the rock, and poured the broth over it all. The moment the angel of God touched it all with the tip of the rod he carried, fire burst out of the rock, and thus the sacrifice which was offered was consumed.[52] This seems to be a clear indication that that rock was a type of the body of Christ, because it is written, *They drank from the rock following them, and the rock was Christ* (1 Cor 10:4). This certainly did not refer to his divinity, but to his flesh, which has flooded the hearts of thirsty people with the perennial river of his blood. So it was then already declared in a mystery that the Lord Jesus would abolish in his flesh, by being crucified, the sins of the whole world, and not only actual misdeeds, but also the greedy lusts entertained in thought. For the flesh of the kid relates to faults of actual commission, the broth to the enticements of greed, as it is written, *The people lusted with a very bad desire, and they said, who will feed us with flesh?* (Num 11:4). That the angel, therefore, stretched out his rod and touched the rock, from which fire came

---

50. See Gn 9:10–23.
51. *On the Holy Spirit*, 1, prologue: PL 16, 703C -704B.
52. See Jg 6:11–21.

out, showed that the flesh of the Lord, filled with the divine Spirit, would burn up all the sins of the human condition. Which is why the Lord too said, *I have come to cast fire upon the earth* (Lk 12:49);

and so on in the rest of the work, in which he is at pains to teach and prove the point.

47. In the moderate style there is that praise of virginity in Cyprian:[53]

> Now our words are addressed to virgins, whose solicitude must be all the greater, the more sublime their honor. Here is the blossom on the Church's boughs, the splendid ornament of spiritual grace, the joyful genius of praise and honor, a work unimpaired and unspoiled, the image of God responding to the utter holiness of the Lord, the more illustrious portion of Christ's flock. The glorious fruitfulness of mother Church rejoices through them, and flourishes in them abundantly; and the more that glorious virginity adds to its numbers, the greater grows the mother's joy.

And in another place at the end of the letter:

> *Just as we have borne*, he says, *the image of the one from the mire, so let us also bear the image of the one from heaven* (1 Cor 15:49). Virginity bears this image, unimpaired wholeness bears it, holiness and truth bear it, those who are mindful of God's discipline bear it, those who combine justice with religion, who are steady in faith, humble in fear, strong to endure everything, meek in bearing with insults, prompt in showing kindness, of one mind and heart in fraternal peace. Each and everyone of these things you, O good virgins, ought to observe, to love, to fulfill, you that give all your time to God and Christ, and so go ahead of the rest of us to the Lord, having chosen the greater and the better part.[54] Those of you advanced in years, act as tutors to the younger ones; those who are younger, give a lead to your peers, stir each other up with mutual encouragement, urge one another on to glory with enviable examples of virtue. Persevere bravely, proceed spiritually along the way, arrive happily at journey's end; only please remember us then, when your virginity finally receives the honor that is its due.[55]

---

53. *On the Dress of Virgins* 3: CSEL 3,189, 11–18.
54. See Lk 10:42.
55. *Cum incipiet in vobis virginitas honorari*, literally, when virginity in you begins to be honored. He is clearly referring to their final crown of glory; but his implication that virginity is not being honored now is strange, since it was highly honored by Christians. But no doubt he is thinking that it is not being honored by society at large.

48. Ambrose also uses the moderate and flowery style of speaking, when he is proposing to professed virgins a kind of model for them to imitate in their way of life; and he says:[56]

> She was a virgin not only in body but also in mind, so that she did not adulterate the sincerity of her affections with any time-serving deceit; she was humble of heart, serious in her words, of a prudent spirit, sparing of speech, always readier to read; not placing her hope *in the uncertainty of riches* (1 Tm 6:17) but in the prayers of the poor; intent upon her work, bashful in her words; looking to God, not any man, as the arbiter of her mind; insulting nobody to the face, wishing all people well, standing up in the presence of her elders, never jealous of her peers; shunning boastfulness, following reason, loving virtue. When did she ever hurt her parents even by so much as her expression? When did she ever wrangle with her companions, ever turn up her nose at the lowly, ever laugh at a cripple, ever turn her back on the needy? Punctiliously attending only those gatherings of men which mercy would not blush at nor modesty pass by. Nothing wild in her eyes, nothing pert in her talk, nothing shameless in her demeanor; not too feeble in her gestures, too loose in her gait, too petulant in her tone of voice, so that the very aspect of her body was an image of her mind, and a picture of her probity. It ought, of course, to be possible to tell a good house by its forecourt, so that it assures you on your first step inside that there is no darkness lurking within, as by the light of a lamp placed inside and shining outside.

> Why should I run through the meanness of her diet, the generous abundance of her duties, the one going far beyond what nature requires, the other falling considerably short of what nature needs? In the one case no time was left idle, in the other days were joined together in fasting—and if ever the will to take some refreshment seemed to triumph, food was forthcoming simply to stave off death, not to provide any pleasure, and so on.

The reason I have quoted this as an example of the moderate style is that he is not here urging his readers to take a vow of virginity, which they have not yet taken, but telling those who have already taken their vow what kind of lives they should live. For the human spirit, after all, to undertake such a great and daunting purpose, it needs to be roused and fired by the grand mode of speaking. But the martyr Cyprian wrote about the dress of virgins, not about undertaking a life of virginity. This bishop, on the other hand, also fired them to this with great eloquence.[57]

49. But I will quote examples of the grand style of speaking from the works of both of them. Both, that is to say, inveighed against women who

---

56. *On Virgins* 2, 1, 7–8: PL 16, 209A-C.
57. These two final sentences seem rather inconsequential.

color their faces with paints, or rather discolor them. The first of the two, when dealing with this subject, said among other things:[58]

> If any professional painter had taken the features of a subject and her beauty and the quality of her body, carefully emulating their natural coloring, and putting his signature to the work; and then someone else had laid hands on the signed and finished portrait, and presumed as if he were a better artist to redesign what had already been designed and painted, it would look like a serious insult to the first painter, and just grounds for indignation. And now you reckon, do you, that in your outrageously bold temerity you can insult God's skill as a craftsman with impunity? For while you may not be a shameless and unchaste woman in human eyes, with your rouge and your make-up, by corrupting and violating what is God's work, you convict yourself of being worse than an adulteress. What you suppose is just adorning yourself, what you suppose is just doing your hair, is really an attack on a divine work, a distortion of the truth. There is the voice of the apostle warning us: *Purge out the old leaven, so that you may be fresh dough, as you are unleavened. For Christ has been sacrificed as our passover. And so let us celebrate the feast, not in the old leaven, nor in the leaven of malice and wickedness, but in the unleavened bread of genuineness and truth* (1 Cor 5:7–8). Can genuineness and truth remain, when what is genuine has been polluted, and what is true has been changed into a lie, adulterated with strange colors and treated with rouge? Your Lord says, *You cannot make one hair white or black* (Mt 5:36), and you, to drown your Lord's voice, wish to prove more powerful. You have the nerve, the hardihood, and the sacrilegious contempt to dye your hair; what an ill omen for the future that you should already be arranging for yourself a flame-colored coiffure!

It would take too long to include everything that follows.

50. The later writer had this to say against such persons:[59]

> Hence arise those incentives to vice, that they paint their faces with exquisite colors, while they dread displeasing their husbands, and from adulterating their features they go on to dream about adulterating their chastity. What mindless folly is this, to change the artistry of nature, to resort to painting it, and while they fear the judgment of their husbands, to lose their own! For the woman who desires to change what she was born with is the first to pronounce judgment on herself; thus while she is taking pains to please another, she is

---

58. Cyprian, *On the Dress of Virgins*, 15–16: CSEL 3,198 -100. It is in my view to Augustine's credit that he never stooped to this favorite theme of some preachers, from the Fathers to the present day; at least no sermon of his on the topic, to my knowledge, has survived. If he did preach any, perhaps he was rather ashamed of them, and took steps to see that they did not survive.

59. Ambrose, *On Virgins*, 1, 6, 28: PL 16, 196–197.

first of all displeased with herself. What truer judge, woman, can we seek of your ugliness than yourself, afraid as you are of being seen as you are? If you are beautiful, why conceal yourself? If ugly, why falsely present yourself as beautiful, since you will gain the favor neither of your own awareness of yourself nor of another's mistaken awareness of you? For he loves another woman, and you wish to please another man, and you get angry if he loves another, though he is being taught all about adultery by you. You are miserably the very teacher of the wrong done to you. Herself the victim of a pimp, she turns to pimping, and although she is a worthless woman, she is still not sinning against anyone else, but against herself. Crimes committed in adultery are almost more tolerable; for in that case it is modesty, in this nature that is adulterated.

It is clear enough, I think, that by this rhetoric women are being force-fully urged not to adulterate their appearance with cosmetics, and to cultivate modesty and bashfulness. Accordingly we acknowledge here neither the plain and calm, nor the moderately ornate style, but quite simply the grand manner of oratory. And in these two writers whom I have chosen to quote, and in other churchmen who speak both worthily and well, that is, as the matter requires, plainly and clearly, or in rather more ornate and flowery language, or with fiery vigor, these three styles can be found throughout their many writings or speeches; and students by assiduous reading or listening can, with practice, acquire the knack and the habit of using them.

More general remarks on the three styles: an experience of his own

22, 51. Nor should anybody suppose that it is against the rules to mix these three styles; on the contrary, to the extent that it can reasonably be done, a speech should be given variety by the use of all of them, because when it continues too long in one vein, it ceases to hold the listener's attention. But when a transition is made from one to another, a discourse proceeds more acceptably, even if it goes on rather too long, although each style has its own variations in the mouths of eloquent speakers, which prevent it from growing cold or stale in the ears of those who are listening. Nonetheless, it is easier to endure the plain style alone for any length of time than the grand manner alone. The fact is that the more profoundly the listeners' emotions need to be stirred if we are to win their assent, the shorter the time they can be held at that pitch, once they have been sufficiently aroused. And that is why we must beware lest, while we are wishing to stir to a still higher pitch feelings that are already running high, they should in fact fall away from the level to which our rousing oratory has brought them. But after introducing some things that can be said more calmly and plainly, you can then profitably return to what has to be said in the grand manner, thus letting the force of your speech alternate like the waves of the sea. From all this it follows that the grand manner of speaking, if you have to speak for any length of time, should not be offered neat, but should be varied by the inclusion of other styles; but the whole speech, all the same, is to be attributed to that style which predominates.

23, 52. For it makes a difference what style is introduced into which in particular and necessary places. Thus it is correct always, or nearly always, to begin a speech that is to be in the grand manner with a moderate opening. And an eloquent speaker is quite capable of saying some things calmly and plainly which could be delivered in the grand manner, so that what he does actually say in the grand manner is rendered grander still in comparison, its brilliance highlighted by what you could call the shadows of the other passages. But if in a speech where any style predominates there are knotty problems to be solved, what is called for is acumen, and this claims the calm, plain style as its own. And thus this style is to be employed even in the other two kinds, when such points occur.

In the same way, when something is to be praised or faulted, but where neither a person's life nor liberty is at stake, and no kind of assent to some action is being sought, the moderate style should be applied and introduced, in whatever other kind of speech the point arises. Thus in a speech in the grand manner the other two styles can also find a place, and the same is true for a discourse in the calm, plain style. The moderate kind of speech, however, sometimes though not always requires the plain style if, as I said, a knotty problem crops up that needs to be solved, or when some matters that could be are deliberately not embellished, but are expressed in plain, unadorned words, in order to throw into relief some more decorative and nicely turned embellishments. But a speech in the moderate style never calls for the grand manner, since it is delivered in order to delight the spirits of the audience, not to stir them to action.

24, 53. Certainly it is not to be assumed that if a speaker is applauded rather frequently and warmly he must therefore be speaking in the grand manner; shrewd arguments in the plain style and embellishments in the moderate can elicit the same response, after all. The grand manner, however, by its very weight frequently makes the voices hush,[60] makes the tears gush. Well anyway, I was once in Caesarea of Mauritania,[61] trying to dissuade the people from their local civil war, or rather something more than civil, which they called "the mob"[62]—for it is not only citizens but also neighbors,

---

60. *Voces premit*, an allusion to Virgil's *Aeneid* IX 324, and balanced against *sed lacrimas exprimit*.
61. Modern Cherchel in western Algeria, on the coast. The event he describes took place in 418 or 419. This text, oddly enough, seems to be the only reference to it in his writings. So the event is dated from the time of his writing this fourth book of *Teaching Christianity*, rather than the other way round. But in Letter 190, written in 418, he does mention that he had just been there on Church business imposed on him by Pope Zosimus.
62. *Caterva*. F. van der Meer, in *Augustine the Bishop* (E.T. London, 1961), 410, or rather his English translator, renders this as "the great row." But the word means

brothers, indeed parents and sons, divided into two parties, ritually fighting each other with stones at a certain time of the year, and each of them killing anyone he could; and I did indeed speak and act in the grand manner, to the best of my ability, in order to root out such a cruel and inveterate evil from their hearts and habits and rid them of it by my speaking. But still I did not consider I had achieved anything when I heard them applauding me, but only when I saw them weeping. Their applause only showed they were being instructed and delighted, while their tears indicated that they were being swayed. When I observed these, I was confident, even before the outcome confirmed it, that I had beaten that monstrous custom, handed down from their fathers and grandfathers and their remote ancestors, which was laying hostile siege to their breasts, or rather was in full possession of them. I soon finished the sermon, and turned their hearts and tongues to giving thanks to God. And here we are, something like eight years or more later, and by the good favor of Christ nothing of the sort has since been attempted. There are many other experiences which have taught me that people have shown by their groans rather than their shouts, sometimes also by their tears, and finally by the change in their lives, what the grandeur of a wise man's speech has achieved in them.

54. People have also frequently been changed by the calm and plain kind of speaking—but so as to know what they were ignorant of, or to believe what used to strike them as incredible; not, however, to do what they already knew should be done and were reluctant to do. For swaying that kind of stubbornness, after all, hard-hitting talk in the grand manner is needed. Again, when praise and blame are being eloquently distributed, while this belongs to the moderate style, some people are so affected that not only are they delighted by the eloquence displayed in praising and blaming, but they themselves also start trying to live in a praiseworthy way and to give up a blameworthy kind of life. But do all who are delighted by this style also imitate the examples given, as all who are swayed by the grand manner proceed to act? And do all who are being taught in the plain style *ipso facto* know or believe to be true what they were ignorant of?

25, 55. From all this one concludes that those two kinds of speaking which are intended to achieve something are supremely necessary for the person who wishes to speak both wisely and eloquently. But the one which engages in the moderate style, that is in order to delight the hearer by its very eloquence, is not to be made use of for its own sake, but in order that matters which are being usefully and properly talked about, even though they do not call for a style that either instructs or moves, because an audience is being addressed which is both knowledgeable and favorable, might the more readily win that audience's assent and stick in its memory.

---

a band or crowd of people, and here possibly alludes to the inhabitants divided up into two rival bands, in what looks like having been almost a ritual blood-letting.

After all, the universal task of eloquence, in whichever of these three styles, is to speak in a way that is geared to persuasion. The aim, what you intend, is to persuade by speaking. In any of these three styles, indeed, the eloquent man speaks in a way that is geared to persuasion, but if he doesn't actually persuade, he doesn't achieve the aim of eloquence. Now in the calm, plain style he persuades his hearers that what he is saying is true; in the grand manner he persuades them to do the things they know should be done and are not being done; in the moderate manner he persuades them that he is speaking beautifully and with many a flourish—and what need do we have of an aim like that? Let those people aim at it who glory in their tongues, and who pride themselves on panegyrics and suchlike speeches, where the audience does not have to be taught anything or moved to action, but solely and simply to be delighted.

We, however,[63] should refer this aim to another one; that is, we should wish to achieve by this style what we wish to achieve when we speak in the grand manner, which is that good morals should be loved and bad morals shunned. This is appropriate when people are not so alienated from such a course that they apparently have to be driven to it by the grand manner of speaking—when, for example, they are already set on it, but need to be prodded into going about it more zealously, or reminded to persevere in it firmly. So it is that we may make use of the embellishments of the moderate style, not just to show off, but sensibly, not content with the aim simply of delighting our hearers, but doing this rather, so that in this way too they may be helped toward the good object about which we wish to persuade them.

26, 56. We have stated above that if the person who is speaking wisely also wishes to speak eloquently, he should so[64] manage those three styles that he is heard with understanding, with pleasure, and with compliance. But this is not to be taken in the sense that each of these three is to be attributed to one each of those, so that it pertains to the calm, plain mode to be heard with understanding, to the moderate mode to be heard with pleasure, and to the grand mode to be heard with obedient compliance, but rather that the speaker should always have these three intentions, and as far as possible act to realize them, even when he is concentrating on just one of those styles. After all, we do not want even what we say calmly and plainly to bore people; and thus we want it to be heard not only intelligently, with understanding, but also gladly, with pleasure.

What in fact are we aiming at, when we support with divine testimonies what we say in our teaching, but that we should be heard with obedient compliance, that is that these testimonies should be believed, with the assistance of him to whom it was said, *Your testimonies have come to be*

---

63. Would-be ecclesiastical orators.
64. Emending *id agere debere* of the text to *ita agere debere*. This makes it possible to treat the *Illa tria* with which the paragraph begins as the object of *agere*. If its object is *id*, then *Illa tria* is left hanging loose, with no grammatical relation to the rest of the sentence.

exceedingly believed (Ps 93:5)? Again, what is the person looking for, who is narrating facts to learners, but to be believed, even though he is talking in the plain, unadorned manner? And who would be willing to listen to him, unless he also held the hearer's attention with some pleasantness of style? Because, of course, if he is not understood, it's obvious to all of us that he cannot be heard either with pleasure or with compliance.

It frequently happens, though, that when the most difficult problems are being solved in the calm, plain mode, and something is demonstrated with unexpected clarity, when from heaven knows what kind of ship's holds, from where they were quite unhoped for, the speaker hauls up and displays the shrewdest judgments, convicting his opponent of error, and proving that what he seemed to be saying so irrefutably is false; especially when his words have a certain grace that is not contrived but somehow or other quite natural, and a number of rhythmic periods that are not just thrown in to show off, but are almost necessary, and distilled, so to say, from the very matter itself; it frequently happens that such spontaneous applause breaks out on an occasion of this kind that you would scarcely suppose the calm, plain mode was being employed. Just because this style, after all, does not enter the arena either dressed up or armed, but engages the opponent as it were naked, it doesn't follow that it fails to grapple him with its sinewy arms, and to overthrow the falsehood resisting it, and to reduce it to nothing by its sheer strength of muscle. How is it, though, that people speaking in this way are repeatedly and loudly applauded, if not because it is such a pleasure to see truth thus demonstrated, thus defended, thus unbeaten? That is why in this calm, plain mode of speaking too, this teacher and speaker of ours ought so to conduct himself that he is heard with pleasure and with compliance, as well as with understanding.

57. Coming now to eloquence in the moderate mode, the eloquent churchman neither leaves it entirely unadorned, nor adorns it inappropriately, nor seeks simply and solely to delight his audience, which is the one and only thing other orators intend with it. Rather, even in his praising of some things or finding fault with others, he wishes his hearers, surely, to comply with what they hear from him by aiming at the former or holding on to them more firmly, while shunning or ridding themselves of the latter. But if what he says is not understood, it cannot also be heard with any pleasure. Accordingly those three objects, that listeners should understand what they hear, should enjoy hearing it, and should comply with it, are also to be aimed at in this mode of speaking, in which giving pleasure has pride of place.

58. Finally, where the need is to move and sway the audience with the grand manner (which is necessary when they admit that what is being said is true and that it is being said very pleasantly, and still do not wish to do what they are being told), the speaker must undoubtedly employ the grand manner. But who will be moved if they do not know what is being said? And who will be constrained to listen if they are not also being enter-

tained? So it is that in this mode also, where stubborn hearts need to be swayed to obedience by the very grandeur of the style, unless the speaker is listened to with understanding and with pleasure, he cannot be listened to with compliance.

The preacher's lifestyle carries more weight than his style of oratory

27, 59. But for us to be listened to with obedient compliance, whatever the grandeur of the speaker's utterances, his manner of life carries more weight. For the man who speaks wisely and eloquently, while living a worthless kind of life, does indeed instruct many who are eager to learn, although, as it is written, *he is unprofitable to his own soul* (Sir 37:19), which is why the apostle says, *Whether from ulterior motives or for the sake of the truth, let Christ be proclaimed* (Phil 1:18). Now Christ is the truth,[65] and yet the truth can be proclaimed even by the not truth, that is, so that things that are right and true may be preached by a twisted and deceitful heart. This of course is how Jesus Christ is proclaimed by those *who seek what is their own, and not what is of Jesus Christ* (Phil 2:21).

But since good people who are believers listen obediently, not to any mere human being, but to the Lord himself as he says, *Do what they say; what they do, however, do not do, for they say and do not do* (Mt 23:3), that is why even those who do not act in a profitable way can be listened to with profit. For they are indeed bent on seeking what is their own, but they dare not teach what is their own, from the higher place, that is to say, of the chair of ecclesiastical authority, which has been established by sound doctrine. That is why the Lord himself, before speaking about such people as I have mentioned, first said, *They sit on the chair of Moses* (Mt 23:2). So it was that chair, not their own but the one of Moses, that was constraining them to say good things, even while not doing good things. So they were doing their own thing in their lives, but were not permitted to teach their own thing by the chair that belonged to someone else.

60. And so they benefit many people by saying what they do not do, but they would benefit far, far more by doing what they say. There are plenty of people, after all, who seek an excuse for their bad lives in those of their very own leaders and teachers, replying in their hearts, or even bursting out with it and saying to their faces, "Why don't you yourself do what you are telling me to do?" Thus it happens that they do not listen obediently to someone who doesn't listen to himself, and that they despise the word of God being preached to them along with the preacher. Finally, we have the apostle writing to Timothy, and after saying, *Let nobody despise your youth*, adding a reason why it should not be despised, and saying, *but be a model for the faithful in word, in behavior, in love, in faith, in chastity* (1 Tm 4:12).

---

65. See Jn 14:6.

28, 61. That such a teacher should be heard with compliant obedience, he may also unashamedly speak in the grand manner, as well as in the plain and the moderate style, because he does not live in a despicable manner. For he chooses to live a good life in such a way that he does not neglect his good reputation either, but takes care, as far as he can, *to act well in the sight of God and of men* (2 Cor 8:21), fearing him and being concerned for them.

In his sermons too he should prefer to please with the substance of what he says more than with the words he says it in; nor should he imagine that a thing is said better unless it is said more truly; and as a teacher his words should be serving him, not he his words. This, after all, is what the apostle says: *Not in the wisdom of the word, lest the cross of Christ should be canceled out* (1 Cor 1:17). The same point is also made by what he says to Timothy: *Do not argue about words; for it is of no use for anything but for the subversion of the hearers* (2 Tm 2:14). Nor was the reason for saying this that we on our part should not speak up for the truth against opponents attacking the truth; in that case where would what he said fit in, where he was showing what sort of man a bishop should be: *That he should be strong on sound doctrine, and capable of refuting those who contradict it* (Ti 1:9)? For arguing about words does not mean caring how error may be overcome by truth, but how your way of saying things may be preferred to someone else's.

Accordingly, the one who does not argue about words, whether he is speaking calmly and plainly, or in the moderate style or the grand manner, is intending that by his words the truth should become clear to his hearers, that the truth should please them, that the truth should move them, seeing that not even charity, which is the end of the commandment and the fulfilling of the law,[66] can in any way be rightly directed, if the things that are loved by it are not true, but false. Indeed, though, just as someone who has a beautiful body and a misshapen mind is more to be grieved over than if he also had a misshapen body, so too those who eloquently utter things that are false are more to be pitied than if they said such things in a shapeless style. What therefore does it mean to speak not only eloquently but also wisely, if not to provide words that are sufficient in the plain style, brilliant in the moderate, vehement and forceful in the grand manner, but still for saying true things that really need to be heard? But if anyone is unable to do both, let him say wisely what he does not say eloquently, rather than say eloquently what he says unwisely. 29, If however he cannot even do this, let him so conduct himself that he not only earns a reward for himself, but also gives an example to others, and so his manner of life can itself be a kind of eloquent sermon.

---

66. See 1 Tm 1:5; Rom 13:10.

Conclusion: Those who cannot compose their own sermons should learn by heart and preach those of acknowledged masters

62. There are, of course, some people who can declaim and enunciate well, but cannot think up and compose anything to say and declaim. But if they take things that have been written eloquently and wisely by others, and proffer them to the people, provided they have that role to play,[67] they are not acting improperly. For in this way too we get the useful result of there being many preachers of the truth without there being many masters, if all say the same thing, taught by the one true master, and there are no schisms among them.[68] Nor should such men be deterred by the words of the prophet Jeremiah, through whom God reproves those *who steal his words, each one from his neighbor* (Jer 23:30). Those who steal, after all, are purloining what does not belong to them; but God's word does belong to those who do what he tells them. In fact, it's the man who speaks well and lives badly that really speaks words that do not belong to him. For any good things that he says seem to be the product of his own wits, but do not go along at all with his morals. And so the ones who God said are stealing his words are those who want to give the appearance of being good by speaking what belongs to God, when in fact they are bad by doing what belongs to themselves.

Nor, in fact, is it they who are saying the good things they do say, if you pay careful attention. How, after all, can they be saying in words what they are contradicting in deeds? It was not for nothing, you see, that the apostle said about such people: *They claim that they know God, but contradict it with their deeds* (Ti 1:16). So in one way it is they who are saying it, and again in another way it is not they who are saying it, since each thing is true that Truth has said. Speaking of such people, *What they say*, he said, *do, but what they do, do not do*, that is, do what you hear from their mouths; do not do what you see in their works; *for they say*, he went on, *and do not do* (Mt 23:3). Therefore, although they do not do, they still say. But in another place where he is chiding such people, *Hypocrites*, he says, *how can you say good things, since you are bad?* (Mt 12:34). And consequently it is not they who say even the things they do say, when they say good things, inasmuch as by will and work they contradict what they say.

Thus it can come about that a learned but bad man may compose a sermon in which the truth is proclaimed, to be spoken by another man who is not learned, but is good; when this happens, he is himself handing over from himself what does not belong to him, while the other man is

---

67. *Si eam personam gerunt*; if they bear the *persona*, the role, or possibly the dignity, the rank—presumably of a pastor. I did wonder if this were not an early ecclesiastical use of the word *persona* in the sense that eventually resulted in the English use of the word "parson" for a beneficed clergyman, or indeed any clergyman.

68. See 1 Cor 1:10; Mt 23:8.

receiving what is in fact his own from someone it does not belong to. But when good men who are believers do this service for good men who are believers, both parties are saying what is their own, because God too is theirs and the things they are saying are his. And those who are unable to compose these good sermons make them their own, when they compose themselves to live according to what they contain.

30, 63. But whether you are at this very moment about to preach to a congregation, or give a talk to any kind of group, or whether you are on the point of dictating something that is to be preached to a congregation, or to be read by anyone who wishes and is able to, you should pray that God may put good words into your mouth. After all, if Queen Esther prayed, when she was going to speak in the king's presence for the temporal salvation of her people, that God might put suitable words into her mouth, how much more should you pray to receive such a favor, when you are toiling in word and teaching for the people's eternal salvation?

Those, however, who are going to say something that they have received from others, should pray for those they receive it from even before they do so,[69] that they may be given what they hope to receive from them; and when they have received it, they should pray both that they themselves may give it out well, and that those they give it out to may take it well; and on the successful conclusion of the talk they must give thanks to the same God from whom they cannot doubt that they have received it, so that he that boasts may boast in the one[70] *in whose hand are both we and our words* (Wis 7:16).

31, 64. This book has turned out longer than I wished, and than I expected. But for the reader or listener to whom it is acceptable it will not be too long, while anyone who does find it too long, and who wants to know what it contains, should read it piecemeal. As for those who are not interested in knowing what is in it, they should not complain about its length. I, for my part, give thanks to our God that in these four books I have set out to the best of my poor ability, not what sort of pastor I am myself, lacking many of the necessary qualities as I do, but what sort the pastor should be who is eager to toil away, not only for his own sake but for others, in the teaching of sound, that is of Christian, doctrine.

---

69. Here it looks as if he is thinking of a clergyman—a bishop, perhaps?—who has commissioned a ghost writer to write his sermons for him, not of the one who fetches down a volume of sermons by Newman, or Bossuet (Cyprian, Ambrose—or Augustine) from his library shelf.
70. See 1 Cor 1:31; 2 Cor 10:17.

INDEX OF SCRIPTURE

(prepared by Michael Dolan)

(The numbers after the scriptual reference refer to the section of the work)

Old Testament

Genesis

1:26–27	I, 22, 20
2:8–9	III, 36, 52
2:9–10	III, 36, 52
2:15	III, 36, 52
10:20	III, 36, 53
10:32–11:1	III, 36, 53
14:18–19	IV, 21, 45
25:25	II, 22, 33

Exodus

3:14	I, 32, 35
12:22	II, 41, 62

Leviticus

19:18	I, 22, 21

Numbers

11:4	IV, 21, 46
13:19	II, 13, 20

Deuteronomy

6:5	I, 22, 21
13:2–3	II, 23, 35
25:4	II, 10, 15

Tobit

4:15	III, 14, 22
8:5–7	III, 18, 27

Psalms

1 :4	III, 37 ,55
5· 12	III, 26, 37
Il :5	I, 23, 23
16:2	I, 31, 34
16:4	IV, 10, 24
27:13	III, 34, 9
33:2	II, 16, 26
34:1	III, 35, 51
35:2	III, 26, 37
35: 14	I, 30, 33
35:18	IV, 14, 31
51:7	II, 16, 24
51:7–8	II, 41, 62

75:8	III, 24, 36
93:5	IV, 26, 56
110:4	IV, 21, 45
111:10	II, 7, 11
119:164	III, 35, 51
121:2	III, 6, 10
132:18	II, 13, 20
139:15	III, 3, 7
143:10	IV, 16, 33

Proverbs

2:6	III, 37, 56
3:34	IV, 23, 33
8:22	I, 34, 38
9:17	III, 24, 36
25:21–22	III, 16, 24

Ecclesiastes

3:5	III, 18, 27

Song of Songs

1:5	III, 32, 45
4:2	II,6, 7

Wisdom

4:3	III, 12, 18
6:24	IV, 5, 8
7:16	IV, 15, 32; IV, 30, 63
13:9	II, 21, 32

Sirach

1 :16	II, 7, 11
7:25	III, 17, 25
12:4	III, 16, 24
37:19	IV, 27, 59
37:20	II, 31, 48

Isaiah

7:9	II, 12, 17
10:22	III, 34, 48
14:12	III, 37, 55
42:16–17	III, 32, 45
58:7	II, 12, 17
61:10	III, 31, 44

INDEX

(prepared by Joseph Sprug)

*Citations are to: Prologue (P), Book(s) (Roman numbers),
and section numbers*

Works of St. Augustine:
A Translation for the 21st Century

New City Press, in conjunction with the Augustinian Heritage Institute, will provide the complete works of Saint Augustine for the first time in the English language. New translations, introductions and notes are written by renowned Augustinian scholars. Foreseen are 49 volumes. See the list below for books already published. Future publication plans available upon request. Standing Order customers receive a 10% discount on each volume in the Works of Saint Augustine series.

Part I — Books

Autobiographical Works

The Confessions (I/1)
  cloth,   978-1-56548-468-9
  paper,   978-1-56548-445-0
  pocket, 978-1-56548-154-1

Revisions (I/2)
  cloth, 978-1-56548-360-6

Philosophical-Dogmatic Works

The Trinity (I/5)
  cloth, 978-0-911782-89-9
  paper, 978-1-56548-446-7

The City of God 1-10 (I/6)
  cloth, 978-1-56548-454-2
  paper, 978-1-56548-455-9

The City of God 11-22 (I/7)
  cloth, 978-1-56548-479-5
  paper, 978-1-56548-481-8

On Christian Belief (I/8)
  cloth, 978-1-56548-233-3
  paper, 978-1-56548-234-0

Pastoral Works

Marriage and Virginity (I/9)
  cloth, 978-1-56548-104-6
  paper, 978-1-56548-222-7

Exegetical Works

Teaching Christianity (I/11)
  cloth, 978-1-56548-048-3
  paper, 978-1-56548-049-0

Responses to Miscellaneous Questions (I/12)
  cloth, 978-1-56548-277-7

On Genesis (I/13)
  cloth, 978-1-56548-175-6
  paper, 978-1-56548-201-2

New Testament I and II (I/15 and I/16)
  cloth, 978-1-56548-529-7
  paper, 978-1-56548-531-0

Polemical Works

Arianism and Other Heresies (I/18)
  cloth, 978-1-56548-038-4
Manichean Debate (I/19)
  cloth, 978-1-56548-247-0
Answer to Faustus, a Manichean (I/20)

  cloth, 978-1-56548-264-7

Answer to the Pelagians I (I/23)
  cloth, 978-1-56548-092-6

Answer to the Pelagians II (I/24)
  cloth, 978-1-56548-107-7

Answer To The Pelagians III (I/25)
  cloth, 978-1-56548-129-9

Answer to the Pelagians IV (I/26)
  cloth, 978-1-56548-136-7

Essential Texts Created for Classroom Use

Augustine Catechism: Enchiridion on Faith Hope and Love
paper, 978-1-56548-298-2

Essential Expositions of the Psalms
paper, 978-1-56548-510-5

Essential Sermons
paper, 978-1-56548-276-0

Instructing Beginners in Faith
paper, 978-1-56548-239-5

Monastic Rules
paper, 978-1-56548-130-5

Prayers from The Confessions
paper, 978-1-56548-188-6

Selected Writings on Grace and Pelagianism
paper, 978-1-56548-372-9

Soliloquies: Augustine's Inner Dialogue
paper, 978-1-56548-142-8

Trilogy on Faith and Happiness
paper, 978-1-56548-359-0

Ebooks Available

City of God, Books I-X, Essential Sermons, Homilies on the First Epistle of John, Revisions, The Confessions, Trilogy on Faith and Happiness, The Trinity, The Augustine Catechism: The Enchiridion on Faith, Hope and Love.

Custom Syllabus

Universities that wish to create a resource that matches their specific needs using selections from any of the above titles should contact New City Press.

About the Augustinian Heritage Institute

In 1990, the Augustinian Heritage Institute was founded by John E. Rotelle, OSA to oversee the English translation of *The Works of Saint Augustine, A Translation for the 21st Century*. This project was started in conjunction with New City Press. At that time, English was the only major Western language into which the Works of Saint Augustine in their entirety had not yet been attempted. Existing translations were often archaic or faulty and the scholarship was outdated. These new translations offer detailed introductions, extensive critical notes, both a general index and scriptural index for each work as well as the best translations in the world.

The Works of Saint Augustine, A Translation for the 21st Century in its complete form will be published in 49 volumes. To date, 42 volumes have been published.

NEW CITY PRESS
of the Focolare

About New City Press of the Focolare

New City Press is one of more than 20 publishing houses sponsored by the Focolare, a movement founded by Chiara Lubich to help bring about the realization of Jesus' prayer: "That all may be one" (John 17:21). In view of that goal, New City Press publishes books and resources that enrich the lives of people and help all to strive toward the unity of the entire human family. We are a member of the Association of Catholic Publishers.

Free Index to *The Works of Saint Augustine*

Download a PDF file that provides the ability to search all of the available indexes from each volume published by New City Press.

Visit http://www.newcitypress.com/index-to-the-works-of-saint-augustine-a-translation-for-the-21st-century.html for more details.

NEW CITY PRESS
of the Focolare
Hyde Park, New York

About New City Press of the Focolare

New City Press is one of more than 20 publishing houses sponsored by the Focolare, a movement founded by Chiara Lubich to help bring about the realization of Jesus' prayer: "That all may be one" (John 17:21). In view of that goal, New City Press publishes books and resources that enrich the lives of people and help all to strive toward the unity of the entire human family. We are a member of the Association of Catholic Publishers.

Further Reading

15 Days of Prayer with St. Augustine, Jaime Garcia, 978-1-56548-489-4, $12.95

Roots of Christian Mysticism, Olivier Clement, 978-1-56548-485-6, $29.95

From Big Bang to Big Mystery, Brendan Purcell, 978-1-56548-433-7, $34.95

A Critical Study of the Rule of Benedict, Adalbert de Vogüé, 978-1-56548-494-8, $39.95

Periodicals
Living City Magazine,
www.livingcitymagazine.com

Scan to join our mailing list for discounts and promotions or go to www.newcitypress.com and click on "join our email list."